# Family games

# Family games

EDITED BY BRIAN BURNS

tangerine
press™

Published by Tangerine Press™, an imprint of Scholastic Inc.
555 Broadway, New York, NY 10012. All rights reserved.

Scholastic and Tangerine Press™ and associated logos are
trademarks of Scholastic Inc.

Copyright © 2001 Amber Books Ltd

ISBN: 0-439-32569-2

Editorial and design by
Amber Books Ltd
Bradley's Close
74–77 White Lion Street
London N1 9PF

Contributors: Nina Hathway, Byron Jacobs, Andrew Kinsman,
Nigel Perryman, Jenny Sutcliffe
Additional material: Molly Perham, Jason Beckford-Ball
Project Editor: Brian Burns
Editor: Molly Perham
Editorial Consultant: Jim Glenn
Design: Colin Hawes

Printed in Singapore

Picture acknowledgements:
All step by step illustrations: Colin Hawes
Chapter opener illustrations: Mike Fuller

# CONTENTS

# INTRODUCTION

For thousands of years, history has recorded that man has been a keen games player. The earliest recorded writings from ancient civilizations frequently refer to simple games such as Tic-Tac-Toe. As civilization has progressed, so has the complexity of its games. The earliest games played were probably of the simple race variety, but many of these have developed and matured through the centuries to become sophisticated modern games such as Chess and Shogi. References to games and game boards have frequently been found etched onto classical remains, such as Hadrian's Wall.

Further evidence of the antiquity of game-playing was unearthed in early 1997, when the remains of a game and board were found at an archaeological site in Colchester – a town situated on the east coast of England and used by the Romans as a garrison town 2000 years ago. This was the first time that a gaming board of such antiquity, with the pieces set out in what appeared to be the starting position, had been found. The board measured 22 x 14in. (55 x 35cm) and appeared to be checkered. The playing pieces, neatly lined up in their initial array, were blue and white glass beads, similar in size to children's marbles. One can only speculate at the rules by which play in this game was conducted.

## MENTAL AND PHYSICAL GAMES

It has often been thought that mental games would never achieve the prominence of their physical counterparts. Events such as the Olympic Games and the soccer World Cup have caught the public imagination in ways that never seemed possible for games such as Chess and Shogi. Historically, this is probably due to the fact that a sporting event played in a large stadium can be witnessed by many thousands of people, whereas a board game would seem to restrict the possibilities for spectators. These days, however, this is no longer the case. Although television can transmit the excitement of an event such as the Olympic Games to more than a billion people, it also has the facility to home in on a small-scale game. This was apparent in 1991 when the Icelandic Bridge team won the Bermuda Bowl (the World Championship of Bridge), the first time that this small country had won any world title. The crucial final ten hands of the match concluded around 5:00 am Icelandic time. Nevertheless, 50 percent of the population stayed up to watch the conclusion on television. It is difficult to imagine any sporting event exceeding this level of spectator interest.

It has often been suggested that board games are simply not as popular as physical ones and that people much prefer an activity involving kicking or hitting a ball to one that involves a mental battle. However, the incredible popularity of board games offers compelling evidence to the contrary. Many top football players, golfers, and tennis players can command substantial fees for playing their games and also for endorsing products. However, top players in games of mental skill are also very well rewarded. For example, recent Chess matches for the World Championship have all had prize funds in excess of $1.5 million, while in Japan, top Shogi professionals can earn in excess of $1 million per season. Ely Culbertson, an erstwhile revolutionary in Russia, Mexico, and Spain, turned his hand to card-playing activities when the family fortune was wiped out in the Russian revolution in 1917. The new game of Contract Bridge provided him with the opportunity he had been looking for. After winning a prolonged match against his main rival, Sidney Lenz, in 1931, he received in excess of US$3 million for a series of short movies.

## GAMES AND TECHNOLOGY

The Internet provides the perfect medium for the relaying of board games to the masses. This was spectacularly demonstrated during the clash in 1997 between world Chess champion Garry Kasparov and IBM's Deep Blue computer. The games were shown live on IBM's World Wide Web site and the final game generated more "hits" than the whole of the 1996 Atlanta Olympics.

The Internet also enables players located in geographically distant locations to compete together in games. Almost all well-known board games are represented on web sites that have facilities for the games to be played in real time. This is a tremendous development, allowing enthusiasts of the more obscure games to find regular opponents.

## THE STRATEGY OF GAMES

Expertise in games is not seen as a purely esoteric ability; it is also recognized as a manifestation of intellectual prowess. The game most frequently used as an intellectual metaphor in literature is that of Chess; many writers have expanded on this theme and incorporated it into their work. Goethe, for example, described Chess as "the touchstone of the intellect." Lenin called it "the gymnasium of the mind." This perception is not limited to literature. In 1990 Bankers Trust, a leading US financial institution, ran a series of advertisements in *Chess Life*, the world's widest-read Chess magazine, seeking applicants for their trading division. They received over 1000 responses, eventually hiring five chessplayers, two of whom were grandmasters.

As this example shows, games are not always merely viewed as entertaining diversions. The strategies employed to achieve success over the gaming board can also be applied in many real life situations. In fact a whole branch of study, game theory, has built up around this idea. A game theorist will study the strategies that players in such "games" adopt. In 1993 the Nobel prize in economics was shared between John Harsanyi, Reinhard Selten, and John Nash. Nash's contribution was the development of his idea which has now become known as the Nash Equilibrium, a key component in the study of game theory.

Whether you wish to play games in order to improve your career prospects, or whether they simply act as an entertaining diversion, *Family Games* will furnish you with fascinating material on the history, rules, and basic strategies of many well-known games.

# PARLOR GAMES

Although few people nowadays may claim to have a room called a parlor, the term "parlor games" is still used to describe a whole range of indoor games that can entertain children and adults alike.

Nowadays parlor games are played mainly at children's parties, but in the past they were popular entertainment for the whole family. Samuel Pepys, the English diarist, records that, on 26 December 1664, he went to bed leaving his wife and household "to their sport and blind man's buff, which they did not leave off until four in the morning …" Under its various names, Blind Man's Buff is probably more often mentioned in English literature than any other informal game, and in one form or another is part of the social history of many parts of the world. It is one of a family of blindfold games that also includes Squeak Piggy Squeak and Pin the Tail on the Donkey.

Hunting games have also been popular. In some, players hunt for hidden objects, while, in others, the seeker hunts for the other players and the game is often played in the dark – Sardines is a popular example.

Luck is the major component of blindfold and hunting games, as it is with guessing games such as Rock, Paper, Scissors, and Spoof. Other games require a degree of ingenuity or dexterity in order to outwit the opponents. Grandmother's Footsteps falls into this category, as do games in which teams of players race to pass objects to each other in different ways and contestants need to strike a balance between speed and skill in order to be successful. Buzz and Buzz-Fizz rely on concentration.

To play acting games well, you need a lively imagination and a little acting ability. Dumb Crambo, much played in the nineteenth century, was the forerunner of games such as Charades. In acting games, amusement derives not only from the players' acting attempts, but also from the often bizarre guesses made by the other team.

This game has been played for centuries – you can see it in many paintings of medieval life. Apple Ducking is still great fun today, for young and old alike. Play it in the kitchen, if you have enough space, or play outside.

*Players: from two upward, depending on the tub's size*
*Equipment: a large tub of water and some apples*
*Difficulty: harder than you would think, especially*
       *if the aim is to stay dry; children love*
       *it, but adults can enjoy the game, too*
*Duration: a one-off game can last half an hour, but*
       *players often want to go back for another try*

*Diagram 1  A game*
*of Apple Ducking*

## BEGINNING TO PLAY

Place a tub of water – an old-fashioned zinc bath is ideal, or a rain barrel from the yard will do just as well – in the center of a large space. If your bathroom is large enough, you could always use the bathtub. Drop some apples into the water – preferably as many apples as there are people taking part – and ask the players to gather around.

## PLAYING THE GAME

The most fun, and the maximum mayhem, comes when everyone plays at the same time – although you might prefer to let players take turns individually. The aim is to get as many apples out of the water as you can without using your hands or elbows: this means that you can use only your head and mouth – and teeth, of course. Getting hold of even a single apple is much easier said than done, though large mouths and sharp teeth are distinct advantages. The winner can either be the first person to get an apple out of the tub, the person who gets the most apples out in a set time, or – if you are taking individual turns – the person who gets an apple out faster than everyone else.

One of the simplest – and silliest – games that there is, Matchbox Race is a standby of children's parties. But it is not only children who enjoy this game, because it has been used to break the ice at many an adult party, too.

*Players:* six or more
*Equipment:* the sleeves of two matchboxes
*Difficulty:* much harder than it would appear, though children have an advantage because they have smaller noses
*Duration:* unlikely to last for more than 15 minutes

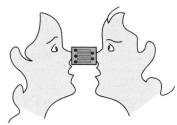

*Diagram 2  A Matchbox Race*

### BEGINNING TO PLAY
Divide the players into two teams and ask each team to stand in line one behind the other, with the players clasping their hands behind their backs. (Depending on the age of the players, and whether they would giggle or be embarrassed, it is worth considering alternating men and women along each line.)

### PLAYING THE GAME
The first person in each line puts a matchbox cover on their nose, and, on the call of "go," passes it down to the next player along the line, using only noses – and so on, to the end of the line. If any player drops the matchbox, it is returned to the first person in the line and the process starts all over again. The first team to get the cover to the end of the line wins.

### HORSE OR CURRANT BUN?
Some people think the entire human race can be divided into two groups according to what type of nose an individual has: according to

the theory, we are all either "horse" or "currant bun." Placing your friends (and enemies) in the appropriate category is a game in its own right, but debating which player fits into which type can add considerable spice to a matchbox race – especially because a succession of "horses" plunging their noses into a matchbox can make it hard for a "currant bun" to get much of a grip.

## PASS THE ORANGE

Oranges are something of a tradition at Christmas, so it is not surprising that this game has always been a part of the Christmas festivities. For earlier generations, a variant of Pass the Orange was traditional at teenagers' parties.

*Players:* *ideally, six or more on either side*
*Equipment:* *two oranges*
*Difficulty:* *this game is far from easy, but it is the ludicrous contortions needed that make it fun, rather than success itself; it is suitable for both children and adults*
*Duration:* *about half an hour*

### BEGINNING TO PLAY
Divide the players into two teams, and ask them to sit in lines, with each player side by side; the teams should face each other across the floor. The first player in each team is then given an orange.

### PLAYING THE GAME
At a signal, the first player on each team puts the orange between his or her feet, and, using only feet, passes it on to the next player. The orange is passed down to the end of the line in the same way, and then returned

back up the line to the first player. Any player that drops the orange must pick it up again – no matter where it has rolled – using feet alone. Any orange that has been dropped has to be returned to the first player in the team, and the process repeated – if this means that players have to shuffle around the room on their bottoms, so be it. The first team to get the orange from one end of the line to the other and back again wins.

**VARIATION**

In another version of this game, the players hold the orange not between their feet, but between their chin and their neck, again, passing it without the use of hands. This version can be quite uncomfortable – in both senses of the word – but used to be very popular at teenage dances, many years ago.

*Diagram 3  Passing the orange between chin and neck*

Winking has weird and sometimes frightening connotations in some cultures. Perhaps this is why this game – though thoroughly domesticated – can still be surprisingly tense and has deliciously scary overtones.

*Players: four or more*
*Equipment: a pack of playing cards*
*Difficulty: with practice, this game can become*
*surprisingly complex; it might be scary for*
*children under seven*
*Duration: about an hour, with a number of adult players*

*Diagram 4  Winking*

## BEGINNING TO PLAY

Select cards from the pack to the same number as there are players – one card must be the Ace of Spades, but the others can be random. Lay the cards down on a table, with the players sitting around it, and ask each player to pick a card, keeping its identity secret. The person who draws the Ace of Spades is "the murderer," but whoever it is must keep their identity secret.

## PLAYING THE GAME

"The murder" is committed by catching the eye of another player and shooting a deadly wink in his or her direction. The victim waits a few seconds so as not to give the game away, before slumping over dead. Any other player who spots the wink can reveal the identity of the murderer and a new game can begin.

## STRATEGIC TIPS

On one hand, players try to avoid eye contact with each other because they do not want to become victims, but on the other hand they want to catch the murderer before they become a victim themselves. Staring fixedly at the table will get you nowhere – you will just become the last victim – but trying to wink at everyone at the table at the same time, if you are the murderer, rarely works. Winking is best played by friends who know each other reasonably well, because then they can try to second-guess the strategies and reactions of the others.

## DUMB CRAMBO

The forerunner to Charades and The Game, Dumb Crambo was an extremely popular parlor game in the nineteenth century, in the days before people had television for entertainment. It is extremely simple, but its very simplicity gives it a rumbustious charm.

*Players:* six or more
*Equipment:* none
*Difficulty:* fairly easy, but the charm of the game lies not in winning, but in the
        pure pleasure of acting, which both adults and children can enjoy
*Duration:* an hour, on average

### BEGINNING TO PLAY
As with The Game and Charades, the players are divided into two teams. One team leaves the room while the other team thinks of a word – usually, but not necessarily, a verb. When the players in the first team are summoned back to the room, they are not told the actual word that has been chosen, but a word that rhymes with it. For example, if the word chosen was "bite," the word given to the opposing team could be "night." This is the only point in the game when the teams actually speak to each other – hence the name Dumb Crambo.

### PLAYING THE GAME

The opposing team is allowed to leave the room for a few minutes to consult, and has to decide on three words that rhyme with "night." The team then returns to the room and mimes the first of their three words: for example, they might mime "fight." Since, in our example, this is incorrect, the members of the first team then boo, hiss, and stamp their feet, and generally express their complete disdain and disgust.

The opponents might then mime "light" – someone might act out lighting a cigarette, for example, or another member of the team might pretend to flick a light switch – to more boos and hisses from the other team. Then they might try "bite," with one person miming a dog that bites the others. Huge applause then comes from the the other team. You only have three guesses at the word, and then the teams swap roles, the spectators becoming the actors, and the ex-actors – trying to think of some really difficult word for the opposing team – become the rumbustious spectators. Remember that not a word must be uttered, apart from the one and only rhyming clue that is given at the start. Even so, the whole point of the game is to make as much noise as possible, and to exaggerate responses to a ridiculous extent.

Many game players have no doubt that this is the best game in existence. There may be room for argument about this claim, but the only way to see whether it is true is to play The Game for yourself.

*Players: a minimum of four*
*Equipment: pencil and paper*
*Difficulty: can be tailored for both adults and children*
*Duration: anything from half an hour to a whole evening*

## BEGINNING TO PLAY
First the players divide themselves into two teams. Then comes the question of which version of The Game to play: the first version is the more relaxed of the two – almost a spectator sport – with only one person in the spotlight at a time; the second version requires everyone to participate at the same time, and is usually chaotic and noisy – and lots of fun.

## A SINGLE PROTAGONIST
In this version, the two teams each compile a list of phrases in secret: they can be titles of books, films, songs, proverbs, or whatever the players can think up – the number of phrases chosen should equal the number of players in the opposing team. Team One then gives the first player from the second team one of the phrases that has been chosen, and that player has to act out the phrase to his or her team-mates, without using words. The team-mates have to guess the answer, while the members of Team One look on and, at least as a rule, snicker. When the phrase has been identified – or the second team has given up, as the case may be – the round is over. The teams reverse roles and the second team takes its turn at trying to outwit the players of the first team. And so the game goes on until both lists are finished. The advantage of this version is that the lists

an be tailored so that they bring out the best, or the worst, in individual members of the opposing team. There is a danger that doing this can bring an element of cruelty to the game, but this need not be the case.

## A JOINT EFFORT

In the second version, players compete in two teams and a quizmaster is elected who belongs to neither team. The quizmaster compiles the list of phrases, and gives the first phrase to one player from each team at the same time. The players then return to their respective team-mates and attempt to act it out. The first person to guess the phrase correctly dashes to the quiz-master to get the next phrase, and so on – until all the phrases have been acted out. The winning team is the one that reaches the end of the list first.

The problem with this version is that there is ample opportunity to cheat, either by watching the other team acting, or by listening to their guesses. But the likelihood is that the players will be too absorbed to do this, because as it is essentially a race, the pressure is on to perform quickly and appropriately. Nevertheless, the quizmaster should keep an eye on events to ensure fair play. This version is very exciting and things become very noisy, as members of both teams shout, cajole, abuse, and mock the actors.

## PLAYING CONVENTIONS

Whichever version of The Game you play, it is important to know the conventions that are used. These indicate whether the phrase about to be acted is a movie title, a book title, a television program, or whatever. They take the form of sign language: opening your palms, for example, signifies a book; drawing the rough shape of an arch with your fingers indicates a play; pulling sound from your open mouth means a musical or an opera; drawing quotation marks in the air says that the phrase is a proverb; drawing a square in the air signifies a television program; and winding an old-fashioned movie camera indicates a movie title.

*Diagram 5 Holding three fingers in the air signifies that the phrase contains three words*

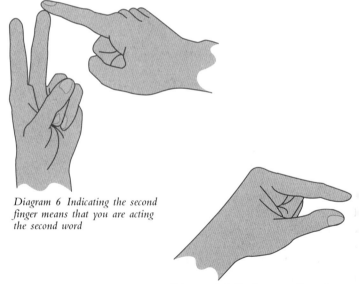

*Diagram 6 Indicating the second finger means that you are acting the second word*

*Diagram 7 Indicating a small word*

By holding the appropriate number of fingers in the air, you tell the others how many words a phrase contains. To indicate which of the words you are acting at any point, you indicate the relevant finger.

To indicate how many syllables there are in the word, you lay the corresponding number of fingers across your forearm. If the word or syllable rhymes with something easier to act, you pull your ear lobe to indicate that it "sounds like" the word you are acting out. Small words such as "in," "of," and "but" are indicated by holding your thumb and forefinger up slightly apart. And, if you are brave enough to act the whole phrase out in one go, you draw a circle in the air with both hands. Your team-mates are allowed to shout out questions, but you can only nod or shake your head in response. There must be no talking, whispering, or even mouthing between the actor and the team.

## AN EXAMPLE

If you are going to act out *To Kill A Mockingbird*, the title of a book by Harper Lee, you start by opening your palms to indicate a book. Then you put up four fingers to indicate the number of words. Next, indicate with your first finger to show that you are acting the first word, and hold up your thumb and forefinger slightly apart to show that it is a small word. If you could not think how to act out "kill," you could pull your ear lobe and act out "pill" or "hill." Again, with "a," you would show that it is a small word. "Mockingbird" could be split into "mocking" (rhymes with "stocking," "rocking," or even "locking") and "bird."

## HINTS FOR SUCCESSFUL PLAY

There is no fun in The Game if you choose a phrase that is too easy to act out. But if you are feeling unkind, it is not difficult to come up with some real horrors. In such uncharitable moments, try these: *Persuasion*, by Jane Austen; *Oscar and Lucinda*, by Peter Carey. Some easier ones are: *Gone with the Wind*; *Three Men in a Boat*; and *A Tale of Two Cities*.

An old favorite for people of all ages, this game was devised as a country-house frolic with amatory overtones. While it is important to have a fair amount of space, a mansion is not necessary.

*Players:* four or more
*Equipment:* a large house
*Difficulty:* easy, though frustrating at times, for people of all ages
*Duration:* half an hour with just four players, but can be several hours
         depending on the number of players and the amount of room

## PLAYING THE GAME

This game is a variant on Hide-and-Seek, so the first thing you must do is to draw lots to decide who is to go off and hide – though sometimes it is easiest to give the most tired and reluctant player the task of hiding, to save them from energetic seeking. Whoever it is leaves the room to find a suitable place in which to hide, and, after a decent interval – five minutes, say, depending on the size of the house – the rest of the players separate to hunt for them. The first player to find the person who is hiding waits until any other players are out of sight and then jumps into the hiding place, wherever it may be – for example, under a bed, in a cupboard, or on top of a child's bunk bed. The two of them wait for the next player to discover them, and so on, until all but one of the players are in the same hiding place together, packed in like sardines in a can – hence the game's name. The last player to discover the rest of the group has to be the next sardine.

## HINTS FOR SUCCESSFUL PLAY

Obviously, the success of this game relies largely on the resourcefulness of the first sardine, who must find a spot in which the rest of the players can hide, no matter how uncomfortably. It becomes progressively harder for each subsequent sardine to find a hiding place that is both difficult to find and also big enough to accommodate the other players.

There are many detective games, but this one has the great advantage of being played with the lights out, which can lend the game a surprisingly exciting sense of tension, suspense, and scariness.

*Players: eight or more*
*Equipment: pencil and paper, and, preferably, a large house – the darker and gloomier the better*
*Difficulty: suitable for adults and older children – but not for the faint-hearted*
*Duration: an hour or more, depending on the number playing and the size of the house in which it is played*

### BEGINNING TO PLAY

Tear some sheets of paper into as many slips as there are players. Mark one with a black cross and another with a circle. Fold the slips over and place them in a hat, then ask everyone to choose one. The player who picks the piece of paper with the cross is the murderer, but must not betray the fact in any way, keeping totally quiet. The player who picks the circle is the detective, and should identify himself or herself to the other players. Then the lights are turned off and all the players except the detective disappear in all directions.

*Diagram 8 Slips of paper marked for a game of Murder in the Dark*

### PLAYING THE GAME

The murderer roams around until he comes across a victim, and whispers "You're dead," or puts his hands around the victim's neck – though this is sometimes going too far in a dark and scary house if people are of a nervous disposition. The victim lets out a bloodcurdling scream, while the murderer slinks away to some suitably innocent and distant location. When the screams are heard by the other players, they must all stay exactly where they are. The detective then hurries to the scene of the crime and switches on the lights, before noting down where everyone is.

The suspects are then summoned to a main room and questioned about their movements and where they were at the time of the crime. The innocent must tell the truth, but the murderer is allowed to lie as necessary – but, if there is a direct challenge that a suspect is guilty, the truth must be told. After all the evidence has been assembled, the detective is allowed just two guesses as to the murderer's identity.

## CHARADES

This classic parlor game has a special appeal for children because it involves dressing up and using props, though adults enjoy it, too. Charades certainly has its devotees – among whom, reputedly, are Britain's royal family.

*Players: six or more*
*Equipment: a dressing-up box, containing old clothes, and a few props*
*Difficulty: as easy or as hard as you wish to make it*
*Duration: from an hour to a whole evening*

### PLAYING THE GAME

Charades differs from The Game in that speech, clothes, and props can be used to help convey the syllables that make up a word or phrase. Otherwise, the two games are very similar. In Charades, two teams are formed and each one chooses a two- or three-syllable word that is acted out to the opposing team, syllable by syllable. Finally, the whole word is acted out. For example, "incubate" could be split, for acting purposes, into "in," "queue," and "bait." The conventions used are the same as those for The Game.

The trick is to disguise each syllable as cunningly as possible and to try to fool the other players with red herrings and high drama. There are really no winners and losers in Charades, unless, perhaps, one team guesses far more quickly than the other or fails to solve the puzzle at all. However, winning is not really the point. Charades is boisterous and noisy, and, as a result, is normally very popular with children. It is simpler than The Game too, and has the advantage that you can dress up – the sillier the props and the wilder and more ridiculous the clothes, the better.

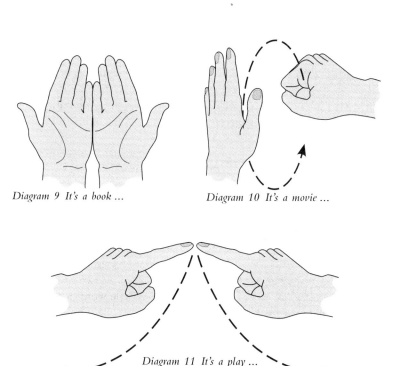

*Diagram 9 It's a book ...*

*Diagram 10 It's a movie ...*

*Diagram 11 It's a play ...*

An ancient game, played all over the world, which is based on the simple principle of anticipation. As with Poker, the game depends on bluff and double-bluff: a knowledge of your opponent's foibles is therefore vitally important.

*Players:* two (but there is a team variant – see Elves, Gnomes, and Giants)
*Equipment:* none
*Difficulty:* adults and children from seven upward
*Duration:* anything from 15 minutes up
    to an hour

## PLAYING THE GAME

Both players put one hand behind their backs and at the count of three bring it out, either in a representation of scissors, paper, or stone. Scissors are represented by a horizontal hand with two fingers extended; paper is indicated by a hand held out horizontally and flat; rock by a clenched fist. The point of the game is that scissors cut paper; that paper covers rock; and that rock crushes scissors. Therefore, scissors wins over paper; paper beats rock; and rock beats scissors. If both players use the same shape, that round is a draw. One of the great advantages of the game is that it can be played anywhere at all – in the car, on a train, or sitting in the garden.

*Diagram 12  Scissors,*

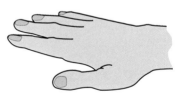

*Diagram 13  Paper,*

*Diagram 14  And Rock*

This game is for the exuberant and uninhibited – it involves two teams charging toward each other across a room, shouting their identities, and brandishing the gestures that match them.

*Players: the more the better, but ideally at least 12*
*Equipment: none*
*Difficulty: easy, but tense for grown-ups and fun for children*
*Duration: half an hour for adults; an hour for children*

## BEGINNING TO PLAY

The principle is like Rock, Paper, Scissors, but the execution is very different. The players divide into two teams and retreat to either end of a room – ideally, it should be large and cleared of furniture. Each team forms a huddle and debates whether all its members should be elves (the same as scissors), gnomes (paper), or giants (stone) – the teams make the same gestures as in Rock, Paper, Scissors to indicate their choice. After making their decision, the teams wait for an umpire to start the game. As with Rock, Paper, Scissors, elves beat gnomes; giants beat elves; and gnomes beat giants. Identical selections mean that the round is tied.

## PLAYING THE GAME

On the umpire's call, each team rushes toward the other, shouting their identity and brandishing the appropriate gestures – if played with sufficient enthusiasm, these gestures may not be very exact. The team that wins stays in the middle of the room; the team that loses retreats to its original position. Both teams then huddle around to choose what they will be in the next round. However, if both teams chose to be elves, say, in a round, and the result is consequently a draw, they both stay in the middle of the room and are forced to choose in secret, by means of nods and winks, what they will be in the next round. The first team to overrun the other, by winning two rounds in a row, wins the game.

Spoof is a guessing game containing an element of bluff that gives it added interest.

*Players:* *two or more*
*Equipment:* *small objects, such as coins or buttons*
*Difficulty:* *chance plays a major part, but bluffing – and the ability to spot bluffs – adds an element of skill. Enjoyable for both adults and older children.*
*Duration:* *as long or as short a time as you wish*

## PLAYING THE GAME

Each player finds three objects that are small enough to be concealed in a clenched fist – coins, matches, or buttons are ideal. The players then put some or none of these objects in their hand and hold their fists out in front of them. Then each player, going around clockwise, guesses the total number of objects that have been concealed. The first player to make a guess can say whatever number he or she pleases, but each subsequent guess must be different from any that has been made previously. When the round of guesses is complete, the objects are counted and the player whose guess is closest to the correct answer is the winner.

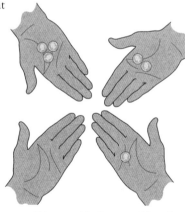

*Diagram 15  A game of Spoof*

## HINTS FOR SUCCESSFUL PLAY

The player who has the first guess has the advantage of being able to guess any number, from zero to three times the number of players. The rest of the players have the advantage of time to try to work out who is bluffing and who is not. But the possibilities are intriguing: does a high number mean that the person guessing holds the maximum of three objects, or is it a bluff? Does a low number mean that the player has put no objects in his or her hand, or is it a bluff?

## IN THE MANNER OF THE WORD

This very popular parlor game, thought to date from the nineteenth century, has a special subtlety that derives from its dependence on adverbs – and so, of course, it teaches young people what adverbs are. It appeals to natural show-offs and tempts even the shyest people to be extrovert.

*Players:* *four or more people*
*Equipment:* *none*
*Difficulty:* *as hard as you make it, but the game is enjoyed by both adults and older children*
*Duration:* *a whole evening, when good friends are playing*

## PLAYING THE GAME

There are two versions of this very popular game, which can be played by any number of people.

## A SINGLE PROTAGONIST

In this version, one person leaves the room and those remaining choose an adverb, for example "slyly," "madly," or "naughtily." When the choice has been made, the person returns to the room and has to guess what the adverb is – they can either ask questions that the others have to answer "in the manner of the word;" or ask any number of them to act out a situation, such as cleaning windows or crashing your car, "in the manner of the word."

Some combinations can be wonderfully inappropriate – such as cleaning windows "naughtily," or directing traffic "slyly."

### A JOINT EFFORT

In the second version, two people leave the room to think of an adverb. When they return, the others have to guess what it is by giving the pair situations to act, "in the manner of the word" – for example, milking a cow, or washing a car. Many people prefer this version of the game because it is less inhibiting: the person acting has someone with whom to share the agony. It also tends to be funnier, because you can tailor the situations to suit the participants. You could try asking your elderly uncle to conduct an orchestra "groovily," or a rock music–loving teenager to play the guitar "loftily."

*Diagram 16  Acting "In the Manner of the Word"*

# BLIND MAN'S BLUFF

There is no record of when this game was first played, but it has
certainly been in existence for many centuries and has been played
by countless generations of children – and adults, too. Try the
original game, or play one of its variations for added spice.

*Players:* six or more players
*Equipment:* a blindfold
*Difficulty:* either easy or hard, depending on the abilities of the "blind man," but
enjoyed by both adults and children
*Duration:* playing for an hour is generally enough

## PLAYING THE GAME

One player is selected to be the "blind man." He or she is blindfolded,
led to the center of the room, and turned around three times – the idea
is to make the blind man disoriented. The other
players scatter around the room. The
blind man then searches for the
other players, who are not allowed
to move their feet, but may twist their
bodies to escape. But once the blind man
has found a body, its identity has to be
established by touch. If the blind man
guesses the person's identity correctly,
that person becomes the next blind
man; if unsuccessful after one go,
the blind man has to try to catch
someone else.

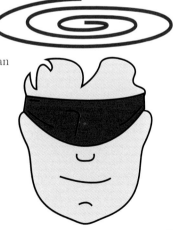

*Diagram 17 A game of Blind Man's Buff*

## VARIATIONS

There are a number of variations to this game, all of which have their own supporters.

### Blind Man's Circle

In this variation, the players walk in a circle around the blind man until he or she claps three times: the players must come to a standstill and the blind man points to the edge of the circle. The player most closely identified by the point must enter the circle and try not to be caught for two minutes. If caught, that player becomes the blind man.

### Blind Man's Staff

Here the blind man carries a stick and the players walk around in a circle that is sufficiently tight for the stick to reach them. When the blind man points his stick, the players stop walking and the one closest to it takes its end. The blind man says, "Who's there?" and the person, in a voice disguised as much as possible, answers: "It's me." If the blind man recognizes the voice, the one who has been identified loses, and changes places. If the blind man gets it wrong, they try again.

### Seated Blind Man's Buff

This is for more risqué gatherings. All the players except for the blind man sit on chairs placed in a tight circle. The blind man sits on the lap of one of the players and has to try to identify the player without touching the body any further. Usually the player who is being sat upon will giggle – but not always. If the blind man guesses correctly, he or she changes places with that person. If not, another lap must be tried.

A deceptively simple game that reveals surprising facts about the players and tends to lead to considerable argument – all of which makes it an ideal after-dinner entertainment.

*Players:* three or more
*Equipment:* none
*Difficulty:* not as easy as it first appears; for adults
*Duration:* 15 minutes for each round, up to an hour at least

## PLAYING THE GAME

Each player in turn has to declare something that he or she has never done, selecting on the basis that there is a probability that everyone else playing has done it. For example, a player might say: "I have never eaten a grapefruit;" "I have never possessed a pair of jeans;" "I have never swum in the sea;" or "I have never had a school meal." If your "I have never …" proves to be unique, you score a point; the first person to gain three points wins the game. It is important that all the players are honest about their claims, because it is almost impossible to prove or disprove negatives, but there is still some scope for challenging claims that seem too extravagant. It can become surprisingly difficult to think of something that you have not done, but that everyone else has – which all adds to the fun of the evening.

# —PAPER & PENCIL GAMES—

Paper and pencil games need only the simplest equipment, so they are ideal for passing the time on long journeys, as well as having a beneficial educational value. Many of them involve making up words, or listing words beginning with a certain letter of the alphabet.

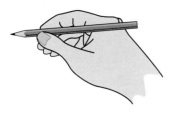

In the game of Crossword, players attempt to make up a word square with words of equal length that read both horizontally and vertically. The game became popular in Britain in the nineteenth century and probably developed from Acrostics – puzzles or poems in which the first or last letters of each line spell a word or sentence. Acrostics date from Roman times – examples have been found at Pompeii, Italy, and Cirencester, England.

Crosswords are a relatively recent invention that combine elements of the acrostic and the word square. The first "word-cross" appeared in a Sunday newspaper, the *New York World*, on 21 December 1913. The name was later changed to "cross-word," and soon the game became a craze in America and Britain. Many party games are based on anagrams. Players are given jumbled letters to turn into words, or they can be asked to make a word by adding one letter to an anagram

Consequences was another popular Victorian game, frequently described in eighteenth- and nineteenth-century literature. It must have been an appealing game in strict Victorian society because it enabled young people to flirt with one another under the guise of a harmless recreation. The fun of the game today comes from the incongruous juxtaposition of sentences, and the fact that it is not a competitive game. While the origins of some of today's paper and pencil games date back to ancient times, others are more recent inventions. Battleships is said to have been developed by British prisoners of war during World War I, and since then has become one of the most popular paper and pencil games for two players.

One of the most enduring of games, Tic-tac-toe is also known as Noughts and Crosses in Britain.

*Diagram 18 A winning strategy*

**Players:** *two*
**Equipment:** *paper and pencil, or any surface that can be marked*
**Difficulty:** *frustratingly difficult for both adults and children to actually win*
**Duration:** *a few minutes for each game, but generally repeats are required*

## PLAYING THE GAME

The great thing about Tic-tac-toe is that it can be played practically anywhere – at home, in the car, on a train, or even on a beach by drawing a grid in the sand. First, draw two pairs of parallel lines at right-angles to each other to make a grid of nine squares. Then, taking it in turns, one player marks an "O" and the other an "X" in one of the nine spaces, the object being to get your Os or Xs in a row of three – up and down, across or diagonally. The player who starts the game has an advantage, so it is wise for the players to start alternately.

## HINTS FOR SUCCESSFUL PLAY

There are around 15,000 possible permutations for the first five moves of the game, but you can nearly always force a draw when playing second. One winning strategy is shown in diagram 18: if you place your "X" in a corner, and your opponent puts an "O" in the corner beneath it, place your next "X" in the opposite corner to your first one. To stop the diagonal line, your opponent will have to place an "O" in the center. You can then place your next "X" in the remaining corner, ensuring that your next go will be the winning one. Even with this strategy, the majority of games are draws. And if your opponent starts, you can only win if he or she fails to spot a line developing. This should not happen, but surprisingly often does.

This word game has two advantages: first, it still has a point even when simple, straightforward words are chosen; second, its scoring system provides entertainment and even a bit of suspense.

*Players:* from two to 20
*Equipment:* paper and pencil
*Difficulty:* depends on the obscurity of the word or phrase chosen; adaptable for both adults and children
*Duration:* depending on the number of players, from half an hour to a whole afternoon

## PLAYING THE GAME
When played by two people, one person thinks of a word and writes down as many dashes as there are letters in that word. For example, "cream" would be:

– – – – –

The other player then has to try to guess a letter. If the guess is "E," for example, the player who set the word fills in the third dash. If the guess is "F," say, or any other incorrect letter, the base of a gallows is drawn, and the letter "F" is written down as a reminder that it should not be guessed again. Any subsequent incorrect guess results in another line being added to the gallows, and, finally, to the person suspended from them – as shown in diagram 19. The game continues either until the word has been guessed or the loser has been hung.

## A TEAM VERSION
If there are sufficient players, divide everyone into two teams and appoint a quizmaster to run things. The quizmaster thinks of a phrase – a well-known quotation, for example, or the title of a book, play, or movie –

nd writes out the necessary number of dashes, separating the individual words with a slash. So *The Full Monty*, for example, would be:

$$- - - / - - - - / - - - - -$$

This sequence is presented to one team as a challenge, and the members of that team try to guess the answer. If they are lucky, in our example, they might guess "E" and "L," with the result that "L" is put in wherever it appears. So:

$$- - e / - - 1 1 / - - - - -$$

When the phrase has been guessed – and it is often easier to guess a phrase, rather than a single word – the team is awarded points according to the number of lines that would have been required to complete the hanged man before their correct guess, and the other team is challenged in its turn.

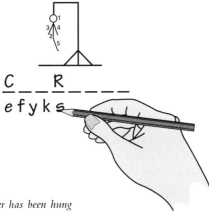

*Diagram 19 The loser has been hung*

This game is deceptively simple, but in fact it demands a high level of concentration and a grasp of the strategy. The advantage constantly swings from one player to the other, and the outcome is rarely certain until the end.

*Players:* two players
*Equipment:* paper and pens of different colors
*Difficulty:* irritatingly difficult; for adults and children over eight
*Duration:* half an hour is usually long enough for a session; otherwise frustration sets in

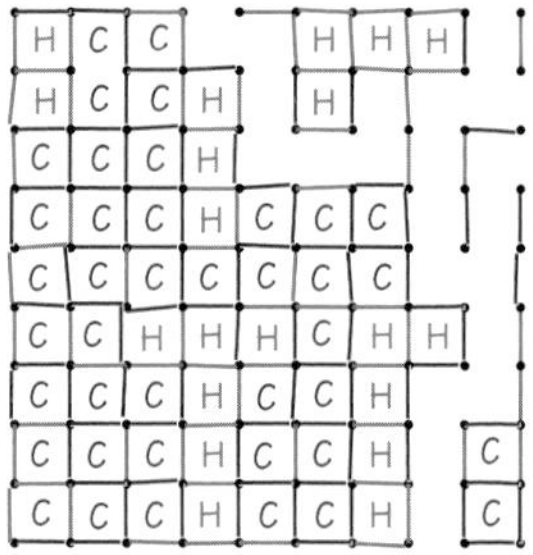

Diagram 20 A game of Boxes

## BEGINNING TO PLAY

Mark out a grid of dots on a piece of paper, using the same number of dots horizontally and vertically – 10 in a row is about right for a 10-minute game.

## PLAYING THE GAME

Using pens of different colors, in order to avoid arguments, the players take it in turns to draw a line between any two dots in an attempt to form a box. When a player completes a box they mark it with their initial, and can then add another line. If this line encloses another box, they mark that one, too, and another line can be drawn, and so on. When all the boxes have been enclosed, each player's boxes are counted, and the one with the most is the winner.

## HINTS FOR SUCCESSFUL PLAY

Strategy and cunning come into play as the game progresses and it gets ever more difficult to draw a line without leaving a square that your opponent can complete. Damage limitation becomes very important – in other words, the position should be examined carefully, so that the line you draw gives your opponent the opportunity to complete the fewest squares possible. Every pair of players will have to lay down their own local rules, which add enormously to the complexity of the game.

## VARIATION

If you become bored with the standard version, make up some local rules. For example, you could decide that the player with the fewest enclosed boxes is the winner, so reversing the approach to the game.

————————— SPROUTS —————————

This demands the same close attention as Boxes and involves similar strategies. However, there are fewer opportunities for inventive rule-making and more for bizarre embroidery.

*Players:* two
*Equipment:* paper and pencil
*Difficulty:* easy to play, but hard to win; for adults and children
*Duration:* about an hour for a session with several games

## PLAYING THE GAME

Draw eight dots – the more you draw, the longer the game – from each other on a piece of paper. Taking it in turns, each player draws a line joining any two dots, or joining a dot to itself, and then draws a dot somewhere along the new line. There are three rules that dictate whether a line is permissible: first, a line cannot cross either itself or any other line; second, no line can be drawn through a dot; third, no dot can have more than three lines leaving it.

The winner is the player who draws the last admissible line.

One way of describing this game would be to say that it is like Scrabble®. It is Scrabble® without the board, the tiles, or the points system. Success depends on knowledge of words and sheer imagination, but is rarely achieved completely in the straightforward version, so it is usual to agree beforehand to vary the rules.

*Players:* two or more
*Equipment:* paper and pencil
*Difficulty:* adults and children
*Duration:* about half an hour in the simplest version

## BEGINNING TO PLAY
Each player lists the letters of the alphabet on one piece of paper, and another plain sheet of paper is used as a board.

## PLAYING THE GAME
The first player (toss a coin or roll dice to see who this will be) writes down a word on the piece of paper being used as the board, spacing the letters out carefully, and then crosses the letters that have been used off their own alphabet list. The next player continues by adding a word to the board and crossing those letters off their list – only the letters that have been added to the board can be crossed off, not those used by the first player. The sequence continues until each player has had a turn, and then the first player has another go, but this player can only use the letters that remain on their alphabet list.

The rules about whether you can use a word are the same as those for Scrabble®. For example, in the example illustrated, the first player has written "MOTHER," the second has used "TOP," using the "T" from "MOTHER," so only the "O" and "P" can be crossed off their alphabet list. The third player has taken the opportunity to cross "Z" off, by adding "ZI" to the "P;" and the first player has added an "N" to the "I" on the second go.

m o t h e r
o
z i p
n

*Diagram 21  A game of Alphabet Race*

It is not too difficult to think of better words than this on the first round, but it becomes increasingly difficult to do so as the game progresses. However, a player who is stuck can say "Pass" and miss a turn. The first player to finish off their alphabet wins, but because players start with only 26 letters, it is difficult to do so. In such cases, the person with the fewest letters left is declared the winner. As you may guess, it is much more frustrating than Scrabble® because you start with only 26 letters.

## VARIATIONS

There is endless scope for varying the rules of Alphabet Race, but it is important that any changes should be agreed in detail beforehand, in order to avoid arguments. One option is to double, or even triple the number of vowels (a, e, i, o, u) available to each player. Alternatively, you could double the whole alphabet, with the exception of letters such as "X" and "Z." The choice is yours.

Said to have been invented by British prisoners of war during World War I, this game has been a favorite for children ever since – and it is easy to play a variation set in the future.

*Players: two*
*Equipment: pencil and paper*
*Difficulty: much luck is involved, and this is more a game for children
        than adults*
*Duration: 15 minutes or so, but the loser normally wants revenge*

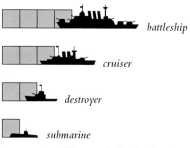

*battleship*

*cruiser*

*destroyer*

*submarine*

*Diagram 22 The vessels for Battleships*

### BEGINNING TO PLAY

Each player draws two 10x10 grids, numbering the squares from 1 to 10 down the left-hand side, and labeling them from A to J along the top. One grid is for the "home fleet" and the other is for the "enemy fleet" – this one is left blank for the moment.

Each player's fleet consists of one battleship (made up of four squares), two cruisers (three squares each), three destroyers (two squares each) and four submarines (one square each). This means each player uses up 20 of the 100 squares in the grid. Each player marks the individual ships of their home fleet on their grid, using a "b" for a battleship, a "c" for a cruiser, a "d" for a destroyer, and an "s" for a submarine. The squares that make up each ship must touch each other, and can do so either horizontally, vertically, or diagonally. However, no two ships can touch each other by even so much as a corner – see diagram 23 opposite.

A coin is tossed to see who starts. After the first game, the loser of the previous one should start any subsequent game.

### PLAYING THE GAME

Each player takes turns to try to hit the enemy fleet, being allowed three attempts on each turn. This is done by calling out the reference for the appropriate square. All direct hits must be declared by the enemy and the type of vessel given honestly.

In diagram 24, the player has called "D3" and missed and then "F6" and missed again. However, the third attempt reveals that part of one of the enemy's cruisers is at B8. This information, as well as which squares are empty, is marked on the first player's enemy fleet sheet. The second player then makes their challenges. The winner is the first player to destroy the enemy fleet.

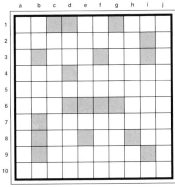

*Diagram 23  The home fleet*

### VARIATIONS
#### Starships

Great fleet actions at sea are a thing of the past, and some children may prefer playing "starships" – it is just Battleships in disguise. Substitute an intergalactic battle cruiser for the battleship; asteroid smashers for the cruisers; starwarp cruisers for the destroyers; and starfighters for the submarines. Or, more sensibly, ask the children for their advice on names.

#### Salvo

This complex version of Battleships demands more thought and analysis by the players. The game uses the same basic grids for home and enemy fleets, but differs in the ships used and the method of play. Each player has one battleship (made up of five squares), one cruiser (three squares), and two destroyers (two squares each). Each player lays out their home fleet according to the same rules as Battleships. But unlike Battleships, in which three attempts at hitting an enemy ship are allowed each turn, in Salvo seven shots are allowed – "the salvo," of which three shots are accounted for by the battleship, two by the cruiser and one by the destroyer. The opposing player notes where the shots have landed on the home fleet grid, but does not say whether a specific shot has been a hit. Instead, they may say: "one hit on a cruiser and one on a destroyer." If a ship has been hit more than once, this information must also be given.

The player on the receiving end of the first salvo then takes a turn, again being allowed seven shots. Meanwhile, the first player has to devise a strategy to develop the information that emerged after the first salvo, by aiming the next round of shots in such a way as to confirm which of the original shots were successful.

A ship is considered to be sunk when all of its squares have been hit, and each player must declare it when this happens. This has a critical impact on the game, because the number of shots in that player's next salvo are reduced by the number of shots that the sunken ship took. So if a player's battleship is sunk, the number of shots in that player's next salvo will be reduced by three, and only four shots will be available. As in battleships, the winner is the first player to sink all the ships in the enemy fleet.

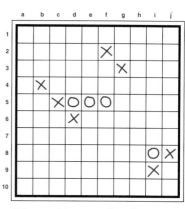

*Diagram 24 Enemy fleet sheet*

This game is said to have been invented by a Mrs. Gugg
member of the fabulously rich American family. It is rath
to play well, but making the attempt is satisfyingly amusing.

*Players:* two or more
*Equipment:* pencil and paper
*Difficulty:* can be quite hard; for adults and older children
*Duration:* 10 minutes a game

## BEGINNING TO PLAY

First, the players decide on five different categories. Any will do, such as
food, drink, bad habits, countries, politicians, objects of hatred, and so on.
This means, of course, that a considerable amount of heated debate
normally precedes the game. Then one player opens a book and picks a
five-letter word at random. Next, each player makes a grid, placing the
categories running down the left and the letters of the word that has
been chosen at the top.

## PLAYING THE GAME

If the word chosen was "TRAIN," for example, the players have to think
up words in each of the categories chosen that start with the appropriate
letter of "TRAIN."

It is usual to set a time limit, during which each player has to write
in as many words starting with the correct letter in the appropriate
category as possible. The more unusual the words are, the better: two
points are awarded for any word that nobody else has got, and only one
point for a word if it has been used by more than one person. The player
with the most points wins.

This word game relies on a familiar device known to those who do crosswords, especially cryptic ones: anagrams.

*Players:* two, or four or more
*Equipment:* pencil and paper
*Difficulty:* can be complex; for adults and older children
*Duration:* allow half an hour per game, plus half an hour to prepare for it

## THE TWO-PLAYER VERSION

The players toss a coin to decide who will draw up a list of categories: they can be anything – movie stars, parts of the body, mammals, fish, and so on. There can be as many categories as you like, although five is usually the maximum for a 30-minute game. Each player then devises an agreed number of anagrams (between two and five) for each category. Again, there is a time limit for doing this, generally 30 minutes. When the lists are ready, each player spells out each anagram in a category and the opposing player writes each one down. The two players have to solve the anagrams they have been given in an agreed time, such as seven minutes per category. The player who solves the most anagrams in the time given, over all the categories, wins; the prize is to compile the next round's list of categories.

---

*MOVIES*
Dogger Flin — Goldfinger
Hubren — Ben Hur
Primo Snappy — Mary Poppins

*POP*
Dan O Man — Madonna
Rum Chap Roul — Procul
Harum
Teeth Bales — The Beatles

*BIRDS*
Pigame — Magpie
Niff Up — Puffin
But Lite — Blue Jay

*FIVE-LETTER WORDS*
Retbe — Beret
Bmthu — Thumb
Steap — Paste

---

*Diagram 25 A completed Anagrams sheet*

This is not the type of crossword that you find in your morning newspaper, but it holds the attention equally well and is something of a challenge to play well.

*Players:* two, or can be played in teams
*Equipment:* pencil and paper
*Difficulty:* surprisingly demanding; for adults and older children
*Duration:* 10 minutes for the two-player version

## FOR TWO PLAYERS

Each player draws a grid of squares, 5x5, on a sheet of paper. Then, taking turns, each player calls out a letter of the alphabet. Both players enter the letter into a square on their grid, in an attempt to form words that may read either across or down. Rules for acceptable words can be agreed beforehand, but generally words must contain at least two letters and cannot be either abbreviations or proper nouns. Once in place on the grid, a letter cannot be moved. When the grids are full, the game is over and scoring begins. Each player receives one point for each word formed, reading either horizontally or vertically; however, the end of one word must be separated by one letter from the beginning of another in order for both words to count. A bonus point is awarded if a word fills an entire row or column. The horizontal and vertical totals are added up, and the player with the most points wins.

## THE TEAM VERSION

As many as five people can play using precisely the same rules as for the two-player version of Crossword. However, the greater the number of people who are playing, the more the game depends on good fortune rather than skill, because each player has to rely more on the letters that are chosen by the others. One way out of this dilemma is to increase the size of the grid used, perhaps to 7x7.

This is a group game that has been played for many generations. It has always been popular with children, but can be fun for adults, too.

*Players: two or more*
*Equipment: pencil and paper*
*Difficulty: easy in principle, but imagination is required for success; for both*
         *adults and children*
*Duration: about 20 minutes, but one game is rarely enough.*

## PLAYING THE GAME
This game normally follows a set format. Variations exist, but this is probably the most common one.

1. One or two adjectives
2. [Name of a male character] met
3. One or two adjectives
4. [Female character] at
5. Where they met
6. He … [what he did]
7. She … [what she did]
8. He said …
9. She said …
10. And the consequence was …
11. And the world said …

The players arrange themselves in a circle. Each player takes a pencil and paper and writes down one or two adjectives to describe a male person, then folds the paper over so that the writing is hidden and passes the paper to the player on their right. This player writes the name of a male person (preferably a teasable friend or known enemy), folds the paper over to hide what was written, and passes the paper to the person on their right again. Then another one or two adjectives to describe a female person are written, followed by the name of the female character. This continues until the final phrase "and the world said ...". Then everyone in turn unfolds the paper they are holding and reads the story out.

The game sounds complicated, but in fact it is simplicity itself. The point is to produce wonderfully inconsequential and incongruous stories, each of which has the appearance of being sensible, that produce lots of laughter but no winners. A typical end result could be as silly as this:

> "The daring but dastardly Mickey Mouse met the ugly Marilyn Monroe on a bike. He gave her a pound of fish; she bashed him over the head with a potato; he said, 'I will never forget this;' she said, 'You always knew how to get around me.' The consequence was a bad thunderstorm; and the world said, 'We always knew it would end in tears.'"

**VARIATION**
Children particularly enjoy a variation of this game called Picture Consequences. The idea is much the same as ordinary Consequences, but in this version of the game you use drawings to create a person – or, more likely, a monster. First, each player draws a head on a sheet of paper. This is then folded over and passed to the next player on the right, who draws a neck. This is then folded over and passed to the right once more, for a torso to be drawn; then legs and, lastly, feet. As you can imagine, some pretty peculiar creatures appear as a result.

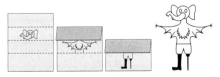

*Diagram 26 A game of Picture Consequences*

# THE POETRY GAME

A delightfully silly game that is really a rhyming and scanning version of Consequences. It is great fun to play and also has the virtue of irritating the pretentious and those who consider themselves poetry experts.

*Players: three to 10*
*Equipment: pencil and paper*
*Difficulty: moderate; adults enjoy it more than children*
*Duration: no more than 10 minutes, but the game can become addictive*

## PLAYING THE GAME

Do not be put off by this game's title: you do not need to have any knowledge of poetry, nor to excel at its composition. Each player is given a pencil and paper. The first player writes two lines of verse, which can either be something remembered or made up – the two lines should have rhythm, but they do not have to rhyme. The paper is then folded to hide the first line and passed to the next player, who writes the third and fourth line, without having looked at the first one; the third line should rhyme with the second line, and, preferably, have the same rhythm. The game continues, with each player being given the last line written and adding two more, until a preset length is reached. Eight lines is usually enough, though more heroic meters can be attempted if you wish. Each poem is then read out loud (with luck) much hilarity and applause.

## AN EXAMPLE

This is a rather weak attempt, but it illustrates the game's potential.

**First player:** I know that I shall meet my fate, Somewhere among the clouds above;

**Second player:** Where there flew a turtle dove, That nowhere could find a place to rest;

**Third player:** She thought she was of all least blest, And laid her down upon a sod;

**Fourth player:** A man came by who bore a rod, With which he set about her frame.

The idea behind this game is eminently simple, and you would think that it was equally simple to play. Don't be fooled, though, because it is really annoyingly difficult.

*Players:* two or more
*Equipment:* pencil and paper
*Difficulty:* surprisingly difficult; for adults and older children
*Duration:* two minutes per game

### PLAYING THE GAME

Short stories can be played by as few as two people, but is more fun with three or more. All the players have to write down the longest sentence they can think of, using words of only three letters or less. The sentence must make sense. The game is as simple and as difficult as that, but the catch is that you only have two minutes. For example:

> "I sat on a bed and I saw a cat but it did not see me, so I got off
> the bed and ran up to it and got a dog and an emu and we all ran
> off in a cab."

If a player seems to be suspiciously good at this game, it may well be that they have played it before and memorized the best answer. If this is the case, you might want to make the game more difficult by reducing the time limit, or specifying that each word must be exactly three letters long – or do both.

Also known as Housey-Housey, this game is the forerunner of Bingo.
No skill is required, but it demands a great deal of preparation.
Children often enjoy it immensely.

*Players: from four to 200*
*Equipment: Lotto cards and numbered discs*
*Difficulty: extremely easy; for people*
*of all ages*
*Duration: up to 20 minutes, depending*
*on the caller*

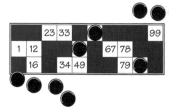

*Diagram 27 A Lotto card*

### BEGINNING TO PLAY

Depending on the numbers playing, there will be a great deal of
preparation unless you buy the numbered discs and individual cards from
a games store. Each player is given one of the cards (see diagram 27), and
the numbers on each card are unique.

If you are going to make the cards yourself, you must follow certain
conventions. Each card is nine rows across and three rows deep. Each
horizontal row contains four blanks and five numbers, so each card
carries 15 numbers in all. The first vertical row is only allowed to contain
numbers between 1 and 10; the second vertical row carries numbers
between 11 and 20; the third one runs from 21 and 30; and so on, with
the last row going from 81 to 90. Then you must make 90 discs, each
carrying a different number between 1 and 90.

### PLAYING THE GAME

A card is issued to each of the players and the discs are placed in a bag,
which is handed to the person who has been designated caller. The caller
takes one disc at a time out of the bag, and announces it to the players.
Any player who has the number can mark it off their card. The first
player to mark all the numbers off their card calls out "Lotto" and wins.

Car games have saved many children from perishing at the hands of their parents, so good ones are very welcome. License plates is completely mindless, but also distracting – at least for a while.

*Players:* two or more
*Equipment:* pencils and paper
*Difficulty:* ideal for children
*Duration:* depends on how busy the road is, but generally 10 minutes a game

*Diagram 28 A game of License Plates*

## PLAYING THE GAME

One of the grown-ups specifies a number of letters and then each player writes down a word that is made up of that number of letters. Then the players have to keep an eagle eye on the road, checking the license plates of every vehicle they see. Whenever one of the letters in their word is seen, that letter is crossed off, and the first player to cross off all the letters is the winner.

## VARIATION

When the children grow tired of this game, you can reclaim your sanity for a while by suggesting a variation. Persuade them to write the whole alphabet down, and get them to cross off each letter as they see it. The winner is the player who crosses off the whole of the alphabet first. And when the pleasure of this variation has been exhausted, try another one: ask them to write down the numbers from 0 to 100, and cross them off as they see them. The first player to cross off all the numbers is the winner.

Many people find this game compulsive, and that's possibly because the most improbable combinations of objects have legs.

*Players:* three to 12
*Equipment:* pencils and paper
*Difficulty:* *difficult to play well, though enjoyed by both adults and children; at its best as an after-dinner game for grown-ups*
*Duration:* *five minutes for a round, but many more are usually requested*

## BEGINNING TO PLAY
Each player is given paper and a pencil, and then one person is elected to pick a letter at random. Next, note the time, because players have just two minutes to write down everything they can think of, starting with the chosen letter, that has legs (or can have them).

## PLAYING THE GAME
Legs might seem to be the simplest game ever invented. Play it once, though, and you will find that it is really quite difficult. In theory, the list can be considerably longer than the one shown in diagram 29. But it is surprising how quickly your mind goes blank, especially when you can see the other players scribbling away feverishly.

When the two minutes are up, everyone stops and one person starts off by reading out their list. Anyone who has the same word on their list crosses it off. The next player then reads out their list, and the process is repeated. When all the lists have been read out, everyone declares how many words are left on their list, and the winner is the person with the most words remaining.

## HINTS AND TIPS
The secret of success is to avoid the obvious and try to think of the more unusual things that have legs, so that you can keep your points. For

example, if "C" was the letter chosen, the majority of players would immediately think of "CAT," but most likely such a commonplace word would benefit nobody. However, you might well keep your points if you came up with "COMMODE," or "CANON," or even "CARABINEER" (a soldier equipped with a carbine).

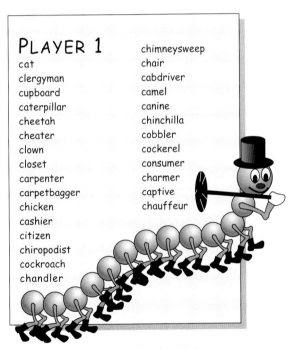

# PLAYER 1

| | |
|---|---|
| cat | chimneysweep |
| clergyman | chair |
| cupboard | cabdriver |
| caterpillar | camel |
| cheetah | canine |
| cheater | chinchilla |
| clown | cobbler |
| closet | cockerel |
| carpenter | consumer |
| carpetbagger | charmer |
| chicken | captive |
| cashier | chauffeur |
| citizen | |
| chiropodist | |
| cockroach | |
| chandler | |

*Diagram 29  A sample list of words with legs*

This is a slightly simpler game than Legs, but it can be just as enjoyable. If anything, this old favorite relies more heavily on general knowledge.

*Players: three or more*
*Equipment: pencils and paper*
*Difficulty: can be played successfully by a mixed group of adults and children,*
*but it is perhaps more successful when played by adults only*
*Duration: 15 minutes*

### PLAYING THE GAME

One person is elected (or take it in turns, if you intend to play more than one round) to select a list of categories. Eight is about the right number, but they should be as varied as possible and as difficult as you wish to make them. Categories might include: five-letter words, composers, novelists, breeds of dog, poets, mountain ranges, trees, dances, countries, actors, film stars, parts of the body, root vegetables, and so on.

A letter of the alphabet is chosen at random (open a book and ask a player to point at a letter without looking at it) and players have 10 minutes in which to write down as many words as possible in each category, starting with the chosen letter. When the time is up, each player's list is read out and points are allotted. Scoring is simple: one point is awarded for any valid entry that is also on someone else's list; and two points are given for a valid entry that no-one else has got. Disputed words must be put to the majority vote. You can agree your own rules about eligibility beforehand, but generally only surnames count, rather than first names or titles. Foreign names – of cities, and so on – only count in their English form.

### VARIATIONS

Children may find this game rather difficult, but it can be made easier by allowing any letter of the alphabet to be used when making entries in the various categories. The categories can be made more simple, too: animals, birds, and pop stars, perhaps.

A slightly more difficult version than this can be played if you write the letters of the alphabet down the left-hand side of a sheet of paper and choose a single category. Then each player must try to write down, within a set length of time, a word within the category starting with each letter of the alphabet. You can agree local rules to cope with problem letters, such as "X" and "Z." A player who achieves a "full house" of all 26 letters before the time is up wins automatically; otherwise, the scoring system is the same as for the straightforward version of the game.

| Categories | D | B |
|---|---|---|
| five-letter nouns | dunce, duvet, diver | bidet, bench, belfry |
| cities | Dover, Denver, Detroit | |
| breeds of dog | Doberman, | |
| | dachshund | |
| novelists | Dickens, Dostoyevsky | |
| composers | Debussy | |
| countries | Denmark | |
| poets | Donne | |
| parts of the body | duodenum, diaphragm, | |
| | disc | |

*Diagram 30  A sample Categories list*

One of the best things about quizzes is that it is just as much fun compiling them as playing them. You can either play quiz games that come ready-made, or make up your own.

*Players: three or more*
*Equipment: paper and pencil*
*Difficulty: as easy or as hard as you like; can be made suitable for any age group*
*Duration: at least an hour to prepare and an hour to play*

## PLAYING THE GAME

There are no hard-and-fast rules about how to play quiz games, so these are just suggestions about how to go about holding a quiz. With only a few players involved, it is best to ask the questions out loud, and allow an agreed time within which each player has to write down the answer. At the end of the quiz, the answers are checked and a point is awarded for each correct one. If four or more players are taking part, it is better to divide them into teams, and allow team members to confer (quietly) about their answers.

Obviously, though, a quizmaster is needed to set the questions, and it is best if they have a few days warning so that there is sufficient time to prepare properly. The first thing to do is to devise a theme.

The most important consideration when selecting a theme is to make sure that it is appropriate for the players, so that it is neither too easy nor too hard, and that no one person will be able to answer the majority of questions, while the others are floundering. For example, it would be pointless setting a quiz on opera when one player is an opera buff and the others dislike opera. A way round the problem is to set a general knowledge quiz, taking questions from a wide range of subjects. That way everyone is sure to know at least some of the answers and it is unlikely that one person will know them all.

In this simple word game it doesn't matter if the younger players drop out as it proceeds, because they enjoy seeing what more can be done.

*Players:* two or more
*Equipment:* pencils and paper
*Difficulty:* harder than you might think at the later stages, but for all ages
*Duration:* as long as you like, but an hour is usually enough

### PLAYING THE GAME

Each player is given a piece of paper and a pencil, and then a letter is chosen at random. Players are given a set amount of time – five to 10 minutes is about right – to build as long a "stairway" as possible, in which each word begins with the chosen letter and each subsequent word is one letter longer than the word that precedes it. The winner is the player with the longest list when the allotted time is up; any spelling mistakes result in disqualification.

PLAYER 1

a
at
ate
aura
askew
aspire
assault
assassin
astrology
attractive

*Diagram 31 A sample game of Stairway*

# —WORD & SPOKEN GAMES—

Word games are a challenge to the imagination, and as well as being fun, they increase a player's general knowledge and vocabulary, making them a useful educational tool at whatever level they are played.

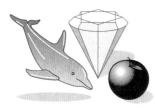

They can be played by one person alone, but are most fun when played with large gatherings of people at parties, or in the classroom. Some games, such as I Spy, are simple enough for young children to enjoy. Others are extremely complex and suitable for adults only – playing a game of Ghosts demands intellectual dexterity, vocabulary skills and the ability to bluff.

There are two basic types of word game. One type consists of words of similar meanings and sounds, word association and puns, and the rearrangement and substitution of letters. The other type usually involves guessing and listing objects and words, often in a particular order. Spoken games are usually of the second type.

Question-and-answer games are among the most commonly played spoken games. The original game of Twenty Questions dates back to the eighteenth century, and is described in Charles Dickens's *A Christmas Carol*, where it is called "Yes or No."

The alphabet provides a natural basis for many types of word game. One of the oldest is I Love My Love, which is mentioned in Samuel Pepys's diary for 4 March 1669. Taking it in turns, each player completes the sentence "I love my love because …" through the alphabet from A to Z.

Word games and word-association techniques are sometimes used by psychologists and educationalists in intelligence and psychological testing. To be really good at word games, you need to be quick-thinking, as well as literate. Even the most erudite of individuals may find themselves stuck for words, which of course is part of the fun.

This game relies not on intelligence, but on a good memory. All too often it is humiliating for adults, because children love it and are usually very good at it.

*Players: two players or more*
*Equipment: none*
*Difficulty: ideal for mixed groups including*
            *children*
*Duration: allow 10 minutes a round*

## PLAYING THE GAME

The game is very simple: the first player starts the round with, "I packed my bag;"

*Diagram 32 I Packed My Bag*

then the next player says, "I packed my bag and put in ...," and adds an item. So it goes on, with each player having to remember what has gone before, in order, as the list gets longer and longer, before packing his or her contribution in the bag. After a few players, it might run something like this:

> "I packed my bag, and put in an apple, two T-shirts, 17 coins, a pair of dumb-bells, a spool of thread, my toothbrush, an imitation leopard-skin coat, a clock, two packs of cards, and a tumble drier."

Whether two or 20 people are playing it is equally difficult to remember the list, but if anyone omits an item, or places it in the incorrect order, that person is out of the round.

## VARIATION

If you are feeling tired – or kind – you can make a rule that items should be in alphabetical order, so:

> "I packed my bag and put in four apples."

Then:

"I packed my bag and put in four apples and a button."

And then:

"I packed my bag and put in four apples and a button and a cat."

And on you go, until only one person is still packing the bag, as each of the other players has dropped out.

## THE DICTIONARY GAME

The object of this game is to make up your own false definitions of obscure words and the opposing team has to figure out which is the correct definition.

*Players: four people as a minimum, but best with six*
*Equipment: a good dictionary, pencils and paper*
*Difficult: as difficult as the imagination of the players can make it*
*Duration: with preparation time, each round takes about half an hour*

### PLAYING THE GAME

The players form two teams, and the members of each team pick an obscure word from the dictionary – it is essential that you use a good dictionary, or you will not find words that are sufficiently obscure. One member of each team writes down the real definition of the word, while the others invent bogus, but convincing, definitions of it. The members of the first team then present their definitions to the other team, whose members have to determine which definition is the correct one; then the second team takes its turn. The game continues for as long as the players wish, with a point being awarded for each successful identification of the true definition and also for each successful bluff.

## HINTS AND TIPS

The key to success lies in the degree of conviction with which both true and false definitions are presented, and in the level of detail given. Specialist knowledge of any kind comes in extremely useful: someone who knows a lot about architecture might convincingly define "stum," say, as a special type of joist used in very large rooms, such as ballrooms and conference rooms. In fact, stum is unfermented grape juice, which is added to fermented wine as a preservative. Here is how the word "placket" might be presented:

*Player one: "A 'placket' was an essential tool of a printing compositor's trade in the days before lithography – when each metal-cast character was placed individually to form words, sentences, paragraphs and, eventually, pages. The assembled characters were held in place by blocks of wood known as 'furniture,' which were fixed as tightly round the blocks of type as possible by a system of screws and ratchets. But before the furniture was tightened, it was banged into place with a small mahogany mallet. So the compositors' room would ring to the sound of 'plack, plack, plack' noises as the final edition was put to bed, giving the mallet its name: a 'placket'. And, to this day, most retired compositors cannot stand watching a croquet game."*

*Player two: "Our great-great-grandmothers found going shopping a rather trying business. After all, in their day women didn't carry purses – or even briefcases – and, until the middle years of the twentieth century, dresses did not have pockets. If you were wealthy, your servants carried everything for you.*

*But where could you put your tram ticket or your loose change – with delicacy, that is – if you were not? As female emancipation took hold, women decided that they would not put up with this any longer, and started instructing their dressmakers to fit their skirts with pockets. And for some reason – we know not what – these were known as 'plackets.' Perhaps a Mrs. Placket started the trend. (In fact, to be technical, the hole in the skirt that gives access to the pocket is called a 'placket-hole.')."*

*Player three: "In the days when knights wore armor and jousted with each other to gain honor for the fair ladies whose favors they wore, accidents were not unknown. All too often, a lance – given momentum by the power of a charging destrier and about a hundredweight of metal – would pierce the breastplate of an opponent, with fatal results. Armor was expensive, though, and thrift was essential in those uncertain times. So, taking the pragmatic view, the breastplate would be cleansed of any unpleasant traces of its previous occupant and repaired, so that it could be passed on, in due course, to the poor man's son and heir. But first the hole made by the lance had to be repaired. The blacksmith-armorer would be consulted, and, having heated up the forge with much bellowing, the breastplate would be patched, hammered and burnished until it was as good as new. And the patch was called a 'placket'."*

The correct definition of a "placket" is a pocket in a woman's skirt. The slit in the skirt that gives access to the pocket is indeed known as a "placket-hole." Much of the rest of the definition, however, cannot be relied upon.

*Diagram 33 Defining objects for the Dictionary Game*

This word game will test even the most literate of players. The rules are quite complicated, which makes performing a series of reasonably easy tasks a fiendishly tricky exercise.

*Players:* best with six or more
*Equipment:* paper and pencil, and a dictionary to settle arguments
*Difficulty:* for adults, rather than children
*Duration:* about 30 minutes a round, with experienced players

## PLAYING THE GAME
The players sit in a circle and the one chosen to play first says a letter – any one that comes to mind. Then the next player, going clockwise, thinks of a word that starts with that letter, and adds another letter to the first one; this must be the next letter with which the word is spelled. (It is sensible to delegate one player to keep a record of the letters as they are added.) Then the third player thinks of a word – almost certainly it will not be the same word that the previous player had in mind – and adds a third letter, and so on, around the circle. So far so good, but the object of Ghosts – and this is where the trickery comes in – is to avoid being the player who completes an English word of more than three letters.

## THE SCORING SYSTEM
Ghosts takes its name from the rule that each player has only three lives – and lives can easily be lost. Any player whose turn it is may challenge the previous player to give the word that he or she was thinking of. If the player who is challenged fails to come up with a word that the other players accept as being valid – a dictionary can be used to check, if necessary – that player loses a life. But if he or she does provide an acceptable word, the challenger loses a life. Any player who completes a word also loses a life, but in this case a new round is started, with a different first letter.

After the loss of the first life, a player becomes a third of a ghost; a second loss makes the player two-thirds a ghost; a third and final loss turns the player into a full ghost. Once you have become a full ghost you are not allowed to join in the game, but you can have great fun haunting the living players noisily in an attempt to get one of them to talk to you. If you succeed, the tricked player joins you in the Other World immediately. Full ghosts can chatter away to each other as much – and as irritatingly – as they like. When all the other players have "passed on," the lone survivor is the winner.

## HINTS AND TIPS

As with most good games, bluffing plays a large part in Ghosts. A player may have no idea of the word that the letters are building towards, but can still confidently call a letter. Remember that only the player who is next in turn can issue a challenge. Some house rules may be needed to control the full ghosts' behavior: are they allowed to pinch and throw things, for example? Are they allowed to make a lot of noise?

## VARIATION

One variation on the basic version of Ghosts is Superghost, also called Fore-and-Aft. In this, letters can be added at the beginning of the words as well as at the end. For example, if the letters so far have spelt F, U, N, C, T, I, O, a player is not forced to finish the word with the letter "N," but can add an "S" to the beginning, thinking of "DYSFUNCTIONAL."

*Diagram 34 Playing Ghosts*

Also known as "Animal, Vegetable, Mineral," this game is an old favorite with both adults and children. Educational and enjoyable, it is best played by those who have a fair amount of general knowledge.

*Players:* four or more
*Equipment:* none
*Difficulty:* most suitable for groups with
similar levels of general knowledge
*Duration:* five to 10 minutes a round, but a
session usually lasts an hour

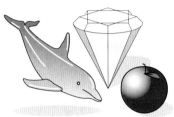

*Diagram 35 Suggestions for Twenty Questions*

## PLAYING THE GAME

This is the classic oral guessing game. One player thinks of an object or a concept and tells the others whether it is "animal," "vegetable," "mineral," "abstract," or "a mixture." It is important that every player fully understands what these classifications mean. For example:

**animal** – includes animal products, such as butter, wool, leather and so on, as well as people and animals;

**vegetable** – includes anything organic but not animal, such as paper, olive oil, and pesto sauce;

**mineral** – means only something that has never been alive, such as paint or the moon;

**abstract** – indicates something non-material, such as the landscape, wickedness, or humor (it is best not to use this category if children are playing);

**a mixture** – means that the word includes elements of more than one of the above; in such cases it is usual to say what the primary quality is.

The players are allowed 20 questions, including direct challenges, to find out what the word is – though an incorrect challenge means that the player who made it is out of the round. If they all fail, the person who chose the word wins. Any player who guesses correctly can choose the next word and be questioned in their turn. If an answer can be shown afterwards to have been incorrect, the player is disqualified.

## AN EXAMPLE

Player one has thought of a pair of leather shoes, and starts the round by saying: "My object is a mixture. It is mainly animal, but there might be some vegetable and mineral" (the player has glues and dyes in mind).

Then the questions start:

**Question one:** "Is it alive?"
**Player one:** "No."
**Question two:** "Can you eat it?"
**Player one:** "No."
**Question three:** "Would you show it to your mother?"
**Player one:** "Yes."
**Question four:** "Can you wear it?"
**Player one:** "Yes."
**Question five:** "Do you wear it on your wrist?"
**Player one:** "No."

And so on.

## VARIATION

You can play the other way round, as a change. In this variation, one player leaves the room and those that remain choose the word. When the player returns, he or she has 20 questions in which to guess the answer. This version can be played as a knockout competition, with each player continuing in the game until they have failed to guess correctly, until the only one left is the winner.

The origins of this familiar game are lost in the mists of time, but it is always a firm favorite. It can be played by young children who have comparatively few words in their vocabulary, but take great delight in using them.

*Players:* two or more
*Equipment:* none
*Difficulty:* only likely to appeal to children
*Duration:* can go on for ever, but patience generally limits the game to
    half an hour

### PLAYING THE GAME

All children love this game, and most adults, playing with children, hate it after a couple of minutes. One player selects an object in the room or, more often, from the car window, and says: "I spy with my little eye something beginning with … C." Nearly always the answer is "Car." The first person to identify the "spied" object has their turn.

### VARIATION

It is possible to play a more interesting version in which the players can ask a number of "yes" or "no" questions about the object, such as: Is it gray? Is it bigger than me? Could I eat it? It may be advisable to limit this game to 10 questions each if you play in a car.

*Diagram 36 I spy …*

This game was known to game players before World War II as "The Box," perhaps because it can feel as if you are in the witness box when you play it. It is enormously versatile and great fun. Nobody knows where the name "Botticelli" came from.

*Players: three or more*
*Equipment: none*
*Difficulty: hard without good general knowledge; for adults*
*Duration: 20 minutes to two hours*

## PLAYING THE GAME

Botticelli can be played anywhere – at home, in a train, or on a long car journey. One person announces the initial of the surname of a famous character, who may be fictional or real, dead or alive. The other players then think of famous people whose surname begins with the same initial letter and, taking it in turns, ask indirect questions about them. The player being questioned has to come up with the name of someone other than the person whose identity he or she has assumed who fits the criteria set by the question. If he or she fails to do so, the player who asked the question can ask a further question, but this time it can be direct and must be answered either "yes" or "no." However, the "player in the box" can disallow a direct question by challenging the player who asked the indirect question to supply an answer if he or she has failed to do so.

Direct questions must be answered truthfully, but indirect questions need not be answered when they hit on the correct character. If, for example, you are Botticelli, you can legitimately answer the question: "Did you paint Birth of Venus?," with "I am not Botticelli." However, the same indirect question can be asked up to three times during a game.

The player who eventually guesses the answer correctly is the winner, and has the privilege of choosing the next mystery person. However, if nobody guessed correctly within 15 minutes, the player who set the

puzzle announces the answer and is allowed to choose another character.
Here is an example of how part of a game might go:

**Player one**: "My name begins with B."
**Player two:** "Did you write *The Thirty-Nine Steps*?"
**Player one** "I am not John Buchan."
**Player two:** "Are you a bivalve sailor?"
**Player one** "Um, um … I don't know."
**Player two:** "Barnacle Bill – so here is my direct question. Are you alive?"
**Player one** "No."
**Player three:** "Are you a composer?"
**Player one** "I am not Beethoven."
**Player four:** "Are you a king of the East who followed a star?"
**Player one** "Er … sorry."
**Player four:** "Balthazar. Are you a painter?"
**Player one** "Yes."

And so on.

## HINTS AND TIPS

To stand any chance of identifying a character, it is vital to get yourself in
a position to ask direct questions – but it is also important that you phrase
your question in such a way that the answer can either be "yes" or "no,"
otherwise the question need not be answered. It is surprisingly easy to
make a mess of this – even people who have played the game for years
sometimes make the dreadful mistake of asking: "Are you alive or dead?"

The art of indirect questioning lies in being either specific or oblique.
There is little point in saying, "Are you a composer?", because there are a
number of composers whose names begin with "B," and you will probably
not get to a direct question (remember that you are allowed to ask the
same question three times). It is best to attach a century, nationality, or
other specific detail to your indirect question in order to pin a player down.

This is a domestic – and original – version of the kind of game made famous by radio and television adaptations. As so often with games that have been popularized, the domestic version has a raw and pure quality generally lost with commercialization.

*Players: **six** or more*
*Equipment: a dictionary*
*Difficulty: as hard as the players wish to make it; for groups with similar levels of knowledge*
*Duration: 20 minutes a round*

## PLAYING THE GAME

In the basic version of this game, the players are divided into two teams and there is a question-master. The question-master reads out a word (making the selection with the help of a dictionary if the game is to be a hard one) and the first player in the first team has to spell it. If this is done successfully, the team is awarded a point; if they are unsuccessful, the question is offered to the first player in the second team, who has the chance to score a bonus point. The question-master then asks the second team's first player to spell a different word. When all the players in each team have had their chance, the team with the most points wins.

## VARIATIONS

Another way of playing is to make it an individual game, with the players accumulating points for themselves. The question-master reads a word to the first player; if they get the answer right, another word is given – the process continuing until a mistake is made, at which point the questions move on to the next player. The player who spells the most words correctly wins.

If you are very good at spelling and find the game too simple, try backwards spelling. This is played in exactly the same way as the ndividual version described above, but the catch is that the players have to spell the words backwards.

Another variation is to ask two teams, with the same number of players each, to stand in a line opposite each other. The question-master then calls out a word to each player in turn, alternating between the teams. Each time a player spells out the word the opposite number on the opposing teams must shout "Right" or "Wrong." Any player who shouts "Wrong" to a word that has, in fact, been spelled correctly has to leave the game; the same thing happens if the shout is "Right" to a word that has been spelled incorrectly. The team with the last player still in the game wins.

## TEAM ONE

necessary ✔

enough ✔

encyclopedia ✔

anenome ✗

laboratory ✔

constabulary ✔

conceive ✔

association ✔

consequences ✔

Mississippi ✔

9/10

Diagram 37 Spelling Round scoresheet

# GAMES OF DEXTERITY

In this section we look at games which, as well as natural ability, require a level of dexterity that demands that players make the best use of basic equipment and uncomplicated rules.

 A perfect example of a game which has endured through the centuries due to its simplicity is Jacks. Played in ancient times, the game's origins lie in many different cultures and this is reflected in the different nationalities that still play the game today. Pick-up-sticks is another old game, once known as Spillikins – the idea behind it could not be simpler, involving, as the name suggests, a set of sticks with different values. This simplicity is also mirrored in a game that so many children know and love – Tiddlywinks. It is argued that the game's origins are Chinese, but it achieved worldwide popularity in the nineteenth century.

Most will recognize the colored balls and green baize of snooker and pool, but there is a much older version of these two popular sports – Carom Billiards, a game much played in the gentlemans' clubs of Georgian and Victorian England, and one which still attracts large number of supporters around the world. Mary Queen of Scots is rumored to have possessed a billiards table and been an enthusiast.

Another pastime familiar from the bar-room is Darts, a game with a fascinating martial history. Originally derived from the medieval English skill at archery, this game of high-precision throwing was once the preserve of the English public house, but has evolved to such an extent that its professional players compete for staggering prize money.

One of the fastest, most eyecatching tests of hand-eye coordination, Ping-Pong has risen to be one of the most popular sports in the world. Also known as Table Tennis, this compact version of Lawn Tennis requires high levels of skill (and energy!) when played by top athletes, yet is versatile enough to be enjoyed by the most leisurely of participants.

This game was known in ancient Greece and Rome, and was certainly played for centuries before that. Part of its appeal lies in the contrast between its inherent simplicity and the level of skill needed for success.

## BRIEF HISTORY

Jacks is also known as Jackstones, Chuckstones, Dibs, Dabs, Fivestones, or Knucklebones. The last name gives a clue to its origins – the game was once played with the small bones from the knees of sheep. The game has evolved over many centuries, with local traditions developing and taking root: for example, a Japanese version of the game is now played in North America, under the name of Otadama, or Japanese Jacks. The two basic games are Fivestones (the traditional version) and Jacks, which is played with a rubber ball. In both games players take turns to attempt throws that become increasingly complex – the sequence of throws being agreed between the players in advance. If a player fails to make a throw, or attempts a throw that is out of the agreed sequence, their turn is over. The winner is the player who achieves the longest and most complex series of throws correctly.

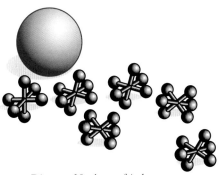

*Diagram 38  A set of jacks*

This is the original version of Jacks, and was known as Tali in classical times. Interestingly, it is still called Tally in some areas in the North of England.

*Players:* two or more, or on your own for practice
*Equipment:* five small stones
*Difficulty:* success only comes with much practice
*Duration:* as long as the players wish

## THE BASIC GAME

Place the five stones in the palm of your hand, toss them in the air and catch them on the back of your hand. Then use the back of your hand to toss the stones in the air, and catch them all in your palm. Also known as the "jockey," this is the basic throw – and it is much harder than it might seem.

## ONE'ERS

If you fail to catch any stones, your turn ends, but if you catch one or more, you can play "one'ers." In this, the stones that have been caught are transferred to your other hand and one stone is retained in your throwing hand. This is then thrown into the air, and you have the chance to retrieve one of the stones that was dropped previously before catching the stone that you threw in the same hand with which you threw it.

If you fail to do this, your turn is over; if you succeed, you can attempt to pick up any other stones that you dropped previously, one by one, in the same way.

One'ers also usually follows a successful basic throw in the sequence of agreed throws for experienced players, when all the stones have been caught. In this case, four stones are dropped to the ground deliberately, and the remaining stone thrown in the air.

## TWO'ERS, THREE'ERS AND FOUR'ERS

Having played one'ers successfully, the next step is generally to play two'ers – though the players can agree any sequence of throws that they like before the game. In two'ers, four stones are dropped to the ground and one stone is thrown into the air. You then have to pick two stones up from the ground with your throwing hand before you catch the stone that has been thrown in the same throwing hand. As you would expect, two'ers is followed by three'ers, in which three stones have to be picked up, and then one stone. Four'ers demands that you pick up all the stones on the ground at the same time.

## VARIATIONS

Experienced players move on from the basic game to challenge each other to attempt complex variations, though the basic game is normally played first, almost as a warm-up. There are endless numbers of these variations, and these are just a few examples.

### Magic

This is played in the same way as one'ers, but only one stone is dropped to the ground and four stones are thrown up – all must be caught after the dropped stone has been retrieved.

### Magic Flycatchers

This is the same as Magic, except that the stones that are thrown up must be snatched out of the air from above.

### Pecks, Bushels, and Claws

The first throw is the same as for the basic game, and if all five stones are caught on the back of the hand and then the palm the player can go straight on to Bushels. If none is caught, the player is out, as is also the case in Bushels and Claws. However, if any stones fall to the ground, one of the stones that was caught must be held between the first finger and thumb of the throwing hand, while any others are held in the same hand. Then the stone between the finger and thumb is thrown into the air, and one stone must be picked from the ground by the throwing hand before it is caught again. The sequence is repeated until all the stones have been picked up.

Next comes Bushels. Again, the first maneuver is the basic throw, and if all the stones are caught on first the back of the hand and then the palm, the player can go straight on to Claws. If not, all the stones that have been caught must be thrown into the air, a stone picked up from the ground and the thrown stones caught, all in the same hand. The sequence is repeated until all dropped stones have been picked up.

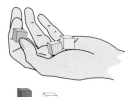

Diagram 39 *A catch in Pecks*

Then comes Claws. The basic throw starts the game, and if successful the player can go straight on to another designated throw, such as "one under the arch." If one or more stones are caught on the back of the hand, in the first part of the basic throw, the player must leave them in position and pick up the fallen stones. This time, however, the stones must be picked up individually, held between each pair of fingers on the throwing hand – without disturbing the stones on the back of the hand. Once picked up, the stones on the back of the hand must be thrown up and caught in the palm, and the stones between the fingers maneuvered into the palm.

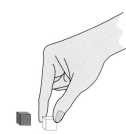

Diagram 40 *Holding the stone for Pecks*

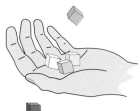

Diagram 41 *Catching the stones in Pecks*

This test of manual dexterity and guile amuses children for hours. The modern store-bought version is derived from the ancient game of Spillikins, in which elaborately carved strips of wood are hooked from a pile with a special tool.

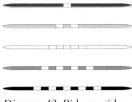

*Diagram 42 Pick-up-sticks*

## THE STICKS

Pick-up-sticks sets can be bought at most toy stores, though they may be masquerading under another name, such as Jackstraws or Jerkstraws. Generally a set consists of about 50 sticks, each about 6in. (15cm) long, made from either wood, metal, or plastic. Colored rings mark the value of each stick, which is usually from one to five.

## PLAYING THE GAME

One player drops all the sticks on to the floor. Taking it in turns, players try to extract a stick from the pile without disturbing any other stick — if another stick moves, the turn is over. Once a particular stick has been touched, no other stick may be touched until the original stick has been taken out of the pile; if successful, a player can then attempt to move another one.

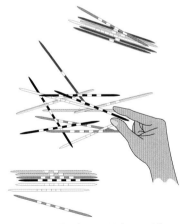

At the end of the game, the points value of each player's sticks is counted, and the player with the highest score is the winner.

*Diagram 43 Playing Pick-up-sticks*

Long a favorite of children, Tiddlywinks is now taken very seriously by large numbers of adults. Regular tournaments are held in both North America and Britain, and there is even a World Championship.

**Players:** *two, with each using two sets of counters; or four, playing in pairs*

**Equipment:** *colored counters, a felt mat, and a cup*

**Difficulty:** *considerable practice is needed to compete at the top level*

**Duration:** *20 minutes for a singles game; 25 minutes for a pairs match*

*Diagram 44 The start of a game of Tiddlywinks*

### BRIEF HISTORY

The first patent application of the game of Tiddlywinks – or Tiddledywinks, as it was then called – was made in 1888, by Joseph Fincher. However, historians of the game, who take the matter extremely seriously, contend that Tiddlywinks had its origin in ancient China, and that it developed in the first half of the nineteenth century from a now forgotten game called Squails.

Originally, Tiddlywinks was played by children in the parlor and by more boisterous types in the tavern – becoming something of a fad in late nineteenth-century America. The fad soon passed, and Tiddlywinks became almost exclusively a children's pastime – until a group of students at Cambridge University, in England, took up the game in 1955. Within a few years, Tiddlywinks was being played seriously at most British universities, and, in 1961, an Oxford University team embarked on a Tiddlywinks tour of America. The game quickly took hold, in particular at the Massachusetts Institute of Technology (MIT). As in Britain, the game spread quickly, and today there is a North American Tiddlywinks Association (NATwA), an English association (ETwA) and a Scottish one

(ScotTwA). Each holds regular competitions and tournaments to decide Singles, Pairs and Teams of Four titles. International events are supervised by the International Federation of Tiddlywinks Associations (IFTwA), which also holds a World Singles and World Pairs championship.

## THE CONVENTIONS

The equipment and rules that follow conform to current internationally accepted practice, but it is worth remembering that pre-1960 Tiddlywink sets may come with different sets of rules. However, older sets can still provide a good deal of enjoyment.

Tiddlywinks has an extraordinary language of its own, and some words, such as "tiddlies," are now more or less obsolete. Unfortunately, there is not sufficient space here to list all of the terms used, but if you wish to find out more, you can do so by accessing one of the many Internet sites devoted to Tiddlywinks, and consult the lexicon. Copies of the detailed rules can also be obtained from the Internet or from national associations.

*Diagram 45*
*The potting shot*

## THE EQUIPMENT

In a singles match, each player uses, separately, two sets of colored disks from a selection comprising blue, red, green, and yellow disks. In a pairs match, each player uses one set, but plays as part of a team with their partner. Blue always partners red, and green always partners yellow.

Each set of disks includes four small, round disks known as "winks." The winks are propelled by a strike from a "squidger," or by pressure from it. The winks are of a standard size: the two small ones are $3/5$in. (16mm) in diameter and the two larger ones are $9/10$in. (22mm). The squidgers may be of any size, provided that they are round, no thicker than $1/5$in. (5mm), and $9/10$–2in. (21–51mm) in diameter. Tournament players choose

a squidger of an appropriate size and with an
appropriate edge that they have personalized
according to the type of shot that they are trying
to make, just as a golfer chooses a club according
to the nature of the shot. Any number of squidgers
can be carried, though only one for each shot.

*Diagram 46 A
squopping shot*

The game is played on a felt mat 72 x 55in.
(182 x 141cm) in size. A straight line (a baseline) is
drawn across each corner, at right angles to the diagonal of the mat and
55in (141cm) from the center of the mat – the field of play consists of all
areas of the mat outside the baselines. A cup (the pot) is placed in the
middle – it is $1\frac{1}{2}$in. (38mm) high, with a $1\frac{1}{2}$in. (38mm) base and a
$1\frac{9}{10}$in. (48mm) diameter top. All of the equipment can be bought as a set
from most toy stores, but if you intend to play seriously check that they
conform to the recognized specifications.

*Diagram 47
A boondock is used
to send a wink that
you have squopped
away from the pot.*

### THE AIM OF THE GAME

At its simplest, the aim of Tiddlywinks is to shoot
all of your winks into the pot (to pot out). In a
pairs game the time limit is 25 minutes, followed
by five extra rounds (finishing with the fifth
round of the first color to play). In a singles game,
the time limit is 20 minutes, again with five extra
rounds following.

However, the game is much more complex than
this, because it involves not only skill but a thorough appreciation of
both strategy and tactics. It is possible to put an opponent's wink out of
play by squopping it – that is, by covering any part of the wink with one
of your winks – and also possible for your opponent to free a squopped
wink. As a result, it is far from common for any player to pot out.
Instead, the aim is to score more points than your opponent.

## THE SCORING SYSTEM

There are seven points to play for in each game, and there are two ways of getting them. If a player pots out, the situation is fairly simple: they are awarded four points, and all squopped winks are unsquopped, with the winks that squopped them being placed alongside the squopped ones, equidistant from the pot and, ideally, $2/25$in. (2mm) away from it. The game then continues, but thereafter any winks that

*Diagram 48  A Bristol is used to move both your wink and one that you have squopped onto an opponent's wink, squopping them both*

are squopped are automatically unsquopped in the same way as described above, and the time limit no longer applies. The next player to pot out gets two points, then all winks are unsquopped as before. The third player to pot out is awarded one point and the remaining player receives no points. The number of points won by the paired colors (or paired players) are then added up and one point is taken from the losing partnership and awarded to the winning one. Another game starts – tournaments are often decided by the aggregate score over a number of games.

More often, none of the players pots out. In such cases the seven points are awarded differently. When the game finishes – the time limit having expired and five further rounds having been played – the score is calculated as follows: any wink that has been potted counts for three time-limit points (these are "sub-points" and determine the final points) and any unsquopped wink counts for one tiddly (so long as it is not still behind the baseline). The player with the largest number of tiddlies is then awarded four points; the next best player is given two points; and the third best gets one point. The number of points for each paired color are then added together to give the aggregate score. If there is a tie in the number of tiddlies, the number of points are added together and divided equally – so if the two colors are first equal, they would both receive three points.

*Diagram 49 A blow-up shot involves shooting your wink as hard as you can at a pile to cause maximum disruption*

## BEGINNING TO PLAY

The winks are placed within the baseline at each corner, with paired colors on opposite corners (it is easy to remember the sequence if you bear in mind that the colors are arranged alphabetically – blue, green, red, yellow – clockwise). Then, taking it in turns, each player has one attempt to squidge one wink as near to the pot as possible – this procedure is known as the "squidge-off." Any wink that is potted wins, otherwise the nearest wink to the pot wins. If two players have winks equidistant from the pot, they each squidge another wink, until the victor is decided. All the winks are put back behind the appropriate baseline and then the winner of the squidge-off (who by convention plays yellow) starts the game.

## PLAYING THE GAME

Before the game starts a timekeeper should be elected, because the clock starts as soon as the player who won the squidge-off takes the first shot. Each color is then played in turn, going clockwise round the mat. Each shot must be played within 30 seconds of the previous one, any further time taken being taken off the time limit at an opponent's request. Only one shot is allowed per turn unless a wink is potted, in which case another shot is allowed. No player is obliged to make a shot during a turn, and can elect to pass. If any wink is squidged off the mat the next turn is forfeit and the wink is replaced in the field of play $9/_{10}$in. (22mm) from the boundary as close as possible to the point at which it left the mat. A turn is also forfeit if no winks of the color playing are available to be squidged – you are not allowed to squidge a squopped wink until it has been unsquopped by a shot from

*Diagram 50 A bomb sho\[t\]*

your partner or paired color. However, if neither partner in a pair has an unsquopped wink their opponents may take a "free turn" and take one shot, taking it in turns, for each wink in play that is neither squopped or squopping, before unsquopping one wink of the colors that had been unable to play by means of a "freeing shot."

There are many ways in which a shot can be made, varying from gentle pressure from the squidger to a firm strike. However, in all cases the squidger must first touch the surface of an unsquopped wink and the movement of the squidger must not start more than 2in. (5cm) above the surface of the wink. If these conditions are not satisfied, or if any wink is damaged, the shot is a foul, and the opponents must either replace the winks as they were before the shot and ask the player to take another shot, or accept the result of the shot as it was played; the clock is stopped during these proceedings.

## HINTS AND TIPS

When they first start to play Tiddlywinks, most people try to pot all their winks immediately. However, they soon see that this is far from easy. A player who attempts to pot out on the first turn will soon find that their winks are squopped by opponents as, inevitably, some or all of them miss the pot. The best strategy in Tiddlywinks is to position your winks fairly close to the pot, so that you can either pot them on your next turn or be in a position to squop an opponent's wink.

After a few rounds, a number of winks have normally been squopped – in fact, squopping winks may have been squopped themselves, as "piles" start to form. Now is the time for great caution: if, for example, you have potted two winks and your other four winks have been squopped, you will be out of the game until your partner (or the other color you are playing, if it is a singles match) unsquops one of your winks.

This form of billiards – in itself, a much older cue game than either snooker or pool – retains its popularity around the world, with large numbers of international tournaments held each year.

*Players:* two, or four in pairs
*Equipment:* table, three balls and cues
(see below)
*Difficulty:* can be played at various
levels
*Duration:* as long as you wish

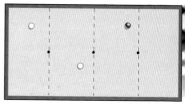

*Diagram 51 A Carom Billiards table*

## THE EQUIPMENT

A carom billiards table is different from the one used to play ordinary billiards. It is smaller (120 x 60in./304.8 x 152.4cm), it has no pockets, and it has a different system of spots and markings (see diagram 51). Three standard billiards balls are used, of which one is red and two are white (one of the white balls is spotted), and the game is played using standard snooker of billiards cues.

## AIM OF THE GAME

To be the first player, or pair, to reach a previously agreed number of points. There are three versions of Carom Billiards, with increasing levels of difficulty, but they share the same basic rules.

## STARTING THE GAME

First, the players or pairs decide who is to take the first turn by a process known as "lagging." The red ball is put on the "foot spot" (see diagram 52) and each player (or a nominated player from each pair) places their white "cue" ball – one of which will carry a spot – on the "head string" on either side of the "head spot," but within 6in (15cm) of it. In turn, the players lagging play their balls off the foot cushion, with the intention of returning them as close as possible to the head cushion. Neither cue ball must disturb the red ball or cross to the other side of the red ball and interfere with the other player's line, otherwise the stroke is a foul and does not count. The player whose ball is nearest to the head cushion starts the game.

## PLAYING THE BASIC GAME

The most simple form of Carom Billiards is called "straight rail carom." The first player to make a stroke has to play a "break shot." The red ball is placed on the foot spot and the "object ball" is placed on the head spot – this is the opponent's ball, distinguished either by a spot or the lack of one, and each player must stick to their ball throughout the game. The "cue ball," which is to be struck with the cue, is placed as for the lagging shot – on the head string, within 6in (15cm) of the head spot.

For this "break shot," and for this shot alone, the player strikes the cue ball and has to make contact first with the red ball. The aim is to make a "carom shot" – that is, to make the cue ball hit the red ball (in this case) and then hit the other white ball (the "object ball"). In the basic game it does not matter whether or not the cue ball bounces off a cushion before doing so.

If the first player makes a successful carom shot, they are awarded a point and can continue playing. However, on any other go but the first one it does not matter whether the red ball or the other object ball is hit first. A point is awarded for any successful carom shot, in which both balls are hit in succession, but a point is deducted if such contact is not made and the player's turn ends. The next player or member of a pair, then takes to the table.

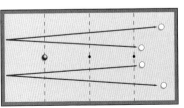

*Diagram 52  Lagging*

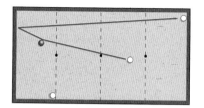

*Diagram 53 Safety shot*

The only exception to this rule is if the player makes a successful "safety shot." To do this, a player must either strike the cue ball in such a way that it comes to rest in contact with a cushion after hitting an object ball, or that the object ball itself comes to rest in contact with a cushion. No point is deducted, but the player's turn ends. However, only one safety shot may be played during any one session at the table: to attempt two safety shots is a foul: one point is deducted from that player's score and their turn ends.

## FOULS AND EXCLUSIONS

There are a number of possible fouls in Carom Billiards as well as failing to make a carom shot. For example, it is a foul to cause the cue ball to fly off the table – the penalty is the deduction of one point and the end of the turn. (The cue ball is put back on the head spot, or the foot spot if this is occupied, or the center spot if both are occupied.). If either of the object balls leaves the table the red ball is put back on the foot spot and the object ball is replaced on the head spot. In this case, however, the player can continue their turn, and still count any previous scores made during that session at the table. But if all the balls leave the table, the turn ends, a point is deducted, and the balls are repositioned as for a break shot.

If the two object balls are touching each other on a cushion, play can continue normally. However, if one of the balls is the cue ball, it must either be played away from the other object ball, or all the balls must be repositioned as for a break shot.

One of the hazards of ordinary Billiards is that it is possible to make up to 75 "cannons" – the equivalent of a carom – in succession when the object balls are stuck in a corner. This tedious problem is avoided in

Carom Billiards because of the rule on "crotch" shots. The object balls are said to be "crotched" when they are both within an imaginary line drawn across each corner $4^7/_{10}$in. (12cm) from the apex of the corner. Only three successive scoring shots may be made in this situation, and any attempt at making a fourth results in the end of the turn.

Otherwise, the normal restrictions of snooker and billiards apply. It is a foul, resulting in the end of a turn and the deduction of a point, to: make a shot while any ball is still in motion; touch the cue ball more than once in the course of a shot; push the cue ball, rather than strike it cleanly; touch an object ball with the cue; use the wrong cue ball; or have both feet off the ground when making a shot.

Since the first Ping-Pong set was marketed, in the 1880s, this game has achieved worldwide popularity. Also known as Table Tennis, it is a highly professional sport with millions of adherents – yet it is simple enough be played on a kitchen table.

*Players:* two (singles) or four (doubles)
*Equipment:* table, net, and paddles
*Difficulty:* can be played by amateurs and
     professionals
*Duration:* a professional game should take
     15 minutes

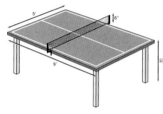

*Diagram 54 A Ping-Pong table*

## EQUIPMENT

The professional game has precise rules about the dimensions of the table: it should measure 9 x 5ft. (274 x 152.5cm), and stand 2ft. 6in. (76cm) high. Tables can be bought from specialized stores, but one can easily be made for home use by cutting a piece of plywood to size and fixing it over an existing table. Mark the end and side lines at the edges of the table with a strip of white paint $^3/_4$in. (2cm) wide. A thinner line, $^1/_8$in. (3mm) wide, runs vertically down the center of the table. The net and its supporting posts and clamps are 6in. (15cm) high – these will need to be bought.

In recent years there has been considerable controversy about the composition and manufacture of paddles (or racquets, as they are called in professional circles). Now the rules forbid the use of any solvent-based adhesives and insist that only adhesives approved by the International Table Tennis Federation (ITTF) should be used to stick rubber to the paddles. Regulations also determine the thickness of the pimpled rubber that is used on the hitting sides of a paddle. It is wise to check that any paddle you purchase conforms to the international standards if you wish to play Ping-Pong seriously.

The balls used in Ping-Pong are light spheres that are made of plastic or celluloid, and these must also conform to the international regulations about exact size and ability to bounce.

## PLAYING SINGLES

Toss a coin to determine who is to serve first. Players must serve near court to opposite court. If you are the server, start play by placing the ball on your open palm, then raise your palm quickly so that the ball rises vertically from it. No spin must be imparted to the ball, which must be in clear sight of the service receiver at all times, and it must rise at least 6in. (15cm) from its starting position and be descending before you can hit it.

The ball must first bounce on your side of the net, then cross over the net without touching it and bounce on the receiver's side before it can be played; only one bounce is allowed. If the ball touches the net, a "let" is called and the serve must be replayed. A let is also called if it is agreed that the receiver was not ready to receive the serve. If the ball does not bounce as described, or if it fails to cross over the net, the point is won by the receiver.

The receiver plays the serve by striking it over the net to the server's side. If the receiver fails to do this, the server has won the point; if the receiver returns the ball successfully but the server is unable to return the ball, the receiver wins the point. Lets only apply during a serve and not during play, when it does not matter whether the ball touches the net. Any player who touches the table with any part of their paddle or body during play forfeits the point.

At the end of each point, the game is restarted with a serve. Each server has five consecutive serves, after which the server becomes the receiver, and vice versa. The winner is the first player to reach 21 points. However, if both players reach 20 points, the winner is the player who first opens up a two-point lead, with the service alternating between players. Competitive matches are generally decided over three or five games. Players must change ends between games.

## THE EXPEDITE SYSTEM

Unless the two players have each reached 19 points, the expedite system comes into force when a game has lasted for 15 minutes but is still not finished. The number of successful return strokes by the receiving player are counted out loud and the receiver is awarded the point if they exceed 13. The serve then alternates between points. In professional competitions, play is halted by the umpire as soon as the 15 minutes is up, even during a rally. The serve then goes to the player who had served to start the rally.

## PLAYING DOUBLES

When playing doubles, the first server in a pair stands behind the right-hand court, and must serve in the same manner as in singles play to the opposite court – in other words to the opponent's right-hand court. The receiver returns the ball, which must be played by the partner of the original server; the partner of the original receiver returns this shot to the original server; and so on (if a player strikes the ball in the incorrect order, that side forfeits the point).

When the point is over, the same player as before serves to the same receiver for the next four points. When five serves are up, the service changes to the original receiver, who serves to the original server. The next player to serve is the original server's partner, serving to the original receiver's partner;

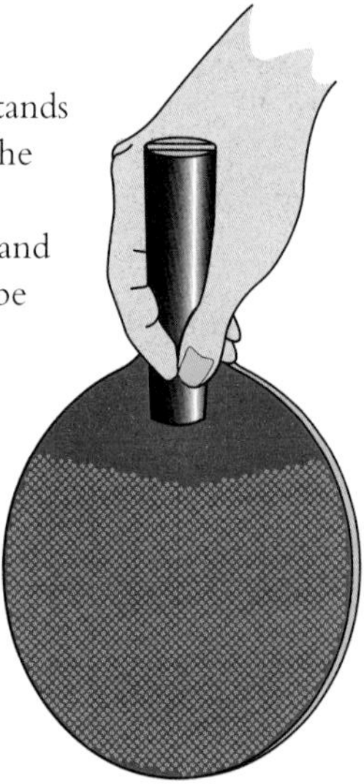

*Diagram 55 The pen-holder grip gives beginners more control*

then the original receiver's partner serves to the original server's partner. All serves are made from the right-hand court to the opposite right-hand court, so the players must move positions between every five serves.

If the expedite system comes into operation the serving sequence stays in force, but each player only serves once before service moves on.

## HINTS AND TIPS

The secret of success in Ping-Pong is an ability to play a wide range of shots (essentially the same as those used in Tennis), to impart spin to the ball and to recognize any spin that your opponent puts on the ball and take appropriate counter measures. As with most games of skill, this ability only comes with considerable practice.

When you are developing your range of strokes, here are a couple you might like to try. Forehand or backhand drives put considerable speed on your shot, making them hard to counter. Stand slightly side-on to the table, tip your paddle towards the net and hit the ball with a slicing, upward stroke, using your entire arm and finishing with the paddle above your head. If you prefer cunning rather than power, try a drop shot that barely makes it over the net, falling so short that your opponent can't reach it.

# OUTDOOR GAMES

This section deals with games that are ideal for relaxed summer days when friends and family can gather to play games that combine skill and application with a little relaxed socializing.

These are games which tax the body more than the mind, although tactics and strategy are usually involved and will need to be carefully considered. Horseshoe Pitching is derived from the European pastime of Quoits, but is a game played mostly in North America. Basically a very simple game, it does require considerable skill to get the horseshoe as near to the stake as possible and be warned – those horseshoes are not light!

Characterized by perfectly manicured lawns and gleaming clubhouses, Lawn Bowls has gained a reputation as a game for those advancing in years – but the truth is somewhat different. This apparently relaxing game requires immense concentration and a high level of skill in order to set the perfectly weighted bowls rolling as near to the smaller "jack" as possible.

Although nothing quite conjures up the image of the a genteel summer pastime as well as the crack of Croquet balls, this civilized game was originally a French invention. Migrating to England in the nineteenth century, it gained a reputation as a game for the aristocracy, but has widened its appeal and is now played all over the world. Similarly popular is Badminton. Played on a smaller court, the feathered shuttlecocks give a false impression of a game lacking in strength, but in fact propelling the light shuttlecocks at high speed requires force, finesse, and precision.

All the games mentioned so far have one thing in common – equipment. But there are games that require only one commodity in order to have a good time – people. Statues, for example, is popular at parties and just requires someone to take the part of Grandma. Hopscotch, a quintessential childhood game for many, calls only for a piece of chalk and some small stones. Simplicity is the byword here so relax and enjoy!.

A game with many thousands of years of history, Bowls is often thought of as a game for the elderly. Nothing could be further from the truth, as an ever younger rollcall of international champions testifies.

**Players:** *for singles, pairs, triples, or teams*
**Equipment:** *a set of bowls, a jack, and a mat*
**Difficulty:** *simple in essence, but considerable skill and experience is needed at the higher levels*
**Duration:** *about 15 minutes for one "end"*

*Diagram 56  A bowl and a jack*

### THE AIM OF THE GAME

To position your bowls as close as possible to the jack, and to prevent your opponent from doing so by blocking the path to the jack, moving the jack or dislodging your opponent's bowls.

### EQUIPMENT AND THE GREEN

Each player uses a set of bowls that consists of four matched balls, which may be made of a rubber composite, plastic or lignum vitae (a hard wood from the West Indies). A bowl must measure $4\frac{5}{8}$–$5\frac{1}{4}$in. (117–133mm) in diameter and weigh no more than $3\frac{1}{2}$lb. (1.59kg). The "crown," or running surface, of one side of each bowl is raised slightly (so that the bowl is not a true sphere) in order to give it bias – as momentum reduces and the bowl starts to slow down it curves or "draws" in an attempt to find its balance. Each bowl in a set carries a distinguishing mark of the same color for ease of recognition.

The bowls are aimed at the jack. This is a smaller ball made of plastic and colored either white or yellow, measuring $2\frac{1}{2}$in. (63mm) in diameter and weighing 8–10oz. (225–285g). The only other piece of equipment needed to play bowls is a mat, 2ft. $11\frac{5}{8}$in. (600mm) by 1ft. $2\frac{2}{16}$in. (360mm).

Lawn Bowls is played on a rectangle of grass called a "green." The green as a whole must be 121ft. 4$\frac{1}{4}$in.–131ft. 2$\frac{1}{2}$in. (37–40m) long, and it is subdivided into individual playing areas, called "rinks". Each rink must be 18–19ft. (5.5–5.8m) wide. The green is bordered by a ditch, behind which is a grassy bank that rises above the playing surface. The center line of each rink is marked out for a distance of 13ft. (4m) from the ditch, and the boundaries of each rink are indicated by the position of markers on the bank.

The condition of the grass that forms the playing surface has a considerable effect on play: the length of the grass, its density, and how much it has been watered and rolled all play a part. Confusingly, a green on which the bowl travels fast – around 12 seconds to run 88ft. 6in. (27m) – is said to be "slow," or "heavy." This is because there is less time available for the bias of the bowl to become apparent in a curve. A bowl takes around 17 seconds to cover the same distance on a "fast" green.

## PLAYING THE SINGLES GAME

It is usual for the players to play a trial end – that is, to bowl a set of four bowls each at a jack – before a game begins, so that they can judge the speed of the green. A coin is tossed to see who will play first. The first to play positions the mat on the center line of the rink, with its back edge 6ft. 6in. (2m) from the ditch. The player then bowls the jack ("delivers" it), keeping the whole of one foot within the edges of the mat – to fail to do so is a foul shot (as it is when bowling any bowl). The jack must travel at least 68ft. 10$\frac{1}{2}$in. (21m) from the mat, must stay within the boundaries of the rink and must not come to rest in the ditch, otherwise it is a foul shot. When the bowl has come to rest, it is positioned on the center line at the length at which it stopped; if this is within 6ft. 6in. (2m) of the ditch, it is replaced on the center line 6ft. 6in. (2m) from the ditch. However, if the jack was delivered with a foul shot, the opposing player is given the chance to position it, though the original player still bowls the first bowl.

When the jack has been positioned, the first bowl is bowled from the mat. The players bowl in turn, keeping the mat in the same position for each shot. A bowl is said to be a "live bowl" and can take part in the play as long as it comes to rest within the boundaries of the rink and travels at least 45ft. 11in. (14m); any bowl that fails to do this is said to be "dead" and plays no further part in the end. The first bowl in an end to touch the jack, or fall over onto the jack within 30 seconds of coming to rest, is known as a "toucher," marked with chalk and counted as a live bowl. It is permissible to hit an opponent's ball off the rink, in which case it becomes dead, unless it is the toucher, in which case it is still considered live. However, if the jack is hit off the rink the jack is said to be dead: the end comes to a halt and is replayed.

When all eight bowls have been delivered, the end is over and the players walk to the jack to determine the score. A point is awarded to the player whose bowl is closest to the jack for each bowl that is closer to the jack than the opponent's closest bowl – as a result, only one player scores after each end. The winner of the end is then allowed to reposition the mat at the end of the rink to which the last set of bowls have been delivered. The mat can be placed wherever the player likes for all ends except the first of a game, as long as it is on the center line of the rink and has its back edge no less than 6ft. 6in. (2m) from the ditch and its front edge no less than 75ft. 5½in. (23m) from the opposite ditch. The winner delivers the jack, and the end proceeds. The game continues until either one player wins by reaching 21 points, or until a previously agreed number of ends have been played. In many champ-ionship matches, the game is over when 25 shots have been played, the winner being the player with the most points at this time.

## MULTI-PLAYER BOWLS

The same basic rules apply, with differences in the order of play. In Pairs Bowls, the players at one end bowl four bowls each, delivering the bowls alternately. They score, and then their team-mates at the other end bowl back all eight, also scoring. Pairs games are normally played to 21 ends. Triples are also played, with three players in each team and each player delivering either two or three bowls and in turn; triples games are usually played to 18 ends. Fours Bowls are played by two teams of four players, with each player delivering two bowls in turn; such games normally run to 21 ends.

## HINTS AND TIPS

There are various different shots that can be made, all with a specific use. A shot that curves the bowl in close to the jack is called a "draw," while a bowl aimed to protect an existing draw or block an opponent"s route to the jack is known as a "guard." A "trail" bowl attempts to carry the jack towards a bowl or group of bowls behind it, while a "yard-on" is a bowl delivered straight and with some force that is intended to break up a "head" – that is, a group of opponent"s bowls around the jack. Which shot to choose depends on skill, experience and an awareness of the strategy of the game.

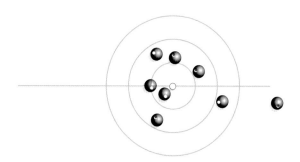

*Diagram 57 Scoring: in this case, A has won two points and B none*

Invented hundreds of years ago in France, where it was known as Paillie Maille, Croquet traveled to England in the early nineteenth century, originally under the name of Pall Mall. Over the past few decades, it has become increasingly popular and versions of the game are played all around the world.

*Players:* two to six
*Equipment:* six Croquet balls and wickets, mallets, nine hoops and two stakes
*Difficulty:* some skill required
*Duration:* about one and a half hours

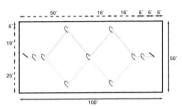

Diagram 58  A Backyard Croquet court

## THE GAME

Backyard Croquet is the simplest version of croquet and is ideal for family games. It is played over nine hoops, or "wickets." More serious Croquet players prefer the added subtleties of one or other of the two six-wicket versions of the game: American Rules Six-Wicket Croquet, sponsored by the United States Croquet Association (UCSA); and Association, or International Rules Croquet, as played in most countries outside the United States and Canada. Full rules of all three games can be obtained in various publications about the sport, many of which are obtainable from UCSA.

## THE COURT

Ideally, Backyard Croquet should be played on a rectangular court 100ft. (30.5m) by 50ft. (15.25m), but it can be played in a smaller space if necessary. The nine wickets are laid out as in diagram 58. The two stakes are put at opposite heads of the two diamonds formed by the wickets: the "turning stake" after the seventh wicket and the "finishing stake" after the fourteenth. Ideally, the boundaries of the court should be

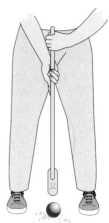

*Diagram 59 An example of a Croquet grip and stance*

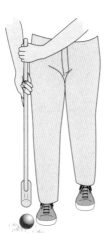

*Diagram 60 An example of a Croquet grip and stance*

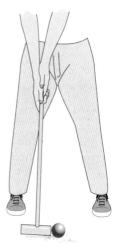

*Diagram 61 An example of a Croquet grip and stance*

marked, but if this is not possible it is sensible to agree beforehand where the boundaries are and any natural features that might mark them.

## THE AIM OF THE GAME

To be the first side to pass all its balls through all the wickets and hit both the turning stake and the finishing stake at the appropriate time with all balls. It is possible to call a halt to a game before this happens if time is running short – in this case the winning side is decided by awarding one point for each wicket that a ball has passed through and one point for each stake that has been hit.

## PLAYING THE GAME

Each Croquet ball carries a different color, and the balls are divided into two sides: "hot colors" are red, yellow, and orange; "cool colors" are blue, black, and green. If six people are playing, all the balls will be used, but with two or four it may be preferable to play with only four balls – blue and black playing red and green. If an odd number of players are taking part, the number of players on that side will have to play the balls alternately, choosing which ball to play. A coin is tossed to see which side starts and which colors they will play. The blue ball is always played first, and the other balls are played according to the order of colors marked on the stakes: blue, red, black, yellow, green, and orange. (After the first round, any ball can be played.) For the first shot a ball is placed the length of one mallet head from the first wicket.

The balls must all pass through the wickets in the strict sequence shown in diagram 8. As each ball passes through a wicket a wicket clip of the same color as the ball is placed on the next wicket that it must pass through.

Only one shot is allowed with each ball during that ball's turn, but bonus shots or "continuation shots" can be won in a variety of ways: first, by passing through the correct wicket successfully; second, by striking the turning stake after the seventh wicket; third, by passing through two wickets with one shot or passing through a wicket and hitting the turning stake in one shot (in both cases two continuation shots are won); fourth, by hitting, or making a "roquet" on, one of the other side's balls. A roquet wins two bonus strokes, but the same ball can only be roqueted once during any one turn, unless the ball that is roqueting passes through a wicket or hits the turning stake in the same turn, in which case the original ball can be roqueted once more.

The first of the two bonus shots arising from a roquet can be used to make a "Croquet stroke": the striker's ball is either placed alongside the roqueted ball and in contact with it, or a mallet's head away from it. The original ball is then struck so that both balls move if required. However, the striker is allowed to place a foot on their ball in order that it does not move while the roqueted ball is dismissed to some other part of the court. (If a ball goes outside the boundaries during the course of play it is replaced on the boundary and played from there.) The second bonus shot can then be played. If the roqueted ball is passed through a wicket as the result of a croquet shot, it is considered to have passed through the wicket fairly but does not win a continuation shot for doing so. Continuation shots only last for one turn and cannot be carried on to another turn. In fact, the only continuation shot that can be played is the last one that has been won – if, for example, a striker's ball roquets another ball straight from the Croquet shot, the striker only has two continuation shots, not three.

When a ball has passed through all the wickets, but has not yet struck the winning stake, it is said to be a "rover." There is no obligation for a rover to be played at the finishing stake, and there is considerable advantage in using it to roquet opponents' balls – the same rules apply as for ordinary balls. However, it can be struck against the finishing stake by any player at any time in the game – at which point it has completed the game and lost its ability to roquet another ball.

## PLAYING A SHOT

There are a variety of ways in which the mallet can be held when addressing the ball, and three conventional ones are shown in diagrams 59, 60 and 61 (page 100). Bear in mind that you are only allowed to strike the ball with the face of the mallet. The mallet is not allowed to touch any ball other than that of the striker, nor to touch a wicket or a stake, nor to be in contact with a ball that is itself in contact with a wicket or a stake. However, the penalties for playing a foul stroke are hardly severe in Backyard Croquet: the balls are simply returned to their original position and the shot is replayed.

## VARIATIONS
### American Rules Six-Wicket Croquet

This more complex version of Croquet is played in North American clubs and tournaments. Only four balls are used, with one side having

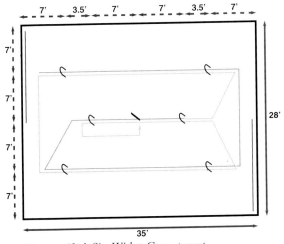

*Diagram 62 A Six-Wicket Croquet court*

blue and black and the other red and yellow. In singles, the players play both balls; in doubles, each player plays the same ball throughout the game. If three players are taking part, one side has two players, each playing their own balls, and the third player plays both balls.

Club courts and tournament courts are 105ft. (32m) by 85ft. (26m), and six hoops are laid out in the positions shown in diagram 62 (page 103), with a single finishing stake in the center of the court. However, UCSA recommends that a smaller court 50ft. (15.25m) by 40ft. (12.20m) is used to learn how to play the game. Whichever size is used, the boundaries of the court should be marked by string and a deadness board should be prominently displayed.

As in Backyard Croquet, a coin is tossed at the start of the game, but the winner can decide either to go first, selecting the blue and black ball, or to go second, selecting the red and yellow balls. The sequence in which the balls are played is as on the stake: blue, red, black, and yellow.

The basic rules of play are as for Backyard Croquet, but with a few differences that significantly affect the character of the game. First, you are not allowed to place either a hand or a foot on the ball being struck during a Croquet shot to immobilize it: whether your ball moves, or how much it moves, depends on the skill with which the shot is played. Second, Six-Wicket Croquet employs the concept of a ball being either "dead" or "alive." This is a fairly complex concept to master, and it is even harder to keep track of an individual ball's state of deadness – which is why a "deadness board" is displayed beside the court. This arrangement of colored flaps is updated at the end of every turn. Your ball is considered to be "dead" on a ball once that ball has been roqueted by your ball and cannot hit that ball again while your ball is dead on it. This means that you are not allowed to hit it again until you have come "alive" on the ball: this happens when you pass through a wicket. The only other way of making one of your balls come alive is to keep a check on when your opponent passes through the seventh wicket: you can clear the deadness of a ball simply by declaring the fact before your turn begins, but you must specify the color of the ball that is being cleared.

The concept of dead and alive also applies to rover balls, but in a different way. A rover can only roquet a ball once in a turn, but can clear itself of deadness first by roqueting two balls and then by passing through any wicket, in any direction. However, a rover cannot at any time roquet the same ball twice in succession. In Six-Wicket Croquet a rover can be struck against the stake to finish its part of the game or can be hit against it by a Croquet shot from another rover.

There are also a number of differences between Backyard Croquet and Six-Wicket Croquet in the rules covering boundaries and penalties. A ball is said to be "out of bounds" if half the ball is over the boundary line and the player's turn ends immediately. The ball is replaced the length of a mallet's head inside the boundary at the point at which it left the court – the exception is when the striker's ball goes out of bounds after a roquet but the roqueted ball is still in play, in which case it is put back in contact with the roqueted ball wherever it may be. The striker's turn ends if a ball is roqueted out of bounds, but the striker's ball is not considered to be dead on that ball; the striker's turn also ends if a ball is played out of bounds by a croquet shot, and any bonus shot is lost.

Some foul shots do not incur a penalty, and the balls are repositioned and play resumes. These occur when a ball is played out of turn or from the wrong position, or when the wrong ball is played. In other cases, the balls are returned to their previous positions but the offender's turn ends immediately. These fouls include: roqueting a ball on which your ball is dead; failing to move a roqueted ball when playing a croquet shot; touching a ball with a mallet when it is in contact with a wicket (this is known as a "crush"); and hitting the ball incorrectly with the mallet.

Whole books have been written about the tactics and strategy of Six-Wicket Croquet. The most important thing to remember is that you must try to stop your opponent from making progress just as much as you try to make progress yourself. The key is to find the correct balance between offense and defense to cope with the level of skill and experience of your opponent

## Association (International) Rules Croquet

This form of Six-Wicket Croquet is played in countries outside North America – Britain, Australia, New Zealand, South Africa, France, and Japan. It is a simpler version of American Rules Croquet – closer to Backyard Croquet in some ways – with different technical expressions and no concept of "deadness."

The equipment used is identical (with the exception of the "deadness board") to that specified in American Rules Croquet. The Association court is the same as the American version except for balk lines at either end of the rectangle: the first shot of each ball must be taken from behind either balk line, rather than the length of a mallet's head from the first "wicket," as in American Rules. (The wicket is named a "hoop" in Association practice, and it is not "passed" but "run.") Games involving three people are not generally played, though there is no reason why they should not be. The black and blue balls still play the red and yellow balls and must be played in order for the first turn only.

The rules for roquet and croquet are the same as in Backyard Croquet, though the striker may not place a hand or foot on their ball while playing a croquet shot; nevertheless, the croqueted ball must move or shake as a result of the strike – the striker's turn ends and the balls are replaced as they were before the roquet if it does so. Since the first shot of each ball is taken from the balk line there is no guarantee that a ball will run a hoop on this shot. Remember that a ball can be roqueted before it runs its first hoop.

# BADMINTON

This game originated in the Far East some 2000 years ago and has been popular ever since. Its rules were laid down by British officers in India in the nineteenth century – some years before Lawn Tennis was invented.

*Players:* two or four
*Equipment:* racquets, some shuttlecocks, a net, and a suitable area to use as a court
*Difficulty:* skillful and athletic
*Duration:* about 20 minutes for one game

*Diagram 63
A shuttlecock*

## THE COURT, RACQUETS, AND SHUTTLECOCK

A Badminton court is laid out as shown below in diagram 64. Serious players always play the game on an indoor court, because the flight of the shuttlecock can be be affected considerably by even the slightest gust of wind. Nevertheless, amateurs can play Badminton perfectly well out of doors, in the garden or in a park. In this case, the only parts of the court that it is important to lay out accurately are the posts and net. The posts must be 5ft. 1in. (1.55m) high, and the net, which should be made of a mesh sufficiently fine that a shuttlecock cannot pass through it, should be 2ft. 6in. (760mm) deep and hung 1in. (2.5cm) below the top of the posts.

Badminton racquets are smaller than Tennis racquets and a little larger than Squash racquets. They are available from most good sports stores – but check that they conform with the international

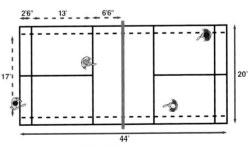

*Diagram 64  A Badminton court*

Badminton Federation (IBF) standards if you intend to play seriously. Shuttlecocks, also known as the "birdies" or "birds," were originally made of 16 feathers stuck into a base of leather-covered cork weighted with lead, but nowadays synthetic substitutes are more widely available. The weight of shuttlecocks approved by the IBF varies from 0.17oz. (4.74g) to 0.19oz. (5.5g), and it is wise to buy the heaviest grade if you intend to play outside in order to minimize wind interference.

## THE SCORING

A point is awarded when the player receiving serve commits a foul or fails to return a shot in bounds. Should the server commit a foul or fail to return, no point is awarded but serve immediately passes to their opponent. According to LBF rules, doubles and men's singles games are won by the first player or side to reach 15 points, while women's singles are won by the first player to reach 11 points. A match is generally decided over three games, though occasionally it is agreed that the winner is the first player to reach 21 points in one game only. At home, you can decide to play up to as many points as you like.

Towards the end of a game of Badminton the "setting" rule comes into force. If the score becomes tied at either of the two scores below the winning post, the player or side that first reached the number of points on which the score is tied has the option of setting the game; this option must be taken or ignored as soon as the scores are tied and before the next serve is made. Setting means that the points so far scored are discarded, the scores are reset to love-all and the first side to reach three points when play resumes wins the game.

So if the game is a men's singles being played to 15 points, and the score stands at 13-12 to player A, player A has the option to set the game if player B wins first the serve and then the next point, making the score 13-13. The same rule applies if the score reaches 14-14. (In women's singles, the relevant scores are 9-9 and 10-10.)

## PLAYING THE SINGLES GAME

A coin is tossed at the start of a game and the winner chooses either at to play at a particular end or to serve first. The server stands in the right-hand service court, with the receiver also in their right-hand court; no part of either player's feet may touch the boundary lines of the service court or be outside them. To start the serve, the server holds the racquet so that it is pointing down and holds the shuttlecock above waist height in the other hand. The shuttlecock is then dropped and must be hit below the waist with the racquet still pointing downwards. The serve is good if it crosses the net and falls between the long and the short service line for singles (see diagram 64, page 107) in the receiver's service court; no "lets" are called during a service. If the server commits a foul while serving, by touching a boundary line or failing to serve into the required area – the serve passes to the receiver.

The receiver loses the point automatically if a foul is committed while receiving service. Otherwise, the receiving player has to return the shuttle-cock to the server. It must only be hit once, and must fall within or on the boundary lines for singles (a shuttlecock is only out if it comes to rest completely over a line). No "let" – in which the rally stops and the point is replayed – is called if the shuttlecock hits the top of the net and falls over into the other side. A let is called, however, if a shuttlecock disintegrates during play, as happens occasionally. (By tradition, though, amateur players offer each other lets if an error is made by mischance.) The receiver wins the rally and takes the next serve if the original server fails to return the ball correctly – clear over the net with one hit and into or onto the boundary lines of the opposite court. Any player who touches the net with racquet or body, or allows either racquet or body to pass into the opponents' side of the court, whether under or over the net, commits a foul and loses the rally.

When each rally has finished, the player who is making the next serve crosses to the other service court, as does the receiver. If three games are being played to decide a match, the players change ends at the end of the first two games. Different rules apply if only one game is being played, however, and also during the third game of a match of three games. If the game is being played to 11 points, the players change ends after one player has reached 6 points; if the game is to 15 points, the change comes when one player has reached 8 points; and if the game is to 21, ends are changed when a player reaches 11 points.

## DOUBLES PLAY

Play starts from the right-hand service court in doubles, as in singles, but only the player in the receiving court may play the shuttlecock. After the serve, either player may play any shuttlecock. On the serve, the shuttlecock must fall within the short service line and the long service line for doubles, and in the receiver's court; as before, on the line is in. Which pair the next serve goes to depends on who wins the rally. However, should the receiving side be next to serve, it is the receiver who serves next, then the receiver's partner after that, should the next point be won. When the original serving side regains the serve, the serve is taken by the original server's partner and so on, alternately.

## HINTS AND TIPS

It is difficult to master the peculiarities of a shuttlecock in flight – practice is the only way to perfect technique. One problem is that, though the shuttlecock moves with some speed just after being hit, it falls fairly slowly. Unless a shot is played with some skill, therefore, an opponent has plenty of time to line up a return shot. There are four basic badminton shots: the lob, in which a player sends the shuttlecock in a high arc to the back of the opposing player's court – especially when that player is near the net; the drop shot, in which the aim is to make the shuttlecock drop to the ground as soon as it has crossed the net; the drive, in which the shuttlecock is hit so that it passes horizontally over the net; and the smash, in which a lob or high shuttlecock is hit as hard as possible towards the ground.

# STATUES

Also known as Grandmother's Footsteps, this game is a staple of children's parties and is guaranteed to make even the most miserable and tearful child cheer up and join in the fun.

*Players:* one person to be "grandmother" and
 as many children as you like, given
 the space

*Equipment:* none

*Difficulty:* as hard as "grandmother" chooses
 to make it; best for under-sevens

*Diagram 65 A game of Statues*

*Duration:* 20 minutes, or until the children become bored

## STARTING THE GAME

An adult or older child takes the part of the "grandmother" and stands facing a wall or some recognizable point in the garden. All the children line behind the grandmother some distance away – 50ft. (15m) is ideal, but anything less will do.

## PLAYING THE GAME

Grandmother starts the game when everyone is ready, and the children have to creep up behind her as quietly as possible, taking whatever route they choose. Every so often, grandmother turns round suddenly. Immediately the children see her start to turn, they must stop moving and freeze into "statues." If she spots anybody moving, she points out the child and that child is out of the game. It is worth announcing beforehand that grandmother's decision is final, especially if she is trying to make a particular child win in order to give him or her a prize. The first child to touch grandmother, or the last child left in the game, wins and is awarded a prize. (In some versions of the game, the child who wins takes over as grandmother, but experience shows that this can lead to disaster and is thus best avoided.) Another round then starts.

This game is an old favorite, and there is a good reason why it retains its popularity: it can be tremendous fun, and even older children enjoy it.

*Players:* four to 20, depending on the number of possible hiding places
*Equipment:* none
*Difficulty:* as hard as the children make it
*Duration:* about 15 minutes

## PLAYING THE GAME

One child is chosen to be the seeker, and stands still with eyes closed for a count of 20 while the other children run off to find hiding places. When the count is up, the seeker shouts: "Here I come, ready or not!," and starts to search out the hiders. The first child to be found becomes the new seeker, but not until the original seeker has found all the hidden children. It is a good idea to put a time limit on each round, after which all the hiders have to reveal themselves – otherwise there is a risk that the children who have already been found will become bored when one player has found a particularly ingenious hiding place.

## SIMON SAYS

Also known as Simple Simon Says or O'Grady, this is an old-established follow-my-leader game that still goes down extremely well at parties.

*Players:* four to 10
*Equipment:* none
*Difficulty:* harder than you might think, especially if played at speed
*Duration:* about 15 minutes

### STARTING THE GAME

One child is selected to start off as "Simon," and the other children form up in front of Simon in a line. (With very young children it is often wise for an adult to take the part of Simon.)

### PLAYING THE GAME

Simon tells the children to perform a certain action – "clap your hands" or "jump up and down" – and performs the action at the same time. If the command is preceded with the phrase "Simon says," the children must carry out the action immediately and any child who fails to do so is eliminated. But if Simon misses the phrase "Simon says" out, the children must not copy the action and any child who does so is out. The winner is the child who is the last left in, and takes Simon's place.

## HOPSCOTCH

This classic hopping and jumping game is a test of balance and agility that has helped while away time in school playgrounds and quiet streets for generations.

*Players: from two to 10*
*Equipment: chalk and a small stone*
*Difficulty: difficult at first, but becomes much easier with practice; best for seven-
to 10-year-olds*
*Duration: up to half an hour, depending on the skill of the players*

### STARTING THE GAME

Once an appropriate site has been chosen – it should be level and either paved or covered with tarmac – one of the players draws a grid on the ground in chalk (see diagram 66 on next page). The grid should be about 4ft. (1.25m) wide and 10ft. (3m) long, though it is not important to be precise. It is worth noting that this is only one type of hopscotch grid and there are innumerable variations on it, and on the rules. It is quite common for one form of Hopscotch to be played on one street and a different version on a neighboring street.

## PLAYING THE GAME

The first child to play throws a pebble, "the puck," into the area marked "1" and hops into it, landing on one foot. The child has to stay on one foot, pick up the pebble and hop back to behind the starting line, without allowing the other foot to touch the ground – though it is permissible to hop from foot to foot. If this has been achieved successfully, the child then throws the pebble into the area marked "2," and hops into it, if necessary using area 1 as a stepping stone.

The first player continues until a foul is committed: this may be done either by throwing to the wrong area, or missing the correct one; by hopping onto a line; or by losing balance and allowing both feet to touch the ground at the same time. When this happens the player's turn is over and the next child starts to play. When each player has made an attempt, the first player has another go, throwing the pebble into the area in which they failed last time. The first player to reach "out" and return to the start line, hopping from area to area with only one foot on the ground, is the winner.

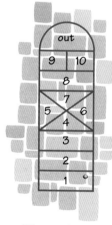

*Diagram 66 A*
*Hopscotch grid*

Children's crazes come and go, but Marbles games have been a constant source of entertainment. There are many different Marbles games, all of which have their adherents.

*Players:* two to six
*Equipment:* five marbles and a "shooter"
          per player, chalk
*Difficulty:* requires a fair degree of skill
*Duration:* 10 to 20 minutes, depending on
          the variation being played

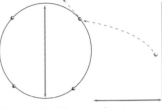

*Diagram 67 Shooting the ring*

## THE MARBLES

Marbles are hard balls, made from plastic or glass, measuring about ½in. (15mm) across. For many games each player also needs a "shooter," or "taw," which is a larger marble about ¾in. (20mm) in diameter. It is one of the traditions of the game that the marbles themselves can be won or lost permanently, with the exception of the shooter. It is as well to make it clear before a game starts whether this rule is going to apply or whether any marbles captured will be returned once the game is over.

## SHOOTING THE RING

The players select a reasonably level area of ground and draw in chalk, or otherwise mark out, a circle about 8ft. (2.5m) in diameter. Each player them places one marble on the perimeter of the circle, making sure that the spaces between the marbles are roughly equal. A line is drawn about 6ft. (1.8m) from the edge of the ring. This forms the shooting line.

First, each player takes their shooter and rolls it to the center of the circle to determine the order of play: the player whose shooter comes to rest nearest the circle's center starts the game; the player whose shooter is next closest goes second; and so on. The first player kneels behind the shooting line – knees must be kept behind the line, but the torso and arms may cross over it. The aim is to hit one of the marbles on the circle's edge with sufficient force that both the target marble and the shooter end up outside the circle. If this happens, the player captures the marble that was hit and has another go. If the shot is unsuccessful – if the target marble is missed or the marble is hit but ends up inside the circle – the turn ends and one of the player's own marbles must be placed on the edge of the circle. However, the player retains the shooter. The game ends when there are no more marbles left on the circle's rim, and the winner is the player who has captured the most marbles.

## RING TAW

As for shooting the ring, a 8ft. (2.5m) circle is marked out on level ground, but then a smaller circle, about 1ft. (30cm) across is drawn inside it. Each player rolls a single marble to the center of the inner circle to decide the order of play, and each places two marbles in the inner circle. The first player attempts to dislodge a marble from the inner circle, shooting from any point outside the outer circle. If successful, the marble is captured, the shooter is reclaimed and another shot is taken from the place where it lay; if unsuccessful, the shooter stays where it is and the player's turn ends. The next player can either attempt to dislodge a marble from the inner circle, as before, or try to hit the first player's shooter. If the attempt to hit a shooter is successful, the shooter's owner must pay a marble. If the shot fails, whatever its target, the shooter stays where it lies. Each player must take their first shot from any point outside the outer circle, but subsequent shots must be taken from wherever that player's shooter lies. The game ends when there are no more marbles in the inner circle and the winner is the player who has captured the most marbles.

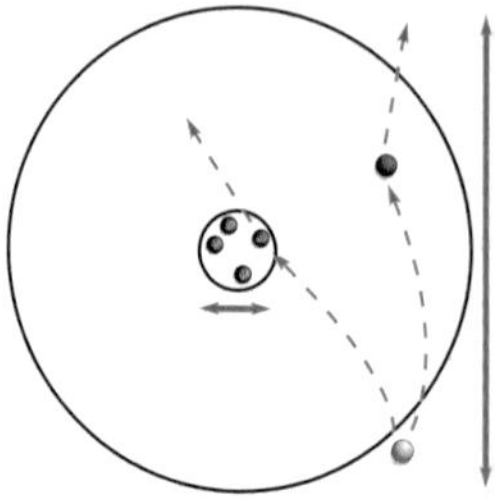

*Diagram 68 Ring Taw*

If you are looking for a fast-moving, exciting, open-air game try Dodge Ball. There are many versions of the game, but in all of them the aim is the same – to hit an opponent below the waist with a soft ball.

*Players:* eight to 20
*Equipment:* a soft rubber ball about 8in. (20cm) in diameter, such as a volleyball
*Difficulty:* speed, agility, and a good aim are needed; suitable for eight- to 10-year-olds
*Duration:* 10 minutes is probably long enough per game

## FREE ZONE DODGE BALL

The players mark out a rectangular playing field 46ft. (14m) long and 26ft. (8m) wide, using chalk if possible, or piles of clothes to denote two goal lines and a center line (see diagram 69, page 119). There are two free zones, one between the center line and each goal line; the areas behind the two goal lines are the end zones.

The players divide themselves into two teams and take their positions in the free zones. The teams toss a coin to decide which one will have the ball first, then play begins. The aim of the game is to get as many of the opposition players into the end zone behind your free zone as possible. Players are allowed to throw the ball to other members of their team, and when a player judges that the moment is right, they throw the ball over the center line with the object of hitting an opposing player below the waist. Any player who is hit must go to the thrower's end zone, and the ball is returned to the thrower's team for play to restart. (A referee of some sort is a good idea for judging near-misses.) However, if the ball is caught before it bounces, the original thrower must go to the opponent's end zone. If the ball misses, it can be picked up by a member of the opposing team, who can attempt to make a hit on any member of the thrower's team. Players in an end zone can still play the ball, which can either be passed to them by a member of their own team by throwing it over the heads of the opposing team or can be retrieved by them if the opposing team misses the ball completely. They cannot move any further forward than the goal line, however.

The game ends automatically if all the members of one team are in an end zone, with the other team winning. Otherwise, the game ends when 10 minutes are up and the winning team is the one that has the most opposition players in its end zone.

## TRAIN DODGE BALL

This version of Dodge Ball is more suitable for younger children. All the children except four form a circle about 23ft. (7m) in diameter. The four children chosen go into the middle of the circle and form a line, putting their hands around the waist of the child in front: the first player in the line is the engine of the train; the second and third are carriages; and the last is the caboose. The players in the circle throw the ball from one to the other, looking for an opportunity to make a hit below the waist on the caboose. The engine tries to kick the ball away or hand it off, or swings the train round to try to avoid it – the carriages are not allowed to fend the ball off. If the caboose is hit, the player who threw the ball joins the front of the line of four and becomes the engine, while the player who was the second carriage becomes the caboose. The original caboose joins the circle of other players. The game continues until each player has had a go at being the engine, and the winner is the engine who keeps the caboose safe for the longest period of time.

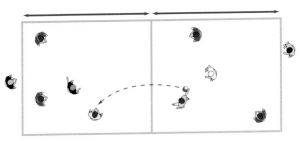

Diagram 69  Free Zone Dodge Ball

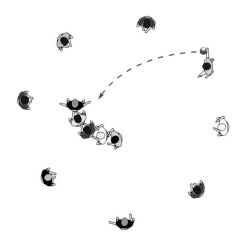

Diagram 70  Train Dodge Ball

# —ONE-PLAYER CARD GAMES—

Few activities can while away idle hours as effectively as one of the Solitaire-style card games. They can be positively mesmerizing, filling the player with a determination to reach a successful outcome

Solitaire games are intended to be played by one person, to pass the time away – as Napoleon did during his exile at St. Helena after the Battle of Waterloo in 1815. The exact origin of card games for one player is obscure, but the name "Patience" (the European name for Solitaire) originated in France. One of the classical French games, La Belle Lucie, survives to this day under various names, including The Fan – because the pack of cards is spread out on the table in 17 fans of three cards each. The craze for one-player card games was brought to Britain from mainland Europe in the 1870s. Queen Victoria's husband, Prince Albert, was an avid player and solitaire games soon became popular in drawing rooms throughout Victorian Britain.

Klondike, one of the most popular games devised in America and said to have originated during the Alaskan goldrush of 1897, is now familiar to computer games players all over the world under the name of Solitaire. It owes its popularity to an unbeatable combination of judgement, luck, attractive layout and fast-moving tempo – all vital ingredients of a good solitaire game. The number of different solitaire games runs into many hundreds. Most are played with one or two packs of cards, some with three packs and just a few with four. Special solitaire cards, which are smaller than ordinary cards, are especially useful when playing in a confined space.

At the start of most solitaire games, the cards are laid out in a prescribed formation that varies from game to game. This formation, or "tableau," together with any other cards dealt out at the beginning of play, forms the "layout."

Also known as Four of a Kind, Hidden Cards, Sundial, or Travelers, this is a game that depends entirely on chance and demands no skill from the player.

*Players: one*
*Equipment: a pack of playing cards with jokers removed*
*Difficulty: no skill required*
*Duration: about five minutes for adults; children, 15 minutes or more*

## THE AIM OF THE GAME

To arrange the cards in 13 piles, each containing four cards of the same rank, as though on the face of a clock – starting with aces at one o'clock and ending with kings in the center.

## LAYING OUT THE GAME

Shuffle the cards and deal them into 13 piles of four cards each. The first 12 piles should be laid out in the shape of a clock-face, with each pile representing one of the numerals on the dial. The thirteenth pile is placed in the center of the circle.

## PLAYING THE GAME

Take the top card from the pile in the center of the clock-face (the king pile). Place it on or under the pile at the corresponding "hour" on the dial – if it is a seven, for example, place it where the hour hand would be pointing at seven o'clock. Jacks and queens should be placed at eleven and twelve o'clock, respectively. Note that the king pile, because the first card is taken from it, only ever has three cards in it.

Next, pick up a facedown card from the pile that you have just added to, and place this in turn in its appropriate place on the clock-face. Take the card from the bottom if you are playing with exposed cards at the top of the pile, and from the top if you are putting the exposed cards

*Diagram 71 Layout for a game of Clock Solitaire*

underneath the pile. If you turn up the last face-down card of any pile and find that it belongs to that pile, take the first available facedown card from the sequence of piles going clockwise. Continue playing until you have four of a kind on each number on the dial, or until you can play no longer because you have turned up a king when the other three are already exposed.

## VARIATION

One variation of Clock Solitaire is designed to overcome the obvious drawback that the game comes to a complete halt once the fourth king is turned up. This version is known as Watch Solitaire and is played in exactly the same way as Clock Solitaire with a single exception. If the fourth king is turned up before the end of the game, the player is allowed to return it facedown to any other pile in which there are unexposed cards, and to take a replacement card from the same pile. Only one replacement is allowed, but the chances of completing the game are increased fivefold.

This game also involves laying out the cards as though on the dial of a clock, and the aim is to end up with the top card on each pile representing the correct number on the dial.

*Players: one*
*Equipment: a pack of playing cards with the jokers removed*
*Difficulty: no skill required*
*Duration: about 5 minutes*

## THE AIM OF THE GAME

To build an ascending sequence of cards of the same suit on each pile or foundation.

## LAYING OUT THE GAME

Shuffle the cards and remove 12 from the pack. These should be in sequence from the two to the king, and should follow a strict rotation of suits: for example, 2K, 3L, 4M, 5N, 6K, 7L, and so on. Place these in a circle, with the nine at twelve o'clock, and the remainder following in clockwise sequence. Shuffle the remaining cards thoroughly and arrange them in five overlapping rows of eight cards each, with the cards facing up. This is the tableau from which cards will be taken to build up the foundations.

## PLAYING THE GAME

The play is straightforward. Any card may be taken from the top row of the tableau and placed on the preceding card in the same suit on the clock-face. For example, if the 5N is uppermost on the clock-face, and the 6N is in the top row of the tableau, the six can simply be placed on top of the five, and the card underneath the six comes into play. To be placed on the clock-face, cards must be in sequence and of the same suit.

There are, however, some additional moves that can be made within the tableau itself. Any card in the top row of the pool can be moved to another column, providing that it forms a descending sequence with the top card in that column. For example, the 6N can be placed on the seven of any other suit. If a column becomes empty, it can be replaced by any card from the top row of the seven remaining columns.

Play continues until each of the piles on the clock-face has the correct card at the top – an ace at one o'clock, a two at two o'clock, and a queen at twelve o'clock.

*Diagram 72 Playing a game of Clock Solitaire*

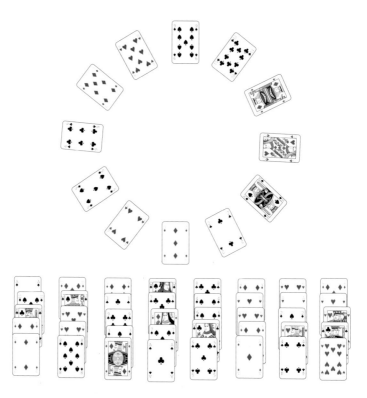

*Diagram 73  Layout for a game of Grandfather's Clock*

# KLONDIKE

Said to have originated in Alaska during the goldrush of 1897, this game will be familiar to many computer users because of its similarity to the game of Solitaire.

*Players:* one
*Equipment: a pack of playing cards with jokers removed*
*Difficulty: a little strategy helps*
*Duration: five to ten minutes*

## THE AIM OF THE GAME

To build four ascending sequences of cards of the same suit, from aces to kings.

## LAYING OUT THE GAME

Shuffle the cards and deal out a row of seven cards, with the first card in the row faceup and the remainder facedown. Then deal a row of six cards on top of the facedown cards in the first row, again with the first card in the row faceup and the remainder facedown. Follow this in similar fashion with rows of five, four, three, two, and finally one card, until you end up with seven faceup cards in seven piles containing from one to seven cards each. This is the tableau. You should have 24 cards left in your hand to form the reserve.

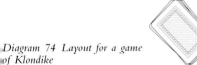

*Diagram 74 Layout for a game of Klondike*

## PLAYING THE GAME

Any exposed aces should be removed from the top row of cards and placed to one side, where they form the foundations. The card beneath the ace is then turned up – there should always be a card faceup at the top of each of the seven columns. If another ace, or a two of a suit in which the ace has already been exposed, is turned up, this can also be added to the foundations. If there are no aces showing, as is often the case, there are two further possibilities.

You may move any card in the top row to any other column provided that it forms a descending sequence with the top card of that column and is of a different color (you can move the 5L onto the 6N or 6K, but not the 6M). Eventually, this will mean that there is a sequence or build of several cards at the top of a column and you may move the entire sequence, or just the top part of it if you wish, to another column provided that the sequence is maintained.

*Diagram 75 Playing a game of Klondike*

If you cannot move any of the cards in the top row, you need to use the cards remaining in your hand – the reserve. There are two different ways of doing this. In the first method, cards in the reserve are turned up one at a time and you may only go through the pack once. When played this way, the game very seldom comes out. In the second method, cards are turned up three at a time, and you may go through the pack three times (or more if you don't want to observe strict rules). In the second method, you may only play the top card of the three you turn up, but once you have played the top card you can play the card beneath it, and then the ones below that, for as long as you can find somewhere to put them. Cards may be placed either directly onto a foundation, providing that they are in ascending sequence and in the same suit, or onto a card in the top row of the tableau if they are in descending sequence and of a different color. Once a card has been played on the foundation, it cannot be returned to the tableau.

If any column becomes empty, you may fill the vacant space with a king, but not with any other card. You may move any sequence of cards built on the king at the same time.

Play continues until you have four piles, each of the same suit, in ascending order, or you cannot move a card and have been through the cards in your hand as many times as permitted.

## HINTS AND TIPS

The opportunities for strategic play are greatly enhanced if you play the version in which three cards are turned up at a time. This enables you to get to know the pack and note the positions of any key cards, and plan your play accordingly. Say, for example, that the middle card of a triplet turned up from the reserve is an ace. It would obviously be beneficial to uncover it so that it can be laid in the foundation. Say the card above the ace is a 4L, and you subsequently turn up a 5K in the tableau. You may decide to leave the 5K exposed, even though you may be able to move the 4M to it from another column in the tableau, or you may be able to lay it onto the 4K in the foundation. Similarly, you may want to delay moving a king to a vacant space in the tableau if you know that you are going to turn up another, perhaps more useful king, from the reserve. And there is quite a lot that can be done by judicious moving of blocks of cards from one column to another to free cards that can then be transferred to the foundation, and perhaps to enable facedown cards to be turned up.

*Diagram 76  A completed game of Klondike*

## KLONDIKE FOR TWO OR MORE PLAYERS

In the two-player version, each player plays their own hand but to common foundations. The player with the lowest card in the left-hand, single-card, column in the tableau plays first. If these are of equal rank, the card in the second column is taken into account. A turn comes to an end when a player turns up a card or cards from the reserve.

If a player is able to move an ace to a foundation and does not do so, the second player may call the end of the turn, provided that he or she does so before the first player has made another move.

If the game is blocked, the winner is the player who has managed to move most cards to the foundation.

Multiple Klondike is very similar to Klondike, except that the players do not take turns: instead, all play simultaneously at their own rate from their own tableaux, and to common foundations. If more than one player is able to play to the same foundation, only the one who gets the card down first is allowed to make the play – the other player must return the card to its original position before continuing play.

Also known as "The Four Winds," this interesting variety of Double-Pack Solitaire is difficult to complete, mainly because success relies largely on luck.

*Players:* *one*
*Equipment:* *two packs of playing cards with jokers removed*
*Difficulty:* *little skill involved*
*Duration:* *about 15 minutes*

## THE AIM OF THE GAME
To build four ascending sequences of cards from aces, according to suit, and four descending sequences of cards from kings, also according to suit.

## LAYING OUT THE GAME
Shuffle the two packs of cards together thoroughly. Lay out 12 cards, following the arrangement shown in diagram 10. Start at the top left-hand corner and lay a card down, faceup, at an angle of 45° to a column of four cards below it, finishing with a card at the same angle at the bottom left-hand corner. Leave sufficient space to the right of this column to accommodate a separate pile for the aces and kings of each suit – you will need to allow for four piles, two abreast. Then lay a card at 45° at the top of a right-hand column, finishing off with a card at the same angle at the bottom right-hand corner.

Move any king or ace that comes up during this stage and use it to form the base of a pile in the area that you have left in the middle, and replace it in the outer columns or corners by another card from the pack. The kings occupy the top two rows, with two kings to each row, and the aces the bottom two. You cannot, however, move any cards from the columns other than kings and aces at this stage. If, for example, you have moved the AK into the middle, you cannot build on its pile with a 2K, should you deal one (see diagram 77, page 132), until the whole

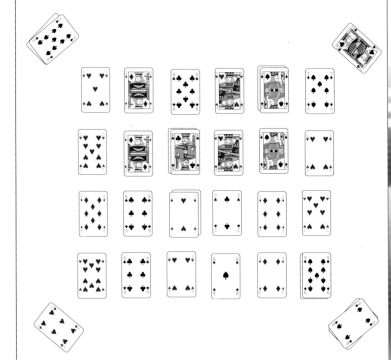

*Diagram 77 Playing a game of Four Corners*

game is laid out. If you find a 2K at a corner, though, you may move it into the centre now.

Each card in a column forms the base of a "depot," while the cards at the corners are known as "corner cards."

## PLAYING THE GAME

First, look at the cards that you have laid out: the idea is to build up from any ace in the center of the arrangement – first a two of the same suit, then a three and so on – and to build down from any king – a queen first, then a jack and so on. The catch is that while you can move any corner card to a central pile, as long as the suit and the sequence are correct, you can only move a card from a depot to a central pile if it is in the same row as that pile. You do not replace any cards that may have been moved from the original layout at this stage.

Next, you repeat the layout sequence, in exactly the same order, placing cards as they come from the top of the deck – again, if an ace or king are revealed, they should be moved into the central area immediately and replaced from the deck. Again, any appropriate corner cards can be moved to the central piles, but cards from the depots can only be moved if they are in the same row as the central pile to which they are appropriate.

Continue to deal out the cards, moving them to the central pile if this is permissible, until your stock of cards is exhausted. At this point, the rules change and the real interest of the game becomes apparent. You are now allowed to move a top card from any depot onto an appropriate central pile; you can also move any of the depot cards or the corner cards to any other depot or corner, in either ascending or descending order in the same suit. However, it is as well to think carefully about the consequences before you move a card: you may be able to move more cards if you move one way rather than another.

If you come to a stop once more, you have a further option, which gives you two more chances to complete the game. Pick up the corner cards and depot cards in the order in which you first laid them down, and form a pack – but do not shuffle them. You can then deal them round the layout to see if you can improve your situation. The rules of the game allow you to do this twice, but no more.

## HINTS AND TIPS

To a large extent, success in this game depends on the fall of the cards. However, it is possible to improve the chances that you will play the game out if you pay particular attention to your tactics during the stage when you have exhausted your stock of cards and the rules of the game are relaxed. Think about the consequences of any move, paying particular attention to what further opportunities any move can give you. Remember, too, that if you build up an ascending sequence in a depot at this stage, it will turn into a descending sequence when you pick up all the outer cards and deal them once more: if you have a 7M in a central pile, for example, an 8M, 9M, 10M sequence in a depot can be moved onto the central pile after they have been turned over to be dealt once more.

Originally a French game called La Belle Lucie, this is a
surprisingly subtle and flexible form of Solitaire.

*Players: one*
*Equipment: a pack of playing cards with jokers removed*
*Difficulty: a little strategy helps*
*Duration: about 15 minutes*

## THE AIM OF THE GAME
To build four ascending sequences of cards of the same suit, from
aces to kings.

## LAYING OUT THE GAME
Shuffle the cards thoroughly, then deal three at a time, faceup, into 17
piles or "fans" of three cards each and one singleton (the only card from
one suit). They can be arranged in any convenient fashion. This forms
the tableau.

## PLAYING THE GAME
The top card of any fan, including the singleton, is available for play.
Those beneath it are blocked until the top card is moved. Move any aces
to one side where they form the foundations.

The remaining cards can be moved in one of two ways. They can be
added to the foundations provided they are in ascending sequence and in
the same suit; or they may be moved to any other fan provided they
form a descending sequence in the same suit as the top card of that fan.
No more than one card can be moved at a time. Once a card has been
placed on a foundation, it cannot be moved back to the tableau. When
all the cards in a fan have been used, the vacant space is not filled by
moving any other card – it remains empty (see diagram 79, page 138).
When there are no further moves you can make, the remaining cards in

*Diagram 78 Layout for a game of Lovely Lucy*

the tableau should be picked up, shuffled thoroughly, and re-dealt in threes as before. Two re-deals are allowed, making three deals in all.

Finally, when you have dealt three times and run out of cards that you can play, one further move is allowed. You may take any card that is blocked by the card or cards on top of it and move it anywhere appropriate on the tableau or foundations. This is known as the "merci" – the French for "thank you."

## HINTS AND TIPS

It is important to remember that each card has only one other card to which it can be moved in a tableau. Once you have moved a card, therefore, it will block the cards beneath it, unless it is subsequently moved to a foundation. Not only will you not be able to move these cards to a foundation, but you will not be able to build on them, either. So take care before you bury cards that might be valuable to you – there may be alternatives that provide a better outcome. A king at the top of a fan also renders the cards beneath it inaccessible.

Remember, cards that are next lowest in sequence to cards that are blocked are effectively blocked themselves, so you can build on these with impunity. Also, you should always move any card to a foundation as soon as possible: if it can be moved to a foundation, there is nowhere it can go on the tableau, and it is merely trapping the card beneath it.

## VARIATIONS
### Trefoil

In a variation of the game known as Trefoil, play is exactly the same, but the four aces are taken from the pack before dealing and put on one side to form the foundations. The first tableau, therefore, consists of 16 fans of three cards each.

*Diagram 79 Vacant spaces in a game of Lovely Lucy*

## Shamrocks

A slightly more complex variation of Lovely Lucy is known as Shamrocks. The layout of the game is identical to that of Lovely Lucy. However, after the deal, any king found above another card of the same suit is transferred beneath the lower card. Building on the tableau also follows different rules. You may build either up or down on any fan, and you need not follow suit. The catch is that no fan may contain more than three cards – a card can only be placed on top of a fan when one has already been removed from it. Empty fans are not replaced and only one deal is allowed, rather than three.

The trick in Shamrocks is to maintain as much flexibility and choice as possible for building on the tableau. The last card in a fan should not be moved until you are sure that you have no further need for it, and cards should not be transferred automatically to the foundations because they may be more useful in the short-term for building on the tableau. As a general rule, the foundations should be kept more or less level.

## MONTE CARLO

Despite its name, this simple, straightforward game of chance is unlikely to have been played at the famous casino. It is also known as Double or Quits, or Weddings.

*Players:* one
*Equipment:* a pack of playing cards with the jokers removed
*Difficulty:* no skill involved
*Duration:* five to ten minutes

### THE AIM OF THE GAME

To arrange the pack into 26 pairs of cards of equal rank.

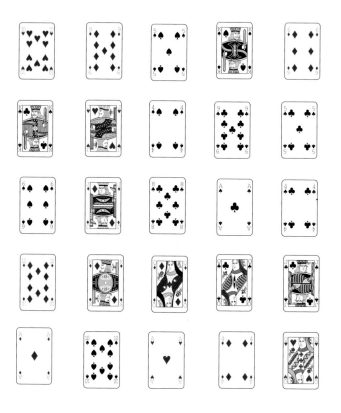

*Diagram 80  Layout for a game of Monte Carlo*

## ,AYING OUT THE GAME

huffle the cards thoroughly, then deal them face-up in five rows each
ontaining five cards. Put the remainder of the pack to one side.

## >LAYING THE GAME

Cards may be picked up from the tableau and discarded if they form
djoining pairs of equal rank. They may be adjoining horizontally,
vertically, or diagonally. Any card is thus considered to have eight
djoining neighbors.

Once all the adjoining pairs have been removed, there will be gaps in
he tableau. Fill these by moving cards to the left, or to the end of the
ow above, so that they still fall in the order in which they were dealt.
When the tableau has been consolidated in this way, use some of the
emaining cards from the pack to build up the array to 25 cards again,
ind discard any adjoining pairs as before. Once again, fill any gaps and
ebuild the tableau with further cards from the pack.

When the pack is exhausted, continue to play, consolidating the
tableau each time all pairs have been discarded. The game ends when
you have 26 pairs of cards in the discard pile, or when you are faced
with the final cards in an unhappy and frustrating combination such as
2-4-2-4.

## HINTS AND TIPS

The only time you have a chance to influence the course of the game in
Monte Carlo is when a card is paired with more than one adjoining
card. In this case, you should discard the pair that will create a further
pair or pairs when the tableau is consolidated.

This unusual game requires a certain amount of mental arithmetic from the player.

*Players: one*
*Equipment: a pack of playing cards with the jokers removed*
*Difficulty: a good grasp of mental arithmetic is required*
*Duration: until your patience runs out*

## THE AIM OF THE GAME
To achieve a total score of 91 on the tableau after assigning each card its appropriate numerical value.

## LAYING OUT THE GAME
Shuffle and deal the cards faceup into 13 piles of four cards each.

*Diagram 81 Layout for a game of Ninety-one*

## PLAYING THE GAME

Each card is assigned its usual numeric value: the ace is one (not 11); two to 10 are the same as their face value; the jack is 11, the queen 12, and the king 13. The total for the tableau is arrived at by adding together the numeric values of all 13 cards at the top of the piles.

To manipulate the total, you move a card from the top of any of the 13 piles to the top of any other pile. You can move cards as many times as you like, but you must keep at least one card in each of the 13 piles. There are many different solutions to the game, including the sequence ace to king. An example is shown in diagram 19.

The game continues until the total is exactly 91, or until your patience finally runs out.

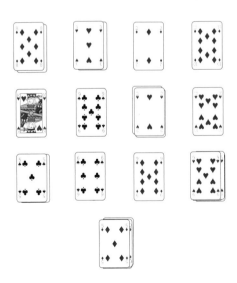

*Diagram 82  Example of cards adding up to 91*

# —CARD GAMES FOR 2 OR MORE—

In non-trick games, points are scored by forming certain combinations of cards, as in Rummy or Cribbage, or by "capturing" them, as in Casino and Scopa.

Along with Bridge and Poker, Rummy is one of the most popular card games. It is a simple game that has lent itself to many variations that can be played by between two and eight players.

Gin Rummy is the most popular of the two-handed versions: from its origins in Spain, the game reached its peak of popularity during World War II, when it was taken up with much publicity by a number of Hollywood film stars, who used it to fill in time between takes. It then became an essential part of sophisticated adult social life.

Canasta, one of the most complex Rummy games, is the most popular form for four players. Taking its name from the Spanish word for "basket," it was introduced to the United States from South America in the 1940s. After becoming the Unites States' most popular card game, it spread to Europe and became very popular there, too. Casino, and the simpler version that is called Scopa, is an unusual game that can be traced back to fifteenth-century France. In the United States, its era of greatest popularity was eclipsed by the Gin Rummy boom of the 1930s.

Cribbage is a very old English game that has hardly changed at all in the past 350 years, since it was first played in clubs and taverns. It is still played using a wooden "noddy" board and pegs for scoring. The best boards are made of fine wood and use ivory pegs to keep score, but bone, wood, or plastic pegs are just as good and used matches are also commonly used to keep score. If nothing else is available, a scoresheet drawn up on paper will also serve the purpose just as well. Originally, Cribbage was a two-handed game, but variations for three and four players are now played

A member of the Rummy family, Canasta was imported into America from Argentina and Uruguay in 1949, and became for a while the most popular game in the history of cards; the fad has passed, but it retains its popularity to this day.

*Players: four, in two partnerships*
*Equipment: two packs of cards with jokers*
*Difficulty: some skill required*
*Duration: about half an hour*

## THE AIM OF THE GAME

Canasta is entirely a point-count game: the aim is to be the first side to reach a score of 5000 – unlike Rummy, there is no great virtue in being the first to "go out." In scoring, cards are allocated the following values:

| | |
|---|---|
| jokers | 50 points each |
| 2s | 20 points each |
| aces | 20 points each |
| K, Q, J, 10, 9, 8 | 10 points each |
| 7, 6, 5, 4 | 5 points each |
| black 3 | 5 points each |

Red 3s are given special treatment: they score 100 points each, or 800 if a side has all four of them, but these are bonus points rather than points earned during play. All jokers and 2s are wild cards: that is, they can stand for cards of any rank.

Points are scored by forming "melds." These are combinations of three or more cards of the same rank – for example, 8, 8, 8, or K, K, K, K. Wild cards may be used, so that 8, 8, 2, or K, K, joker, 2, are also valid melds. A meld, however, must contain at least two natural cards and must not contain more than three wild cards. Combinations held in the hand are not melds and have no scoring value. They must first be laid down or "melded," with the cards faceup on the table.

A meld containing seven cards is known as a canasta, and players should aim to make as many canastas as possible because they have the highest scoring value. Natural canastas – with no wild cards – score higher than mixed ones. Wild cards and red 3s may not be melded, but black 3s may be melded when a player is going out.

## BEGINNING THE GAME

Players cut for partners, with the two higher cards playing the two lower cards. Any player cutting the joker cuts again, as do players showing identical cards. The highest card deals first.

Cards are dealt in a clockwise fashion, facedown and one at a time, starting with the player to the dealer's left. After each player has received 11 cards, the remaining cards are placed in the middle of the table and the top card is turned faceup beside them (the "upcard") to form the basis of the discard pile. The remaining cards are the "stock."

## PLAYING THE GAME

The player to the dealer's left begins play by laying down, faceup, any red 3s in the hand, and drawing a replacement from the stock. They then pick up the upcard or a card from the top of the stock. At this stage, the player is entitled to meld if able to do so (see opposite). The turn ends with the discarding of a card from hand onto the discard pile. Play then passes to the player on the left.

Any player dealt a red 3 must immediately lay it down and take a replacement from stock. The same applies to red 3s taken from stock during play. Only red 3s acquired by capturing the discard pile (see page 148) are not replaced, although these, too, must be laid down. If a red 3 is the first card to be turned up, another card is turned up to cover it. The same applies if the first upcard is a black 3 or a wild card.

Play continues in this way, with each player drawing, melding, and laying off as desired, and discarding, until either one side "goes out" (see page 150) or until there are no more cards left in the stock. When the stock is exhausted, play continues using the discard pile. If the upcard can be placed on an existing meld, the player must take it. There is, however, no obligation to take the upcard to make a new meld – that is for the player to decide. Once there are no players willing or able to take the upcard, the deal is at an end. If the last card is a red 3, the card is turned up and the player who drew it is then entitled to make as many melds as he wishes. In this situation, however, no discard is made, and the deal ends immediately.

One rule of play is that no player may draw from a discard pile containing only one card. By convention, a player with only one card left in hand is required to announce "Last card" while discarding.

## MELDING

Melding is laying down a set of three or more cards of the same rank. Any player can meld in turn, after drawing a card and before discarding. However, this does not apply to the initial meld. In this case, the total point value of the meld must come to at least a certain minimum, depending on cumulative scores from previous deals. The initial meld requirements for different cumulative scores are:

| Cumulative score | Requirement |
| --- | --- |
| minus | 15 |
| 0 to 1495 | 50 |
| 1500 to 2995 | 90 |
| over 3000 | 120 |

If a player uses a card from the top of the discard pile to make an initial meld, the value of this card can be added to the value of the meld to make up the initial requirement.

In the first deal, the initial requirement is obviously 50, since both sides have a cumulative score of zero. If a player is found to have insufficient points in an initial meld, and provided the next player has not drawn a card, the player is obliged to rectify the situation, either by increasing the value of the meld, or by withdrawing it. The initial meld requirement for that side is increased by 10 points, and there is a 100-point penalty for each exposed card that is taken back into the hand. The same penalty applies for any incorrect meld.

Once one player in a side has melded, the other partner can meld without meeting the initial requirement. A side can only meld one set of cards of a particular rank. A meld of 5, 5, 5, cannot be laid down separately if 5s have already been melded: the cards must be "laid off" on the existing meld. Players can lay off cards on their own and their partner's melds whenever their turn comes, but they cannot lay off on their opponents' melds. Partner's melds are laid side by side on the same part of the table, and not kept separately on opposite sides of the table.

When a meld contains seven cards, it becomes a canasta. The cards are collected into a single pile, with a red card on top if the canasta is natural, and a black card if it is mixed. Cards may be laid off on a canasta, including wild cards, but the limit of three wild cards in any meld must be observed, and the addition of wild cards to a natural canasta converts it to a mixed one of lower value. Canastas are not only desirable because of their very high values (300 for a mixed and 500 for a natural canasta), but also because no side can go out without at least one canasta – and many canasta players insist on two.

## CAPTURING THE DISCARD PILE

Winning at Canasta is a matter of adding as many cards to your hand as you can, and the way to do this is to capture the discard pile. This means taking the top card of the discard pile and combining it with two or more cards in your hand to form a meld. Once you have done this,

*Diagram 83  Melds and canastas*

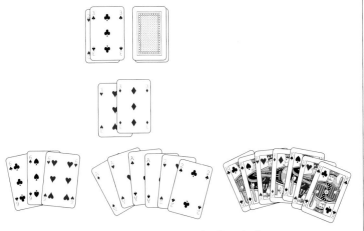

*Diagram 84  Capturing the discard pile*

you are entitled to pick up the remainder of the discard pile and add it to your hand.

In the official version of the game (Canasta is one of the few card games to have official rules), the discard pile has two alternative states – "frozen" and "unfrozen." The pile is frozen to any side that has not made an initial meld, and it is frozen to both sides if it contains a red 3 (as the initial upcard) or a wild card (as the initial upcard or as a discard).

The difference between these two states depends on whether you follow the official rules or adopt generally accepted practice. Officially, when the pack is unfrozen, a player may take the upcard (and capture the discard pile) if it can be laid off on an existing meld, or if it can be melded by matching it with a pair in hand, one of which can be a wild card. If the pack is frozen, then it can only be unfrozen and captured if a player matches the upcard with a natural pair in hand. In the more widely played unofficial version, the upcard can only be taken by a matching natural pair, whether the discard pile is frozen or not. In this case, the only advantage of the initial meld is that further melds (and discard captures) can be made without meeting the initial meld requirement.

Whichever version you play (and it is as well to sort this out before the game begins), the pack can be "stopped" for any individual player if the previous player discards a black 3. The "stopped" player can only draw from stock. As soon as the black 3 is covered, the pack is no longer stopped. Black 3s, for this reason, are referred to as "stop cards."

## GOING OUT

When a player lays down all his or her cards in the form of melds, that player goes out and there is no further play. Players going out do not have to discard: they can add the final card to a meld if they are able to do so.

A player going out who has not previously melded is said to be going out "concealed" and earns additional points. Going out concealed still requires that the player has enough points to meet the initial meld requirement, and must meld at least one canasta if his or her partner has not already done so.

It is legal, but not necessary, to ask your partner "May I go out partner?" before going out. Your partner must then reply "Yes" or "No" and you are bound by the reply. This routine is often used as a device to warn your partner to meld as many cards as possible because you intend to go out in the next round, and the reply is automatically "No." Only cards that have been melded contribute toward the final score: cards remaining in the hand have negative value.

Going out is usually a defensive measure, designed to stop your opponents from making too many points. The side with the bulk of the cards has the best chance of scoring canastas, and will delay going out until most of the stock has gone.

## SCORING

After a player has gone out, the scores are tallied and written down. The "basic count" is calculated first, according to the following scores.

| | |
|---|---|
| For each natural canasta | 500 points |
| For each mixed canasta | 300 points |
| For going out concealed | 200 points |
| For going out unconcealed | 100 points |
| For each red 3 | 100 points |
| For all four red 3s | 800 points |

If a side has no melds, its red 3s count minus 100 (or minus 800 if they have all four). If a side is found to have failed to lay down a red 3, it is penalized 500 points. It is therefore possible for a side to end up with a minus score at the end of a deal.

After the basic count has been concluded, each side counts the points in its melded cards and adds them to the basic count. Finally, the value of all unmelded cards in both partner's hands is totalled and subtracted from the score. The result is the final score. This is written on the scoresheet and added to the cumulative total from previous deals. The first side to reach 5000 wins the game.

---

# CASINO

This unusual game has its origins in medieval France and is still popular in Italy and eastern Mediterranean countries. It has more in common with traditional Chinese "fishing" games than with most other Western card games.

*Players: two, but can be adapted for three or four*
*Equipment: one pack of playing cards with the jokers removed*
*Difficulty: requires skill; suitable for adults and older children*
*Duration: about half an hour*

## THE AIM OF THE GAME
The aim of the game is to capture cards from the table by "matching" them in specified ways with cards from the hand. Certain cards have scoring value: aces score one, and 2 to 10 score their face or "pip" value. Court cards (king, queen, and jack) have no value. The player with the highest score at the end of the game is the winner.

## PLAYING THE GAME
The cards are cut, and the player with the lower card becomes the first dealer. Cards are dealt two at a time, first facedown to the non-dealer, then faceup to the table, and finally facedown to the dealer. A second round of two cards is dealt in the same way, so that each player has four facedown cards, with four faceup on the table.

*Diagram 85 Capturing and a sweep*

Play begins with the non-dealer placing a card faceup on the table. This card can be used to capture matching cards from the table. For a card to match, it must either form a pair with a table card of the same rank, or its value must be equal to the combined values of two or more table cards. A card can match several cards or combinations of cards simultaneously. If the table cards are, for example, A, 2, 5, 8, and you have an 8 in your hand, you can capture the 8 by pairing, and the A, 2, 5, by matching their combined value. You will also have captured all the cards on the table at once, making a "sweep."

Captured cards are placed in a pile, facedown, in front of the player. Sweeps are indicated by turning the hand card face-up on top of the captured cards. Court cards can only be captured by pairing since they have no value. A player can capture a single court card to make a pair, or three court cards to make a four, but it is not permissible to capture two court cards to make a three.

## BUILDING

If you cannot capture cards from the table, there is another option known as "building." The purpose of a build is to position cards for capture the next time around, and you must have a card in your hand capable of making the capture. If, for example, you have a 9 and a 3 in hand and there is a 6 on the table, you can play the 3 on the 6, announce "building 9," and capture both cards the next time round with the 9. There is, of course, always the danger that your opponent will also have a 9 and will therefore capture the build before you do.

It is important that you announce clearly the value of the build in order to distinguish between "single" and "multiple" builds. If, for example, you make a build of A, 3 from the table with a 4 from your hand, you can announce either "building 4s" – a multiple build – "building 8" – equal to the announced value, so if you intend to capture the build with a 4, you should "build 4s" rather than "8," and vice versa. A single build can be duplicated, becoming a multiple build.

For example, you can play a 3 from your hand onto a 6 from the table, and then add a 9 from the table, saying "building 9s." Alternatively, you can add to an existing build of nines by laying a 5 from hand on a 4 from table and then add these to the build.

Obviously, multiple builds may have a total value well in excess of 10. However, their announced value – the value of the basic building block – can never exceed 10.

There is another important difference between single and multiple builds. A single build can be increased in value, provided its value does not exceed 10, and provided the player making the increase has a hand card of equal value to the new total value of the build. If one player places a 4 on a 3 from the table to make a build of 7, the opposing player can add a 2 and announce "building 9." If the first player does not have a 9, there is little that can be done, unless they have A, 10 in hand and can therefore add the ace to the build, announcing "building 10." A build can only be increased with a card from hand, and not with a card from table. The value of a multiple build cannot be increased.

Once you have made or increased a build, you cannot trail a card on your next or subsequent turns (unless, of course, the build has been captured by your opponent). You must either capture it, start a new build or add to an existing build. When both players have played all four cards in their hands, a new round or four cards each is dealt, two at a time as before. The table receives no more cards in the second or subsequent deals. The game ends when neither player has any more cards in hand and there are none left in the stock. Any cards remaining on the table are

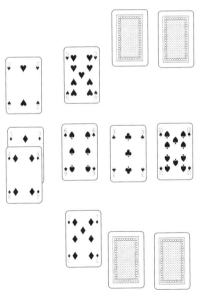

*Diagram 86 Building*

taken by the player who made the last capture. This does not count as a sweep, unless the final cards are taken by a sweep in the course of normal play.

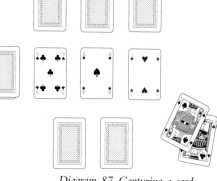

Diagram 87 *Capturing a card*

## SCORING

Players do not continue to play until an agreed score is reached: each deal is regarded as a separate game. Points are scored as follows:

| | |
|---|---|
| For capturing most cards | 3 |
| For capturing most spades | 1 |
| For capturing L10 (Big Casino) | 2 |
| For capturing N2 (Little Casino) | 1 |
| For each ace captured | 1 |
| For each sweep | 1 |

If there is a tie for most cards or most spades, neither player scores a point.

A simpler game than its close relative, Casino, Scopa is particularly suitable for children. The name comes from the Italian for "scoop" or "sweep," referring to a characteristic aspect of play.

*Players: two*
*Equipment: one pack of cards, with the 8s, 9s and 10s removed, leaving 40 cards in all*
*Difficulty: suitable for children*
*Duration: about half an hour*

## THE AIM OF THE GAME

The aim of the game is to capture cards from the table by "matching" them with a card from hand. Each card is given a value: aces count as one; 2 to 7 are given their face, or "pip" value; jacks count as eight; queens count as nine; kings count as 10. Points are scored by capturing the majority of cards and also by capturing certain specific cards. Capturing all the cards on the table at once – a "sweep" – also scores. The winner is the first to reach an agreed score, usually 11.

## BEGINNING THE GAME

Players cut for deal and the player with the lower card deals first. Three cards are dealt, facedown and one at a time, to each player, starting with the non-dealer, followed by four cards faceup on the table. The remainder of the pack is placed facedown beside the table cards: this is the "stock." Play begins with the non-dealer.

## PLAYING THE GAME

Each player has two options – to capture, or to "trail." To capture a card, or cards, from the table, a player must play a matching card faceup on the table. There are two ways in which a card can match: it can form a pair with another card of the same rank; and it can match any combination of two or more table cards that have the same total face value. For example, a jack in your hand can match another jack on the table, or it can match 5, 3, or A, 5, 2, on the table. But it cannot match both at once. If the table cards are A, 5, 2, J, and you play a jack from your hand, you are obliged to capture the jack, rather than the combination – the pair always takes precedence. You do not have to play the jack at all if you do not want to: you can play any other card in your hand instead.

If you lay down a card that does not make a capture, you "trail" the card. It simply stays faceup on the table, where it is available for capture by either player. It is generally accepted that a card cannot be trailed if it can make a capture. If it is able to capture any of the table cards, then once it has been played it must do so.

Players place captured cards facedown in a pile. The exception is in the case of a "sweep." A sweep means capturing all the cards on the table at once. When this happens, the hand card used to make the capture is turned faceup on top of the pile, making it easy to count the number of sweeps at the end of the deal. Since the number of table cards varies during play, it can sometimes be quite easy to make a sweep.

Once you have made a sweep, your opponent can only "trail" a card, because there is nothing there to capture. If you can do this by pairing, then you have made another valid sweep.

When both players have exhausted their cards, three further cards are dealt to each of them, face-down as before. In all, there are five deals of three cards each in a game. The game ends when neither player has any cards in hand and there are none left in stock. Any cards remaining on the table are deemed to have been captured by the player of the last card and are added to the other captures. This does not, however, constitute a sweep, even if the player could have made a valid sweep in normal play.

## SCORING

At the end of the game, players add up the points they have scored using the system in the table below.

| | |
|---|---|
| For capturing 21 or more cards | 1 |
| For capturing 6 or more diamonds | 1 |
| For capturing L7 (the "sette bello") | 1 |
| For "primiera" (see below) | 1 |
| For each sweep | 1 |

The primiera is arrived at in rather a peculiar fashion. From the pile of captures, each player extracts the highest card in each suit. However, the cards have different values in the primiera: 7 = 21; 6 = 18; A = 16; 5 = 15; 4 = 14; 3 = 13; 2 = 12; and K, Q, J = 10. The values of the four cards are totaled, and the player with the highest total wins the point for primiera. If a player has no cards in one or more suits, he or she cannot win the point. If the scores are equal, neither player wins a point. Once both players have totaled their scores, they add them to their scores from previous games. The first to reach 11 points is the winner, and the game comes to an end.

This is the ideal game to play when your opponents claim that they never receive any good cards, because the idea is to lose any trick that contains a heart. Doing so, however, is not nearly as easy as it sounds.

*Players: three to seven*
*Equipment: one pack of playing cards*
*Difficulty: not difficult, but some skill helps*
*Duration: about half an hour for a round*

*Diagram 88 The 2s are removed to ensure equal cards for each player*

## THE AIM OF THE GAME AND SCORING

The basic game of hearts, along with its numerous variations, is played to the fundamental rules of Whist. The main difference between the two games is that in Hearts the aim is to lose any tricks in which a heart is played. (In some variations, players must attempt to lose tricks containing the queen, king, and ace of spades as well.) Aces are high, there are no trumps, and players must follow suit if they are able to do so.

A player winning a trick containing a heart scores one penalty point for each heart in that trick. Any player who fails to follow suit when able to do so is fined 13 penalty points; the hand ends and all penalty points previously incurred during it are canceled.

At the start of a game, the players agree a number of penalty points that will finish the game – either 50 or 100 is usual. When a player reaches that score, the game is over and the winner is the player with the lowest number of penalty points.

## PLAYING THE GAME

The pack of cards is adjusted according to the number of players so that each person has the same number of

*Diagram 89 Discard a high heart if you cannot follow suit*

7 points

10 points

13 points

Diagram 90
Penalty cards

cards: with three players, one card of value 2 is removed; with four or six players, no cards are removed; with five players, two 2s are removed; with seven players, three 2s are removed. The M2 is always left in the deck.

The pack is cut and the person with the lowest card deals. The cards are dealt facedown and one by one, starting with the player on the dealer's left and working clockwise. The players pick up their hands and the one to the dealer's left plays the first card. Going clockwise, the other players must follow suit if possible; if not, any card can be rejected – it is a good idea to lay down the highest heart in your hand, to avoid the risk of it winning a trick if the suit is hearts. A card in the wrong suit cannot win a trick, whatever its face value.

The winner of each trick collects the cards, marks down any penalty points incurred and then plays the next card. Play continues until no cards are left. At this point, the players add up their scores and a new round starts, with the deal moving to the player to the left of the one who dealt the previous round.

Diagram 91 Discarding two clubs leaves a void in clubs. NA is discarded instead of NQ because it may win a spade trick, and the NQ can be discarded on a club trick

## VARIATIONS
### Black Maria

This variation on basic hearts is the most popular form of the game in Europe – a "black Maria" is the British slang name for a police van. In this game, players are not only penalized for winning tricks with hearts, but also for the ace, king, and queen of spades: NA costs seven points; NK costs 10 points; and NQ (the Black Maria) costs 13 points.

The game starts in the same way as basic hearts, but after the deal you select three cards that you do not want and pass them facedown to the player on your right. All the players do this at the same time, so that nobody can see what cards they have received before deciding which ones to discard. Beware passing off the NQ; often it is better to give yourself a void and get rid of unwanted point-cards during play.

## American Hearts or Black Lady

In this widely played variation NQ carries a penalty of 13 points, but capturing all the hearts plus the NQ – "shooting the moon" – reverses the usual scoring. All 26 points are lodged against each of the opponents. (Falling short – even by one point – is of course a disaster.) In order to avoid any advantage in the exchange of cards after the deal – some players have rather predictable strategies – cards are passed off in successive hands: left, right, across, and hold (no pass). Players generally add up point-cards in their piles after play, rather than keep a running score.

 *1 point*

 *2 points*

 *11 points*

*12 points*

*13 points*

## Spot Hearts

This variation gives penalty points for each heart card according to its face value.

*Diagram 92 Penalty points for Spot Hearts*

Derived from the ancient French game of Triomphe, Euchre became the national game of the United States in the 1800s. Jokers were first introduced to card games in the United States in the 1860s, specifically for use in Euchre, where the joker is known as the "benny." The game's popularity waned with the introduction of Whist and Bridge, but it is still a favorite in Australia and England's West Country.

*Players: four in two partnerships*
*Equipment: one pack of cards with 2s to 8s removed and a joker*
            *included (25 cards)*
*Difficulty: some skill required*
*Duration: about 45 minutes for a round*

## THE AIM OF THE GAME AND SCORING

Euchre has elements of both Whist and Bridge. Play follows the same rules as whist, but it also has a bidding system. It also has a somewhat arcane system of nomenclature.

Players bid for the right to try to win three tricks, and are awarded one point if they do so. No extra point is awarded for winning four tricks, but two points are awarded if five tricks are won (this figure is increased to four points if one member of the partnership plays alone). If only two tricks or less are won, two points are awarded to the opponents. A game is won

*Diagram 93 Two 3s and two 4s from the pack are reserved by each partnership for use in scoring*

by the first side to win five points.
Matches are divided into legs, however,
and a leg is won by the first side to win
21 points. The match itself is won by the
first side to win two legs out of three.

## TRUMPS

The order of trumps is different from
that of other games. The joker, or benny,
is the highest trump card, followed by

*Diagram 94 The trump sequence
with diamonds as trumps*

the jack of the trump suit – this card is known as the "right bower." The
jack of the same color is the third highest trump, and is known as the
"left bower." In descending order, the other trumps are the ace, king,
queen, 10 and 9 – the ace, therefore, is the fourth highest trump card.
The other non-trump suits are valued from ace down to 9, though the
suit of the same color as trumps will not have a jack.

## STARTING TO PLAY

The 25 cards are shuffled by the dealer and then cut by the player to the
dealer's right. Five cards are dealt facedown to each player in two rounds,
with three cards in the first round and two in the second. The remaining
five cards are placed facedown in a pile in the center of the table and the
top card is turned faceup (see diagram 95). This card shows the suit that
might be trumps. If the card turns out to be the joker, the dealer then
nominates trumps, but does so before looking at his hand.

## BIDDING

The player sitting to the left of the dealer has the first opportunity to bid.
After viewing your hand, you must decide whether it is possible to win
three or more tricks if the turned-up card were to be trumps. This decision
will be affected by the fact that on the first round only, the dealer has the

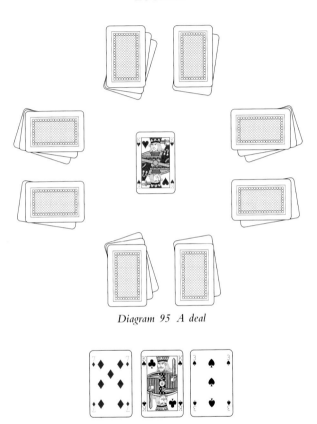

*Diagram 95 A deal*

*Diagram 96 A sample deal*

option of picking up the trump card after the bidding is complete and discarding a card, placing it facedown at the bottom of the pile in the center of the table. If you decide that three tricks cannot be won with that hand and the suit that is trumps, you say "pass." If you decide that three tricks can be won, you say "I order it up." You are then known as "the maker" and must immediately indicate whether you will play the hand alone or with the help of your partner. If you decide to play alone, you say "up, down;" if in partnership, you say just "up." Bidding stops as soon as one player "orders it up" and declares their intentions, and then play starts.

If all the players pass, another round of bidding starts, but this time each player is allowed to say which would be their trump suit of choice – and this time the dealer is not allowed to pick the upturned card up from the center pile. If you wish to play the hand alone with spades as trumps, for example, the bid is "alone spades" or "spades, down." If you wish to play in partnership, the bid would be "spades, up." Again, bidding stops as soon as a player bids for a game and plays starts. However, if no player has bid for a game at the end of this round the cards are reshuffled and dealt again, by the player to the left of the previous dealer.

## PLAYING THE GAME

The partner of a maker who has declared "down" or "alone" places their cards facedown on the table. The opponents then have the option of playing alone or together, though if one of the two players is the dealer and the upturned card has been picked up, that player must take part.

The opening lead is played by the player on the left of a lone player if there is one, or by the player on the dealer's left if there is not. Play obeys normal trick rules: the players must follow suit wherever possible; and the highest card or highest trump wins the trick. When all five tricks have been decided, the hand is over and the scores are noted. The deal then moves one player to the left and another hand is started. The process continues until a game, leg, or match has been won.

## HINTS AND TIPS

As each hand has so few tricks there is little chance of planning a strategy once play has started, so it is in the bidding that a hand of euchre is won or lost. Considerable thought is needed at this stage. For example, if you are the dealer and you deal yourself a hand consisting of NK, N9, KQ, MA, and MJ, and the turned-up card is a diamond (see diagram 19) it would be very unwise to bid. This is also true if the turned-up card is a spade or a club, because even then your NK will only rank as the fifth highest trump. But if MK is turned up, you hold the second, fourth, and fifth highest trumps and could win the hand by picking up the MK and discarding KQ, because you will then have two void suits that can be trumped.

Your position at the table is also significant when playing euchre. If the first two players pass, this indicates that they have weak hands. This means that the third and fourth players have to be sure that they can win without much assistance from their partners. If all the players pass on the first hand it is likely that the dealer is weak in the suit that was turned up and does not feel sufficiently strong to win three tricks even if the turned-up card – the MA, say – is added to the hand. In diagram 97, the dealer's opponents should examine their hands to see if they could make a game in diamonds, while dealer and partner should look more to the two black suits.

*Diagram 97  The dealer's hand*

This is the extremely popular American version of two-handed bezique, the difference being that the 8s are taken out of the double pack, as well as the 2s to 7s. Both games are derived from the German game Binokel.

 11 points

 3 points

 10 points

 2 points

 4 points

 0 points

Diagram 98 Scoring

*Players:* two
*Equipment:* two packs of playing cards
with identical backs; pencil
and paper
*Difficulty:* complex and skillful
*Duration:* 45 minutes to several hours

## THE OBJECT AND SCORING

To win tricks and combine, or "meld," cards, and so score points over two phases of play. Points are obtained from winning tricks according to whether the trick contains high-value cards. The total number of points available from tricks is 250 points.

In addition, 10 points are awarded to the player who wins the last trick in the second phase of play. The points scored by melds (combinations of cards that can be placed on the table after winning a trick) are as follows:

| | |
|---|---|
| a flush (all the trump cards minus the 9) | = 150 points |
| four aces of different suits ("a hundred aces") | = 100 points |
| four kings of different suits ("eighty kings") | = 80 points |
| four queens of different suits ("sixty queens") | = 60 points |
| four jacks of different suits ("forty jacks") | = 40 points |
| the king and queen of trumps (a "royal marriage") | = 40 points |
| NQ and LJ – ("pinochle") | = 40 points |

a king and queen of any other suit (a "marriage")  = 20 points
a 9 of trumps on its own (a "dix")  = 10 points.

Points won for melds are counted as the melds are placed on the table. The points for tricks are worked out at the end of each hand, but the number is rounded up or down to the nearest 10. The player who reaches 1000 points first wins the game, but if both players exceed 1000 points after the same hand the winner becomes the first player to reach 1250 points, and so on.

## STARTING TO PLAY

All cards with a face value of from 2 to 8 inclusive are removed from both packs, leaving 48 cards for play. The cards rank as follows, from high to low: ace, 10, king, queen, jack, 9. The players cut the cards to decide who is to deal first, the winner being the player whose card is highest — the ranking of cards for the cut is the same as that for the game. After the first hand the deal alternates between the two players.

The dealer shuffles the deck, hands it to the other player to be cut, and then deals four cards at a time facedown in three rounds, so that each player has 12 cards. The next card in the deck is turned faceup in the center of the table and determines trumps for the hand. Traditionally, the remaining cards in the deck, known as the "stockpile," are placed crosswise on top of the trump card. If the card that has been turned up proves to be a 9, it is now a dix, because it has become the 9 of trumps. When this happens the dealer is immediately awarded 10 points.

## PLAYING THE GAME: THE FIRST PHASE

The player who did not deal leads. As in whist, a trick is won by the highest card in the suit that was led, or by the highest trump. However, in the first phase of a hand of pinochle the player to whom the lead is made does not have to follow suit. For example, a player does not have to respond to a MJ lead, say, with a MK if it is the only heart in the hand: the player might want to reserve the MK for a meld later and can play a card from any other suit instead.

When a trick has been decided, the winning player picks a card up from the stockpile and places it to one side, and the loser does the same. The winner then leads the next trick, and so on. However, the winner also has the option of placing a meld on the table before picking up from the stockpile and so scoring points; the loser does not have this option. Melding is governed by some fairly complex rules, which are described below, but it is important to note here that any melds that have been put down on the table are still considered to be part of the hand of the player who put them there. As a result, a player can pick up a card from any of their own melds and play it during a trick. To put it another way, each player's hand contains 12 cards at all times.

First-phase play continues until only one card is left facedown in the stockpile. At this point no more melds are allowed and the player who won the last trick can choose to pick up either the faceup card that designated trumps or the remaining facedown card, but in either case the opponent must be shown the card. The hand now moves to the second phase of play.

## PLAYING THE GAME: THE SECOND PHASE

At the start of the second phase of the hand, the players pick up the melds that they have laid down during phase one, so that they are again holding 12 cards. The player who won the last trick in the first phase leads and play continues as before – but this time the players must follow suit if they are able to do so, and in the event that they cannot they must play a trump if they have one. If the lead is a trump, the receiving player must play a higher trump if possible. There is no stockpile in this phase of the hand and points are calculated from the winning tricks when all cards have been played. A new hand then begins as before.

## MELDING RULES

The following rules govern melds and melding:

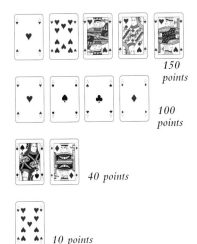

1. A meld can only be put down when a player wins a trick.
2. Only one meld can be placed on the table at once; another trick must be won before a player puts a second meld on the table.
3. Melds that are not put down on the table do not score points.
4. A player has the option of adding to melds that are already put down on the table. For example, if the NK and NQ of

150 points

100 points

40 points

10 points

*Diagram 99 Meld scoring*

spades (a marriage) has been put down, another meld can be scored by adding cards to it: another three kings would make eighty kings, while another three queens would make sixty queens; if a LJ was added, a pinochle would be scored. However, a player cannot add another card to form the same type of meld as the one already on the table: for example, if a pinochle is on the table, a player is not allowed to add another LJ to make another pinochle.
5. A player may move cards around between melds after they have been put down on the table, but only when at least one card has been put down from the hand.
6. A card cannot be picked up from a meld, played in a trick and then put back on the original meld at a later stage; nor can the original meld be reformed by adding the second card of the same value or suit, as appropriate, from the deck. If a player does this, they lose the points

that were scored for the original meld. It is therefore important to remember what melds have already been played.

7. One – and only one – meld has two scoring possibilities: if a player puts down a flush, the score awarded is 150 points, but if the king and queen of trumps are placed down first, 40 points are scored for the royal marriage; when the ace, ten and jack are added on the next occasion that the player wins a trick, 150 points are scored, making a total of 190 points.

8. The first dix to be melded is put in place of the upturned trump card, which is taken into the player's hand and can be used if wanted to form a meld immediately. When the second dix appears it can be placed down on the table alone, winning 10 points, and the player can then put down another meld straightaway.

*Diagram 100 Melding rules: (a) marriage was the first meld; (b) three queens added to the marriage give sixty queens as a second meld*

Pronounced "peekay," this is one of the great
card games and has remained virtually unchanged
since it was first played in sixteenth-century
Europe. It even retains an arcane, and sometimes
bewildering, language of its own.

**Players:** *two*
**Equipment:** *one pack of cards; pencil and paper for
recording scores*
**Difficulty:** *hard; requires considerable concentration and
great skill to play well*
**Duration:** *half an hour for one game of six deals*

*Diagram 101
The deal for a
game of Piquet*

## THE AIM OF THE GAME

Piquet is a very complex and subtle game whose
elements do not necessarily follow from one to
another in a logical order, so it is sensible to read to the end of this
description before trying to start a game.

One game, called a "partie," consists of six hands that are dealt
alternately by each player. The object is to accumulate more points than
your opponent during these six hands. (It is worth noting that if the
loser has failed to reach 100 points they are said to be "rubiconed" and
the winner is awarded a bonus.) There are two ways of scoring points:
through declarations made after the discards but before play, and during
play by leading or winning a trick.

## STARTING THE GAME

Remove the 2s to 6s from the pack, leaving a 32-card deck in which
aces rank high. Cut the deck to decide who will deal first: the winner is
the one with the highest card, and can choose to deal or to receive.
(Usually the choice is to deal first, because there is a slight advantage to

be gained from receiving on the sixth hand.) In each deal the dealer is known as "the younger" and the receiver is called "the elder." So each player is the elder or the younger in alternate games. Having shuffled the cards, the younger deals 12 cards to each player, starting with the elder and alternating between the two. The eight cards that remain after this deal, known as the "talon," are then placed face down in the center of the table.

## PLAYING THE GAME

In the first stage of the game the two players pick up their hands and examine them. On rare occasions a player will have a "carte blanche" – that is, no court cards (a king, queen, or jack). If this is the case, the player must declare the fact. If the younger has a carte blanche, the cards are placed one after another faceup on the table as soon as the elder has discarded. If the elder has a carte blanche, how many cards will be discarded is announced so that the younger can decide which and how many cards to discard and put them on the table, before seeing the elder' hand. A player with a carte blanche wins 10 points.

Whether or not one or other player has a carte blanche, the elder has the option to first discard up to five cards; the discards are placed facedown in a pile alongside the player who discards them. When played under English rules, at least one card must be discarded; under American rules this is not a requirement. Any cards that are discarded are replaced from the talon. If the total of five cards are not exchanged, the elder is allowed to look at the remaining cards in the talon up to the fifth card – so, if

*Diagram 102 Counting points*

three cards are discarded and replaced from the talon, the elder can examine two more cards from the talon before replacing them. The younger can then discard the same number of cards as are left in the talon – according to English rules (but not to American), at least one card must be discarded. The younger can examine the remaining cards in the talon later, after the elder has led the first card. In practice, it is to the elder's advantage to discard five cards – generally those of a lower value, unless a void in one suit is desired – because this stops the younger from discarding more than three unwanted cards. The discards are not used again in the hand, but each player can look at their own discards during play for reference purposes if so desired.

## DECLARATIONS AND SCORING

Before play starts, declarations must be made by means of a question-and-answer routine. Scores can be made in three ways: through points, sequences, and sets. It is important to note that both players must tell the exact truth at all times.

 *11 points*

## POINTS

The elder adds up the number of cards in the longest suit and declares it. If, for example, there are five cards in one suit, the declaration is "point of five." If the younger cannot match this, the elder scores five points – a

 *10 points*

 *10 points*

*Diagram 103 Counting points*

point for each card. But if the younger has more than five cards in a suit, the reply will be "not good," and the younger will score one point for each card. If the younger has an equal number of cards in one suit, the reply is "equal, counting." The elder then declares the number of points according to the value of the cards, with an ace counting 11 points, court cards 10 points each and the other cards their face value. Again, the younger replies "good," "not good" or "equal" as appropriate. The player who has the highest number of points is the winner and scores one point per card, as before. If the count is equal, neither player scores.

## SEQUENCES

The next declaration is in respect of the number of cards in sequence in any one suit, with three cards in a run being the minimum number that can be declared. Again, the elder declares first and has to use the correct terminology, saying "I have a quint," for example. The names for the different sequences and the scores that are awarded to them if a successful declaration is made are:

A "tierce" for three cards, scoring three points.
A "quart" for four cards, scoring four points.
A "quint" for five cards, scoring 15 points.
A "sixieme" for six cards, scoring 16 points.
A "septieme" for seven cards, scoring 17 points.
A "huitieme" for eight cards, scoring 18 points.

As before, the younger replies to the declaration. However, in this case the response to the same sequence is "to?" and the elder has to name the highest card of the run – for example, the reply might be "quint to queen." If the highest card is an ace, the reply is "quint major," and "quint minor" if the highest card is a king. The highest card wins, and the points are awarded; if both highest cards are equal, no points are scored.

It is not necessary for the elder to declare all sequences at this point or even the highest one, as long as at least one sequence is declared. The elder can note down and receive the appropriate number of points for any further sequences that have not been declared. It might be advantageous to disguise a long sequence if a shorter one is available for declaration in order to have a better chance of scoring points by winning tricks (see Hints and tips).

## SETS

Finally, the elder declares any sets of cards of the same face value, but of different suits – only "trios" (threes) or quatorze (fours) can be declared, and only if their value is between ace (high) and ten. A quatorze beats a trio, but otherwise the set of cards that has the highest rank wins: three points in the case of a trio and 14 points for a quatorze. It is not possible for elder and younger to be equal during this declaration, unless neither has anything to declare. As in the case of sequences, the winner need only declare for one set, but can score for any others in the hand.

## PIQUE AND REPIQUE

At the end of the declarations, the elder leads the first card and scores one point for doing so, saying "one for leading." However, before the younger responds, the points that have been won up to this point are added up and noted, by sections in the order in which they were scored: carte blanche, points, sequences and sets. If either player has accumulated 30 points without the opponent having scored at all in the sections so far counted, they have a "repique" and win a bonus of 60 points (the elder is not allowed to use the one point for leading in this calculation).

A "pique" can only be scored by the elder, because achieving one, as opposed to repique, depends on the use of points awarded during trick play. If the point awarded for leading tips the scales, so that the elder now has 30 points and the younger has none, the elder is awarded a bonus of 30 points. Even if the elder does not have as many as 30 points, they can still achieve pique and be awarded a 30-point bonus if they accumulate up to 30 points through play during tricks without the younger having won a point.

## TRICK PLAY

Once points have been totaled and it has been established whether there is pique or repique, the younger can reply to the elder's lead and trick play begins. This follows simple rules: there are no trumps; the players must follow suit if they can; the players may discard a card if they cannot follow suit; the highest value card wins the trick; and the winner of the trick leads the next one, with both players calculating their running total of points before the new trick and stating it. One point is awarded for each winning trick that has been led, and two points for any winning trick that has been led by the opposing player; an additional point is awarded to the player who wins the last trick. The player who wins the most tricks – seven or more – wins an extra 10 points, and a player who wins all 12 tricks is said to have made a "cabot" and scores 40 points.

After the six deals comprising the partie, the player with the highest score is awarded a bonus of 100 points, plus the number of points they have scored, minus the number of points scored by the opponent. However, if the opponent has not managed to accumulate 100 points, the winner scores 100 points, plus their own score, plus the opponent's score: the loser is said to be "rubiconed."

## HINTS AND TIPS

The elder can discard more cards, so has a much better opportunity to improve a hand than the younger does. As a result, the elder can usually afford to play more offensively, while the younger has to take a more defensive approach.

During declarations, neither player has to declare a winning combination if they do not want to do so. A player might wish to confuse the opponent and increase the chance of winning more points during trick play. For example, the elder could declare a sixieme, even though it is a huitieme (this is not, of course, an untrue declaration). The reasoning for this is that as the elder leads the first trick, they could cabot the younger by winning all twelve tricks. Nevertheless, any declaration must be the exact truth: you cannot declare a trio of jacks unless you hold three jacks, but you can do so if you hold a quatorze of jacks.

*Diagram 104
Counting points*

*Diagram 105  Sets*

*Diagram 106  Sequences*

# CHILDREN'S CARD GAMES

These games are easy for children to play amongst themselves, or with adults, and give a great deal of enjoyment while developing their concentration and coordination.

 For many adults, memories of childhood vacations are bound together with learning to play simple card games. Rainy days, especially on vacations, can be made to fly by with just a set of ordinary playing cards. As soon as a child can spot that two cards have the same rank or face value, they are old enough to start playing cards. Snap is one of the simplest and most well-known card games for children. Special Snap cards can be bought, but the game is just as much fun with standard playing cards, and this is a good way of familiarizing young children with them. Beggar my Neighbor is another easy game, requiring virtually no special skills, and is most fun when played fast and furiously.

Much of the fun in children's games is that they are fast-moving and involve making a lot of noise. Go Boom falls into this category – young children delight in shouting out exuberantly when they have won. Cheat is always very popular, too, especially when it is understood that to play it well you have to lie without being found out. Spit is more suitable for older children because it requires great concentration and speed, but still involves a great deal of shouting, thus being the cause for much hilarity.

Pelmanism and other card-matching games are an excellent way of improving concentration. For older children it is fine to play with a standard pack, but for young ones you can buy special cards printed with colored pictures, patterns, or symbols. In games of this sort, a child who is concentrating can often remember more cards than a grown-up player, a fact that some adults find most embarrassing – and almost all children find very satisfying.

Most families with children have played this classic card game. It is always amusing and invariably annoying – and it can be very irritating when the children win.

**Players:** *two or more*
**Equipment:** *one pack of cards for two or three players; two packs for four or more players*
**Difficulty:** *easy if you concentrate*
**Duration:** *five minutes*

*Diagram 107 Playing Snap*

## STARTING TO PLAY

The dealer shuffles the cards thoroughly, and then deals them facedown to each player in turn until all the cards have been dealt out – it does not matter if this means that some players have more cards than others.

## PLAYING THE GAME

The player on the dealer's left turns the top card of their pile face-up and places it next to the pile. The player to that person's left does the same, and so on, around the table. If any two cards on a face-up pile have the same value (suits are irrelevant) the first person to say – or yell – "Snap" takes both piles and adds them to the bottom of their facedown pile. Play then continues, with the player to the left of the one who cried "Snap" turning another card face-up. If a player runs out of facedown cards they can still call "Snap" when appropriate, in an attempt to get back into the game. However, any player who has neither a facedown pile nor a face-up one is out of the game. Any player who makes a mistake by yelling "Snap" when there are not two cards of the same value on display has to pay a forfeit of one card from their facedown pile to every other player. The game is won by the player who captures every card on the table.

A member of the same family of card games as Snap, this is a game in which success depends on speed of hand and quickness of eye. But Slapjack is so easy that even very young children can master it.

*Players: two or more*
*Equipment: one pack of cards, or two packs when there are four or more players*
*Difficulty: the only skill required is the ability to recognize a jack*
*Duration: 10 minutes*

#### STARTING THE GAME
The dealer shuffles the cards thoroughly and deals them facedown, one by one, to each player until the supply is exhausted. It does not matter if some players have more cards than others. Each player picks up their pile of cards, but is not allowed to look at them.

#### PLAYING THE GAME
The player on the left of the dealer places one card face-up in the center of the playing area, which can either be a table or the floor. Going clockwise, each player in turn adds another card as quickly as possible to the pile until a jack is put down. At the sight of a jack, each player has to try to be the first to slap their hand down on the pile and cover the jack. The player who succeeds takes the pile and adds it to the bottom of the pile that they are holding. It does not matter if a player runs out of cards as it is possible to get back into the game by being the first to slap a hand on a jack. The game ends when one player has won all the cards that were dealt.

*Diagram 108 A game of Slapjack*

Spit is a race between two people that depends on speed, luck, timing, and considerable powers of concentration. It is quite normal for a game of Spit to degenerate into complete chaos.

*Players:* two
*Equipment:* one pack of cards
*Difficulty:* requires alertness and speed; for older children
*Duration:* 10 minutes

## STARTING TO PLAY

The deck is cut by all the players and the one with the highest card (aces rank low throughout the game, so the highest card is a king and the lowest is an ace) acts as the dealer, though there is no advantage to being the dealer. The cards are shuffled thoroughly and dealt alternately to each player until the whole pack is finished.

Both players then place the first five cards in their pile facedown in a row in front of them. Another row is placed on top of the first, starting with the second card of the first row, so four cards are laid down by each player in all. A further row is then laid down, starting with the third card of the first row, and so on, until one card is placed on the last pile in the row. This procedure uses up 15 cards from each player's hand.

The remainder are placed in two stockpiles, one for each player, in the center of the table. The top card in each player's row of piles (the first card of row one, the second card of row two, and so on) is then turned face-up. The top card of each stockpile is turned face-up and placed alongside it – this forms two discard piles.

## PLAYING THE GAME

To start the game, the two players say "One, two, three, Spit" in unison. On "Spit," the two players start to build on either of the two discard piles, working as quickly as possible. They do this by placing any face-up card from the rows in front of them, regardless of suit, but in either ascending or descending order, on the top card of either discard pile. When a card is taken from the rows, the card beneath is turned face-up. For example, if the top card on a discard pile is M7, either a 6 or 8 of any suit can be added to that pile. However, an ace or a king must be covered by either a 2 or a queen because aces are low.

An ace cannot be covered by a king, or a king by an ace. The players also have the option of building in either ascending or descending order on face-up cards in the rows in front of them.

If neither player can put a card down, either on the discard piles or their own row, play stops. Another card from each stockpile is then placed on its discard pile. Play resumes after another shout of "One, two, three, Spit."

The first round ends when both stockpiles are empty, at which point each player tries to slap their hand on the smallest of the two discard piles, shouting "Spit" at the same time. The discard piles are now turned over and form the new stockpile and play resumes with another round.

## FINISHING THE GAME

There are now two ways to proceed. Which one you choose depends on whether you want to have a short game or a longer one. In one version of the game, the player who finishes their stockpile first is allowed to choose the smallest stockpile for the next round. The problem is that it is likely that the player who wins this round, and so obtains the smallest stockpile, is likely to finish their stockpile first in the next round, too (though it is not inevitable). It is therefore preferable to continue as for the first round, with play continuing until both stockpiles are exhausted and each player then having to slap a hand on the smallest pile – this at least gives the losing player the chance to get back into the game. The game is won when one player eventually gets rid of all their cards, both from the stockpile and their hand.

*Diagram 109 A game of Spit*

A fast and furious game for children that requires no skill, but is great fun.

*Players:* two or more
*Equipment:* one pack of cards, or two with more than four players
*Difficulty:* depends wholly on luck
*Duration:* 10 minutes

## PLAYING THE GAME

The cards are shuffled thoroughly and dealt face-down to all players, starting from the dealer's left. The players can pick their cards up to put them in a neat pile, but they must not look at them.

The player to the dealer's left turns the top card in their pile card face-up and places it in the center of the table. If the face value of the card is between 2 and 10, the next player, going clockwise, puts the top card from their pile on top of it, and so on around the table. If the card turned up and put down is an honor card (king, queen, or jack) or an ace, the player whose turn it is must place four cards on top in the case of an ace, three cards if the card is a king, two for a queen, and one for a jack. As long as no honor card or ace is put down while this is happening, the player who put down the ace or honor card picks up the pack and places it at the bottom of their own pile. The same player then puts the top card of their pile down to continue the game. If, for example, an ace is put down by player A, player B must play four cards; but if any card up to and including the fourth card is an honor card or ace, then no more cards are played and player A must put down the number of cards applicable to that card. (A jack is therefore the most useful card, because there is less chance of the opponent playing an honor card or ace with only one card to be played.)

As soon as any player runs out of cards they are out of the game. The winner is the last player left to have cards.

*Diagram 110  A game of Beggar my Neighbor*

This extremely simple game can be enjoyed by very young children, who find the idea that the loser becomes the "Donkey" very amusing.

*Players:* three to six
*Equipment:* four cards of equal face
value for each player (for
example, four aces, kings,
queens, and jacks if there
are four players)
*Difficulty:* can be enjoyed by very
young children
*Duration:* five to 10 minutes

*Diagram 111 Cards for a game of Donkey*

### PLAYING THE GAME

The dealer deals four cards to each player. The players pick up their hands and examine them, and then each player has to discard one card – if, for example, a player has two jacks, a king, and a queen, either the king or the queen can be discarded, because it is sensible for that player to try to collect four jacks if two are already held. When all the players have made their choice, each player discards one card, placing it facedown in front of the player to the left, who picks it up. The player making the discard will receive a card from the player on the right.

Play continues in this way, with each player attempting to collect four of a kind. The first one to do so places the four cards on the table, without making any fuss about it. As the other players realize what has happened, they also place their cards – whatever they are – on the table. The last player to react loses the game and becomes the "Donkey."

The cards are then scooped up and shuffled, and the game is repeated – ideally, until all the children playing have had a turn at being the "Donkey" to avoid any tears.

Like several other children's games, the well-known game of Go Fish is simple enough, relying as it does on a large dose of luck. Its arcane phrases and element of strategy make it an entertaining game nonetheless.

*Players: two to five*
*Equipment: a pack of shuffled cards*
*Difficulty: luck plays a major part*
*Duration: five to 10 minutes*

## STARTING THE GAME

If there are two or three players, each player is dealt seven cards; if four or five are playing each player is dealt five cards. The rest of the deck is placed facedown in a pile in the center of the table and forms the "fish pond." All the players examine their cards and decide which four cards of the same value they are going to collect. The player to the left of the dealer starts the game.

## PLAYING THE GAME

The first player asks the player on their right for a card – for example, a jack, because they already have two jacks. If that player has a jack, it must be handed over and another request can be made. If there is no jack, the reply is "Go fish," and the player making the request must take a card from the "fishpond" and add it to their hand. If it happens that this card is the same as the one originally requested, the player must say "I fished upon my wish," and can then request another card from the player on their right. If the card is not the same, that player's turn is over. Play then moves clockwise, and the next player can make a request of the player to their right (the one who has just finished playing).

As players collect fours of a kind, they place these cards on the table in front of them and are allowed to request another card from the player on their right. The winner is the player who first succeeds in putting all their cards down on the table in sets of four. It is unusual for anybody to achieve this, however, so the winner is normally the player with the mos sets of four on the table when the fishpond is exhausted.

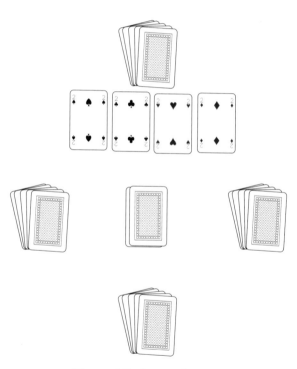

*Diagram 112  A game of Go Fish*

# GO BOOM

Young children love this game, probably because of the amount of noise that can be made as the winner announces his or her success.

*Players: two to 12, though the game works better with three to four*
*Equipment: one pack of shuffled cards, or two if six or more people are playing*
*Difficulty: straightforward, even for very young children*
*Duration: 15 minutes*

## PLAYING THE GAME

Seven cards are dealt facedown to each player. The remainder of the pack is placed facedown in a pile in the center of the table. The players can pick up their cards and examine them. The player to the left of the dealer starts the game, leading with any card of their choice and placing it face-up on the table. The next player, going clockwise, follows by playing a card either of equal value (aces are high, so the lowest card is a two) or of the same suit. For example, if the first card played is a M5, the next player must play either a heart or a 5 of another suit.

Play continues around the table until a round has been completed – that is, everybody has played a card – or until a player cannot match the previous card. If this happens, the player has to pick cards up from the central deck one at a time until a card that can be played is turned up; cards that cannot be played are added to their hand. (If the central pile has been exhausted, a player who cannot play must pass.) After each player has played a card, the cards put down during the round are examined, and the winner is the player who has put down the highest card during the round. If two players have played the same highest card, the winner is the one who played the highest card first. The cards that had been played during the round are then discarded, and the winner of the trick leads off the next round with a card of their choice.

The winner of the game is the first player to get rid of their cards, or – if all the players have to pass during a round – the player with the fewest cards held. Traditionally, the winner announces success with a loud and exuberant yell of "Boom!"

## VARIATION

The game can be continued when the central pile has been exhausted by picking up the cards discarded at the end of each round, shuffling them, and placing them facedown to form a new pile.

*Diagram 113 A game of Go Boom*

Also called I Doubt It, Cheat is a game of bluffing and outrageous lying.

*Players:* three or more
*Equipment:* one pack of cards
*Difficulty:* easy, but requires the ability to keep a straight face
*Duration:* five to 10 minutes

## STARTING TO PLAY

The cards are shuffled and dealt one at a time, facedown, to all of the players – it does not matter if some players have more cards than others. The players pick up their hands and sort them out by value from high to low, irrespective of suit. It is important that all the players make sure that nobody else can see their cards.

## PLAYING THE GAME

The whole point of Cheat is to get rid of all your cards through minor bluffing or outrageous lying, when necessary or appropriate, about their value. The player to the left of the dealer starts the game by placing a card facedown in the center of the table while naming its value – the player has the option of telling the truth or lying. The next player, going clockwise, puts another card facedown on top of the first card and also says what its value is – the claim may be true or false, but it must be higher than the value of the previous card. Each player around the table takes it in turn to put down a card and either lie or tell the truth.

If one player suspects another of cheating, and as the game progresses this becomes more and more likely, that player yells "Cheat" and the card that has just been played is turned face-up. If the person who played the card did cheat, they have to pick up the pile on the table and add it to the bottom of their hand. If it turns out that the claim as to its value was accurate, the player who made the false accusation has to add the pile to their hand. If more than one player shouts "Cheat" at the same time, the player nearest to the left of the person accused is deemed to be the accuser. It is therefore perhaps wise to err on the side of caution and wait for braver or more foolhardy players to take the risk. The first player to be left without any cards is the winner.

## VARIATION

Instead of putting one card at a time, the rules can be varied to allow two or even three cards of the same value to be put down in one go if a player wishes to do so. For example, a player might claim to have put down three queens: this sounds outlandish, but it could just be a clever double-bluff.

## HINTS AND TIPS

Success in Cheat depends on the ability to look either innocent or guilty, as appropriate, in order to fool the other players. As a result, children who excel at the game often grow up to be extremely good Poker players.

## PELMANISM

Also known as Pairs and Concentration, Pelmanism tests both memory and concentration, and this game is an excellent way to improve both these skills. A child who is concentrating hard can often remember more cards than an adult.

*Players:* two or more
*Equipment:* one pack of cards
*Difficulty:* easy, but requires concentration and good observation
*Duration:* five minutes

## STARTING THE GAME

The cards are shuffled and spread out facedown on a table or the floor. They can either be placed in neat rows or at random in any position – the latter method makes the game more difficult.

## PLAYING THE GAME

The first player turns over any two cards of their choice, keeping them in exactly the same position as they were when facedown. If the two cards make a pair of the same face value – two jacks or two 7s, for example – the player wins them. The same player can then turn up another two cards at random, continuing until the cards turned up are of a different face value. Having given all the players time to see which cards have been turned face-up, the player then turns the odd cards facedown again, in exactly the same position as they were before. The next player to the left then has a turn.

At the start of the game it is more luck than a good memory that allows pairs to be collected. However, as the game progresses and more cards have been revealed, concentration and memory start to play the major role. But the game becomes progressively easier as the number of cards on the table diminishes. The player who has the most pairs when all the cards have been picked up wins the game, and is the dealer for the next game.

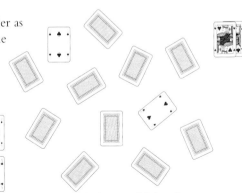

*Diagram 114 A game of Pelmanism*

# BOARD GAMES

The first games played on a board were primarily games of chance. Players competed to complete a circuit of the board by throwing dice to determine the number of moves that could be taken at any one time. The only element of choice was which piece to move, or how many pieces to move from one position to the next.

Increasingly, chance was combined with strategy. Games of strategy seem to have emerged when societies increased in complexity to such an extent that there was a need for diplomacy. In the ancient Chinese game of Weichi, from which Go is derived, players attempt to surround each other's pieces using a blockading kind of warfare. Chess has been likened to a battle between social orders, with the status of each member – from pawn to king – being carefully stated. But unlike Weichi, the aim of Chess is to capture and exterminate the enemy.

Some board games are symbols of personal success and achievement. Mancala, the strategic game of the African continent, first played in ancient Egypt, involves each player having a number of pieces distributed about the playing board. With each move, a player must make estimates involving numerical skill and judgement in order to capture the opponent's pieces.

Many board games were intended to be educational, especially during the eighteenth and nineteenth centuries, when scores of games were designed to impart useful information. Scenes from the past, famous people, and battles were all popular subjects. Some games were based on maps of different parts of the globe, illustrated with landscapes and animals. The boards of these were beautifully colored by hand or stencil, and are now popular collector's items. Today, of course, many board games can be played on a computer screen and are more popular than ever.

The hunt game of Fox and Geese is believed to have originated in Scandinavia. It is played in many different forms, in much of Europe, and Asia.

**Players:** *two*
**Equipment:** *board and 14 or 18 pieces*
**Difficulty:** *mainly strategy*
**Duration:** *usually less than half an hour per game*

## BEGINNING TO PLAY

Fox and Geese boards may be either cross-shaped or round. The pieces may be either counters or pegs that fit into small holes. In the original

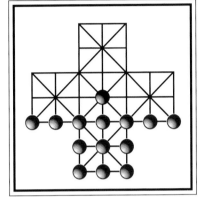

*Diagram 115 Starting position for a game of Fox and Geese (14 pieces)*

version of the game 14 pieces are used, one fox (marked in black) and 13 geese (marked in red).

Sometimes 18 pieces are used instead of 14, in which case the game starts with the position in diagram 116 (page 198). The fox is in the center of the board, but the fox player can in fact choose any vacant square at the start of the game in this particular variation.

The players draw lots to determine who will be the fox and who will be the geese. The fox makes the first move and the players then move in alternation.

## MOVING

In the standard game both fox and geese move in identical fashion, one square forward, backward or sideways on each turn. However, only the fox is allowed to capture, which it does by leaping over an adjacent goose and landing on a vacant square beyond it in similar fashion to draughts. Also, just as in Checkers, it is possible for a fox to make several captures in one turn by a series of short leaps. The geese are not allowed to leap, but will try to crowd the fox into a corner. In the 18-piece game the rules are identical, except that the geese are not allowed to move backwards or diagonally. In some variations of the 18-piece game the fox is not allowed to move diagonally, which has led to the removal of the diagonal lines. However, this makes his task too difficult.

## WINNING THE GAME

The fox wins if it manages to capture so many geese that there are not enough left to trap it, or if it reaches the geese's end of the board. The geese win if they can immobilize the fox by surrounding it.

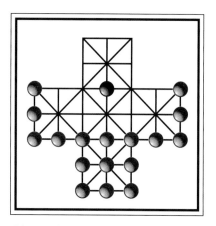

*Diagram 116 Starting position for a game of Fox and Geese (18 pieces)*

The game of Solitaire was invented – purportedly – by a prisoner in the Bastille during the French Revolution. The French version takes place on a board with 37 holes, but the American form uses a simple adaptation of the Fox and Geese board.

*Players: one*
*Equipment: board and 32 pieces*
*Difficulty: easy to grasp strategy*
*Duration: usually less than*
*15 minutes per game*

## BEGINNING TO PLAY

Fox and Geese solitaire takes place on a standard Fox and Geese board on which there are no diagonal lines. The pieces are arranged as in diagram 117, with every point occupied by a piece except one (usually the center point).

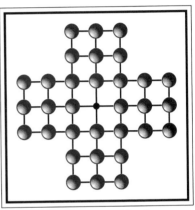

*Diagram 117 Starting position for a game of Fox and Geese solitaire*

## MOVING

There is only one type of move in this game: a short jump over an adjacent piece, removing that piece from the board. These jumps can be horizontal or vertical, but not diagonal.

## WINNING THE GAME

The object of the game is to remove all the pieces from the board except one, which should end up in the central hole (or some other designated point).

Cows and Leopards originated in Sri Lanka (then Ceylon) and has many similarities to Fox and Geese.

*Players:* two
*Equipment:* board and five or seven pieces
*Difficulty:* mainly strategy
*Duration:* usually less than half an hour per game

### BEGINNING TO PLAY
The game takes place on a 12x12 Chess or Checkers board. In the initial position the cows are arranged on the back rank, while the leopards can be placed on any black square on the board. In England, a similar game is often played on an 8x8 board, but it is still known as Fox and Geese.

### MOVING
In Cows and Leopards, the cows can move one square forwards along a diagonal on any turn, in a similar fashion to an uncrowned piece in Checkers. The leopard, on the other hand, can move two squares both diagonally forwards and backwards. Neither piece can jump or capture. In the English version, the fox can only move one square at a time, in similar fashion to a king in Checkers.

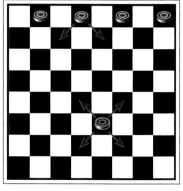

*Diagram 118 Starting position for a game of Cows and Leopards*

### WINNING THE GAME
The cows win the game if they are able to hem in the leopard, leaving it without a legal move. The leopard wins if it manages to break through the line of cows to reach the cows' end of the board.

Wolf and Goats is another form of Fox and Geese that is played on a Checkers board.

**Players:** *two*
**Equipment:** *board and 13 pieces*
**Difficulty:** *mainly strategy*
**Duration:** *usually less than half an hour per game*

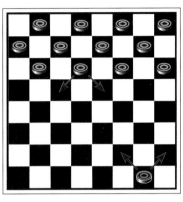

*Diagram 119  Starting position for a game of Wolf and Goats*

## BEGINNING TO PLAY

In Wolf and Goats, the goats are placed in exactly the same formation as one would see at the start of a game of Checkers, while the wolf may be placed on any of the black squares on its back rank.

## MOVING

In Wolf and Goats, the goats can move one square forwards along a diagonal on any turn, just as in Cows and Leopards. Although the wolf can only move one square either diagonally forwards or backwards, in this game it can capture goats by jumping over them and landing on the square immediately beyond.

## WINNING THE GAME

The outcome of a game is determined in exactly the same way as Cows and Leopards: the goats win if they are able to hem in the wolf, leaving it without a legal move. The wolf wins if it manages to break through the line of goats to reach the goats' end of the board.

Halma was invented in the 1880s. It can be played by two, three, or four players.

*Players: two to four*
*Equipment: board and 64 pieces*
*Difficulty: very strategic*
*Duration: usually less than one hour per game*

## BEGINNING TO PLAY

Halma requires a 16x16 Checkerboard, marked out with camps in each corner. In the two-player version, each player has 19 pieces, arranged as in diagram 120 (below). The thicker or double line marks the boundaries of each camp. In a three- or four-handed game each player has 13 pieces as shown in diagrams 121 (opposite) and 123 (page 204).

The players draw lots to decide who will move first and then take alternate turns. In a three- or four-handed game the players act alone, taking turns in a clockwise direction. In a three-player game it is a slight disadvantage to be the one heading for the empty camp, so players should take turns to be the odd man out.

## MOVING

In any turn of play, only one piece may be moved. There are two ways in which a piece can move: the "step" and the "jump." With a step, a piece can move to an adjacent square in any direction – vertical, horizontal,

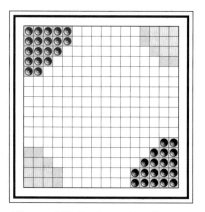

*Diagram 120 Starting position for a game of Halma (two players)*

or diagonal; backwards or forwards. Alternatively, if there is a piece in an adjacent square – whether it be a fellow or enemy piece – it may jump over that piece to an empty square immediately beyond it in similar fashion to a capture in Checkers. Having made such a leap, that piece can jump again until all its jumps have been exhausted. However, pieces are not captured in Halma – they remain on the board, even if they have been jumped over. Furthermore, unlike in Checkers, it is not compulsory to jump when one is able.

## STRATEGY

The ideal strategy in halma is to construct "ladders" across the board to enable your rearguard pieces to traverse rapidly from one side to the other through a series of hops. The ladder technique is illustrated in diagram 123 (page 204), where the white piece is able to move down the board with a series of jumps. Of course, one should also try to block one's opponent from building ladders and take care to remember that one's own ladders can be used by the opponent, too! It is often fatal to advance your scouts and neglect your rear men, as the stragglers may become cut off from the rest of the army.

## WINNING THE GAME

The first player to occupy the opposite camp is the winner.

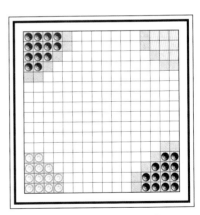

*Diagram 121 Starting position for a game of Halma (three players)*

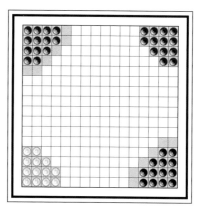

*Diagram 122  Starting position for
a game of Halma (four players)*

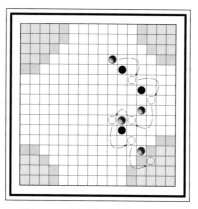

*Diagram 123  The ladder technique*

The American game of Chinese Checkers is neither Chinese nor Checkers – but a modified form of Halma played on a six-pointed star. It was patented in the United States around 1880 by J. Pressman & Co., New York, as Hop Ching Checkers.

*Players:* two to six
*Equipment:* board and 90 pieces
*Difficulty:* very strategic
*Duration:* varies, but usually less than one hour per game

## BEGINNING TO PLAY

The Chinese Checkerboard takes the form of a six-pointed star, as illustrated in diagram 124 (below). In the two-player game, each side has 15 pieces. If there are more than two players, only 10 pieces are used for each player. With three players the camps are arranged so that each player is heading towards an empty camp, but with four or more camps the players can choose whichever camp they like. Each player plays alone; there is no teamwork.

## MOVING

Moves in Chinese Checkers are identical to those in Halma: "steps" and "jumps." The strategy of the game is also similar, with the players trying to construct and block ladders.

## WINNING THE GAME

Just as in Halma, the winner is the first player who manages to occupy the opposite part of the star.

*Diagram 124 Starting position for a game of Chinese Checkers (two players)*

Backgammon is the ultimate race game and has been enjoyed around the world for over five thousand years. Although the play is highly skillful, the fact that the moves rely on the fall of the dice introduces a large element of luck. In the long run, the better player will always win, but the beauty of the game is that even a novice can win the odd game against a world champion.

*Players:* two

*Equipment:* *Backgammon board, 30 pieces (15 black and 15 white), four dice and a doubling cube*

*Difficulty:* *the basic moves are simple, but the strategy can become very complex. The balance between luck and skill is finely tuned and gives the game an enduring fascination*

*Duration:* *games can be over very quickly or can develop into long wars of attrition. A typical social game takes about 10 minutes*

## BRIEF HISTORY

Backgammon is a game of great antiquity, having been played almost everywhere in the world for thousands of years. It originated in the Middle East and has even survived long periods in the doldrums due to banishment by the Church.

## THE BOARD AND PIECES

The Backgammon board consists of a board of 24 points, 12 on White's side of the table and 12 on Black's. The points are alternately colored light and dark. The pieces have a set

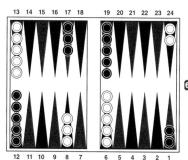

*Diagram 125 Starting position for a game of Backgammon*

starting position as shown in diagram 125. White is playing on the side of the board marked by points 1-12, while Black has the side marked 13-24. The points indicated by 1-6 are known as White's inner table, while 19-24 represent Black's inner table. Similarly, points 7-12 are the outer table for White, as are points 13-18 for Black. White plays in a counterclockwise direction

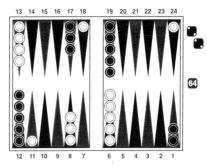

*Diagram 126 The position after White's first move*

around the board, moving pieces from higher- to lower-numbered points. Black's play mirrors this movement, with pieces moving in a clockwise direction from the lower- to higher-numbered points.

There can be any number of similarly colored pieces on any point. Although White already has five pieces on the 6 point, it is possible to place more pieces there. However, pieces from opposite sides cannot share a point, so Black cannot (temporarily at least) bring any pieces to the 6 point.

## THE AIM OF THE GAME

Backgammon is a simple race game. The object is to move the pieces around the board toward your inner table. Once all 15 of your pieces have arrived in the inner table, they can be "borne off," i.e.

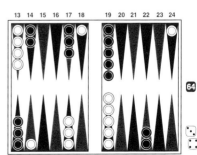

*Diagram 127 The position after Black's first move*

removed from the board. The first player to remove all his pieces from the board is the winner.

## BEGINNING TO PLAY

Players move alternately, the throw being determined by the roll of a pair of dice. To start the game, both players throw one die and the player rolling the higher number moves first, with the two dice counting for the initial play. For example, if White rolls a 6 and Black rolls a 2, then White (having rolled the higher number) starts the game with 6-2. If the players roll the same number, then the dice are rolled again. It is not permissible to start the game with a double.

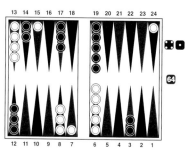

Diagram 128 *The position after White's second move*

## THROWING AND MOVING

The values on the two dice indicate how far around the board a player can move a piece. The numbers on the dice can be added together to move just one piece, or they can be used separately to move two pieces. In White's opening position given above (6-2), two possible moves with this throw are:

1. Moving a piece from 24 to 16 (using the entire roll to move one piece).
2. Moving one piece from 24 to 18 and one from 13 to 11 (using the dice separately).

Let us assume that White chooses the latter option, resulting in the position in diagram 126 (page 207).

Now Black rolls 2-2 (indicated in diagram 126 by the two dice adjacent to Black's inner table). When a doublet is rolled (the same number being shown on both dice), the total for the roll is doubled, as if four dice had been thrown and all had yielded the same value. Therefore, it becomes possible to move up to four pieces. Thus with the 2-2 roll Black now has numerous options, including the following:

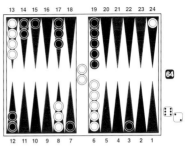

*Diagram 129 The position after Black's second move*

1. Moving a piece from 1 to 9 (using the entire roll to move one piece).
2. Moving a piece from 17 to 23 and one from 1 to 3 (breaking up the roll into a 6 and a 2).
3. Moving a piece from 1 to 5, one from 12 to 14 and one from 19 to 21. The number of points moved still totals eight, but this has now been broken down into 4, 2, and 2.
4. Moving two pieces from 1 to 3 and two pieces from 12 to 14. Now four pieces have moved, each advancing two points.

## CLOSED POINTS

Let us assume that, from the previous diagram, Black chooses to play 2-2 by taking the last option, moving twice from 1 to 3 and also twice from 12 to 14. This results in the position in diagram 127 (page 207), where White has just rolled 4-3 in reply.

Any point that has two enemy pieces on it is "closed." This means that, for the moment at least, it is inaccessible to White's pieces. In the above position, Black's last move has closed the 3 and 14 points. Therefore, White

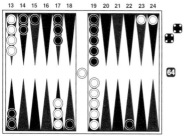

*Diagram 130 The position after White's third move*

cannot move the piece on 18 to 14 nor is it possible to move a piece from 6 to 3. However, White could consider moving the piece on 18 to close the point on 11. Although moving 4-3 would not be possible – this would necessitate landing on the 14 point – White can take the move as 3-4, moving to the 15 point, and then onwards to 11.

Building up a series of closed points is one of the fundamental aims in Backgammon. If one player's back pieces are stuck behind a succession of enemy-held points it can be difficult, or even impossible, to free these pieces. Sometimes a player is fortunate (or skillful!) enough to build up a succession of six closed points. As long as these points can be maintained, any enemy pieces stuck behind them cannot escape.

### HITTING AND REENTERING

Any piece that sits alone on a point is called a "blot," and a blot is always in danger of being hit by an enemy piece. When a piece is hit, it moves to the bar (the central partition between the inner and outer tables). This piece must then re-enter the game via the opponent's inner table. The player with the piece on the

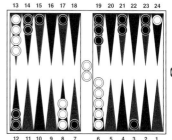

*Diagram 131 The position after Black's third move*

bar cannot make any other moves elsewhere on the board until this has been achieved. Let us assume that from diagram 127 (page 207), White used the roll of 4-3 to move from the 11 to the 7 point and also from the 18 to the 15 point. The position is now as in diagram 128 (page 208), with Black having rolled 4-1 in reply.

White has blots on the 7, 15 and 24 points and with a roll of 4-1 Black can hit two of these. This Black does, moving from 3 to 7 and from 14 to 15, both moves hitting White blots. These two pieces are now placed on the bar and White rolls 6-2.

White must now immediately reenter these pieces into the game via Black's inner table (i.e. points 19-24). Rolling a 1 will enable White to place a piece on the 24 point (the 24 point being the 1 point from Black's point of view). Similarly, the roll of a 2 permits White to place a piece on the 23 point; a 3 would grant access to the 22 point, and so on.

White in fact rolls 6-2. With the 2, White places a piece on the 23 point. However, to White's dismay, the 6 is not playable, as the 19 point is closed. White's other piece, therefore, has to remain on

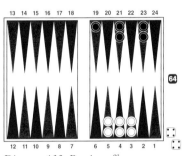

Diagram 132 Bearing off

the bar for the time being. White is not permitted to use the 6 elsewhere on the board while a piece is out of play on the bar.

Black now rolls 4-4. This is an excellent roll which allows Black a very powerful play. Black can move two pieces from 17 to 21 and two pieces from 19 to 23, hitting White's blot, which has just reentered the game, and sending it scuttling back onto the bar. The position is now beginning to look very promising for Black.

White again has two pieces on the bar, while Black has created three closed points in the inner table. With a roll of 2-2, 4-4, 6-6, 2-4, 2-6, or 4-6, White will have to miss a turn completely as the pieces on the bar will be unable to reenter play. Black is now well ahead in the race to get

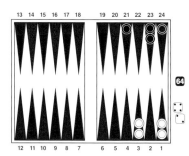

*Diagram 133 Position after Black's play*

around the board and the pieces in Black's outer table (on the 14, 15, and 17 points) indicate good chances to close out further points in the inner table.

## BEARING OFF

The ultimate aim in Backgammon is to "bear off" all your pieces before your opponent. However, you cannot begin to bear off until all your pieces have negotiated their way around to your inner table. During bearing off, the pieces move in the normal way except that the pieces can move beyond the player's 1 point to an imaginary 0 point. When this occurs, the piece is removed from the board.

It is only possible to bear off when all of your pieces are in your inner table. What sometimes happens is that White, for example, begins to bear off while Black still has pieces stationed in White's inner table. It is then possible that White will leave a blot that will get hit. When this piece reenters the game, White must maneuver it round to White's inner table before continuing to bear off.

It is possible to use a larger number than necessary to bear off a piece, provided that one cannot make a move with this number which does not bear off. For example, suppose that White only has pieces on the 4, 3, 2, and 1 points and rolls 6-2. The 2 can be used in the normal way to bear off a piece from the 2 point, but the 6

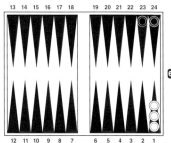

*Diagram 134 The final position, with Black firm favorite*

can be used to bear off a piece from the 4 point – the highest available point. However, if White has pieces on the 6, 2, and 1 points and rolls 4-3, he cannot bear off and is obliged to make moves from the 6 point. The play in diagram 132 (page 211) should help to clarify these points.

Both players are in the process of bearing off and White rolls 4-4. This enables White to bear off two pieces from the 4 point but then the remaining play must be to move the two pieces from the 5 point to the 1 point. Black now rolls 6-3 in reply. There are two ways to play this move:

1. Black can use the 6 to bear off a piece from the 19 point and then use the 3 to move from the 21 point to the 24 point.
2. An alternative line of play is to use the 3 to move from the 19 point to the 22 point. Black then has no way to play a 6 from the 19 point and is thus allowed to bear off a piece from the 21 point.

If we assume that Black chooses the former play, the situation is now as in diagram 133 (opposite). With a big double, White could win the game immediately, bearing off all four pieces. However, White rolls the more modest 4-2, using the 4 to bear off from the 3 point and the 2 to move from the 3 point to the 1 point.

Black could now also win the game with a 6-6, 5-5, or a 4-4. A roll of 3-3 would leave Black tantalizingly short of immediate victory. The first play would be to move from the 21 point to the 24 point, bearing off two pieces from the 23 point and one from 24. This would leave Black with a solitary piece on the 24 point. However, let us assume that Black also rolls a more modest number, in this case 5-2. This roll enables Black to clear the 21 and one of the pieces from the 23 point, resulting in the following position.

Now it is inevitable that Black will be able to complete bearing off with the next roll. Even the smallest possible roll of 2-1 will enable Black to clear the inner table. Therefore, White must finish off with the

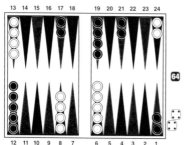

Diagram 135 *A wonderful roll for White*

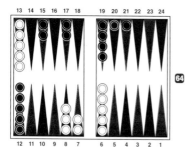

Diagram 136 *A straight race*

next roll and to do this needs a doublet, as this is the only way to bear off more than two pieces at once. Black is now the firm favorite to win the game because the probability of White rolling a doublet is only 1 in 6. White's chances of winning are therefore approximately 17 per cent, while Black has an 83 per cent chance of success. Black should win the game, but the dice can be very cruel!

## SCORING

Normally, the winner of a game of Backgammon scores one point if a match is being played. However, there are two exceptions when the winner can claim more. If a player wins by bearing off all their pieces while the opponent has not yet borne off any, they win a "gammon," which scores double points. An even better result is to bear off all the pieces while the opponent, as well as not having begun to bear off, still has one or more pieces left in the winner's inner table. This results in a "Backgammon," and scores triple points.

Gammon is a reasonably common occurrence and the possibility of it happening plays a large part in a player's strategy. Backgammon is very unusual and can be seen as a lucky bonus when a mere gammon was looking inevitable.

### THE DOUBLING CUBE

Every Backgammon set has a peculiar die bearing the numbers 2, 4, 8, 16, 32, and 64. The doubling cube is an ingenious method of increasing the tension during a Backgammon game by allowing one player to insist upon an increase in the stakes if they feel that the position is favorable to them. At the start of the game, the doubling cube is put in the middle and is available to both players. Conventionally this is shown, as in the previous diagrams, by having the cube on 64 and placed in the middle of the board. At this stage the game is being contested for one unit. Play continues normally until one player decides that he has a good chance of winning the game, and maybe even achieving a gammon. When this happens, the player can then offer the cube to his opponent.

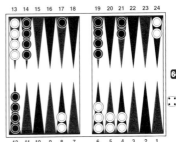

Diagram 137 White's pieces remain stuck on the 24 point

Let us assume that White holds the advantage and wishes to do this. White takes the cube from the middle, turns it so that the 2 is face-up, and places it on Black's side of the board. If Black feels that White will win, the game can be conceded and Black loses one unit. There is no further play and a new game begins. Alternatively, Black may want to continue the game. In this case, Black accepts White's double and the game continues. Now, however, the stake is two units and Black may suffer a loss of two units (or even four if White achieves a gammon) instead of escaping with the loss of a mere one unit.

However, by accepting the double, Black now gains possession of the cube. If at a later stage the play should turn in Black's favor, Black can then offer the cube back to White, insisting on an increase in the stakes from twofold to fourfold. White now has the choice of conceding the game

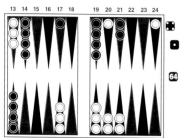

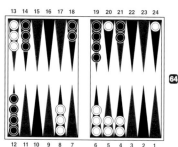

Diagram 138 *White's inner table begins to look powerful*

Diagram 139 *Black is unable to exploit White's blot on the 20 point*

and losing two units or continuing with the stake now at four units. This process can proceed indefinitely, with the stakes increasing exponentially from 2 to 4 to 8 to 16, etc. Games where the cube reaches 2 or 4 are quite common, 8 is rare, and 16 exceptional.

## GAME STRATEGIES

We have already seen how closing out points with two or more pieces can restrict the opponent, so making points is a fundamental aim in backgammon. It also means that your own pieces are secure from being hit. The best points to try to make are the high numbered ones (3, 4, 5, and 6) in your inner table, as these also impede your opponent from reentering pieces should you manage to hit their blots. Other good points are (from White's point of view) 7, 8, and 9, as these can act as landing points to bring pieces around to the inner table. It is also very useful if you can make an advanced point on the opponent's board.

Consider the position in diagram 135 (page 214), where White has just rolled 4-4. This enables White to advance two pieces from 24 to 20 and two from 8 to 4, achieving good points on both boards. The benefit of having the 20 point is that it is a good anchor for White. If White has to leave blots elsewhere on the board at a later stage, and these are hit, there will always be a secure point to re-enter these pieces. The pieces on 20 also put pressure on Black's outer table (the 14 to 18 points) and make it difficult for Black to create points there.

## THE RUNNING GAME

A running game occurs when both sides have successfully freed their back pieces. Contact between the two armies is then either no longer possible, or extremely unlikely. The contest turns into a straight race and whoever rolls the better dice will win. The position in diagram 136 (page 214) is a typical case in point. Neither side has any pieces remaining in the opponent's half of the board, with the exception of the 12 and 13 points. However, this contact is basically irrelevant, as these pieces will inevitably bypass each other. The game is a straight race. If all Backgammon games ended up as such straight races, the game would not be very interesting. Fortunately, this does not happen very often and complex interaction between the forces is far more common.

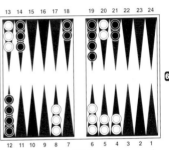

Diagram 140 *White is in a good holding position*

## THE HOLDING GAME

If your opponent manages to free their back pieces while you do not, they will, all other things being equal, have a useful advantage. They can hope to close points in their inner and outer table and your back pieces

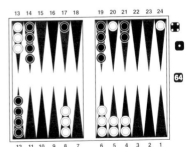

Diagram 141 *Black rolls 4-1 and attacks*

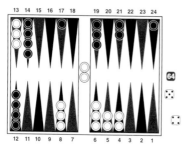

*Diagram 142 White needs a good throw*

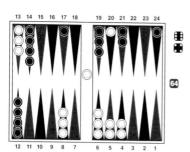

*Diagram 143 Black puts White under great pressure*

may become suffocated. However, you can fight back. If you are unable to free the back pieces, the next best course of action is to try to establish an advanced point in your opponent's half of the board. The ideal spots to aim for are the 5 and 7 points.

Consider the position in diagram 137 (page 215). The Black back pieces have escaped, while White's remain stuck on the 24 point. If White now plays passively, Black will be able to bring up pieces from the outer board and close off useful points. Therefore, a good way for White to play the 5-4 roll is to move 13 to 8 and from 24 to 20. This entails a certain risk as Black now has a few very powerful rolls, such as 6-1, 6-3, and 3-1, all of which would close out the 20 point, while simultaneously hitting White's blot. However, it is better for White to put up a fight than to simply leave the back pieces where they are and watch them become entombed. Additionally, it is more likely that Black will roll a combination which does not allow such a powerful play.

Black actually rolls 4-1 (see diagram 138, page 216) and cannot now hit the white blot on 20 without leaving a blot that White would have an immediate chance to hit. White's own inner table is beginning to look powerful and Black does not relish the thought of having to extricate a piece from this area. Black therefore decides to play solidly by using pieces from 14 and 17 to build the 18 point. White now rolls 3-1 and uses this to build the 20 point. Having achieved this aim, White now has an excellent "holding" position (see diagram 139, page 216) and is well in the game. White's pieces on 20 pressure Black's outer table and make it awkward for Black to bring pieces round. Furthermore, White may soon roll a big double, such as 6-6 or 5-5, and escape with the back pieces completely to compete in a straightforward running game.

## THE ATTACKING GAME

Let us consider again the position from the previous section where Black had to consider how to play the roll 4-1 (see diagram 141, page 217). In the previous example, Black played safely by making the 18 point. However, an alternative line of play was to launch an attack by hitting both White blots with a piece on the 19 point, reaching the position in diagram 142 (opposite).

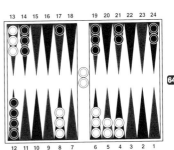

Diagram 144 White is in big trouble

White now has two pieces on the bar and only four of the six entry points are available. With a roll of 5-4, White's move is forced: one piece can be brought back into the game on the 20 point, while the other must remain on the bar because the 21 point (the place of entry for a 4) is blocked.

Black now rolls 6-4, a strong throw that can be used to move a piece from 14, hitting White's blot on 20, and then

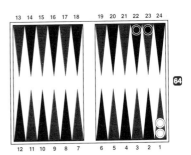

Diagram 145 An endgame position

moving on to close out the 24 point. White is now in big trouble: two pieces are still on the bar and Black has closed out three points in the inner table. Furthermore, the Black forces are poised to move around and close out further points. If White does not get a good roll immediately, there is a danger of being shut out of the game completely. This is the sort of position where a gammon result becomes a very real possibility.

## CUBE STRATEGY

A good understanding of probability and statistics is very important in backgammon, especially in endgame positions where the cube comes into play. Consider the position in diagram 145 (page 219). It is Black's turn to play.

Black will be able to bear off both pieces provided the roll does not include a 1. However, if the roll does include a 1, Black will not be able to bear off and White will win. Out of the 36 possible rolls of the dice, 25 will win for Black and only 11 will lose (1-1, 1-2, 1-3, 1-4, 1-5, 1-6, 2-1, 3-1, 4-1, 5-1, and 6-1 are the unfortunate rolls). Black therefore wants to raise the stakes and offers White the cube. Should White accept?

One way to work this out is to assume that this position is played 36 times with Black receiving each of the possible 36 rolls. We can then see what happens with White's different courses of action:

1. White concedes the game. On all 36 occasions White loses one unit and thus ends up losing 36 units.
2. White accepts the cube. On 25 occasions, White will lose and the cost will now be two units, yielding a total loss of 50. However, on the other 11 occasions White will win, and these will yield a profit of 22. White's net loss will therefore be 28 units (50 − 22).

It is therefore clear that, in the long run, White will be better off accepting Black's offer, even though the chances of losing are still greater.

Ludo is a modified form of the Indian game of Pachisi, which was enormously popular with the sixteenth-century Moguls. First patented in England around 1896, it remains popular with children worldwide.

*Players: two to four*
*Equipment: board, 16 counters (four each of four different colors) and a die*
*Difficulty: ideal for children; mainly luck*
*Duration: usually less than half an hour per game*

## BEGINNING TO PLAY

Players choose which color they wish to play with. Each player starts with four counters of the same color in their yard, as in diagram 146. The first player to

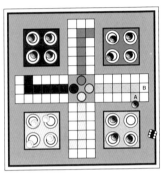

Diagram 146 *The starting position for a game of Ludo*

throw a six starts the game by advancing one of their counters to point "A."

## MOVING

Once a counter has entered the game, it can be advanced in a clockwise direction according to the throw of the die. The object is to race each counter around the board to point B and then run up the middle cells of the arm to be borne off in the center. New counters can only enter when a six is thrown, but a six results in another throw. Enemy counters can be captured and returned to their yard by landing on the cell that they occupy. Counters on the same side can be piled and advanced as if they were a single counter, but this means they can also be captured as a single counter.

## WINNING THE GAME

The first player to advance all their counters around the board and bear them off in the center is the winner.

Like Ludo, Snakes and Ladders has always been a favorite game for children. It is a game that relies entirely on luck and therefore enables young players to compete on equal terms with their elders.

*Players: two or more*
*Equipment: board, four counters and a die*
*Difficulty: ideal for children; all luck*
*Duration: usually less than 20 minutes per game*

## BRIEF HISTORY

Snakes and Ladders is based on the Indian game Moksha Patamu, which was used a means of religious instruction. The board stands for the symbolic moral journey through life to heaven, with the ladders representing virtuous acts that shorten the soul's road to nirvana (the state of ultimate perfection) and the snakes representing sins that lead to reincarnation in a lower animal form, thereby delaying nirvana.

## BEGINNING TO PLAY

Each player selects a different colored counter. Play takes place on a 10x10 board with approximately 10 snakes and 10 ladders scattered around it, such as in diagram 147 (opposite). The first player to throw a six starts the game. Other players do not enter the game until they have thrown a six themselves.

## MOVING

Counters are moved according to the throw of the dice. If you land on a square with a ladder, you can advance up the ladder (say from 28 to 84), but, if you land on a snake, you have to slide down to the bottom of the snake (say from 49 to 11). If you land on an opponent's counter, that counter is sent back to the first square.

### WINNING THE GAME

The object of the game is to reach the 100 square with an exact throw. (If you overthrow 100, you have to travel back down again from that point; thus a throw of six from square 96 means the counter advances to 100 and then back to 98.) The first player to land exactly on the 100 square is the winner.

*Diagram 147 The board used for a game of Snakes and Ladders*

Chess is the classic war game, combining elements of art and science. It is a game of pure skill, requiring both strategy and tactics.

*Players:* *two*
*Equipment:* *board and 32 pieces. Tournament games also use a Chess clock*
*Difficulty:* *although Chess is a difficult game to master, it can be enjoyed by all ages*
*Duration:* *tournament games will typically last between four and five hours. However, with a Chess clock, games can be played much more quickly and tournaments where games are completed in one hour, or even 10 minutes, are frequently held. A leisurely social game will probably take between 30 minutes and one hour*

## BRIEF HISTORY

Chess is one of the world's oldest board games. Since its invention in India around AD 600, it has experienced many changes in the rules and the movements of the pieces to arrive at the version we know today. The original Indian version of Chess featured pieces directly based on warfare, such as infantry, cavalry, elephants, and chariots. These have metamorphosed into the modern pieces: kings, queens, rooks, bishops, knights, and pawns. The queen was once a male minister or adviser to the king, but when the game reached Europe this piece became a queen and much greater powers were conferred on her.

Until the twentieth century, Chess was regarded mainly as a pursuit for the leisured classes; now it is played by many millions of people.

Before the breakup of the Soviet Union, Chess was the national sport in Russia and, until recently, Russian players have dominated world chess. Russia remains the strongest nation, but many other countries, including the United Kingdom and the United States, are fast gaining ground.

Every now and again, the classic confrontational nature of a major Chess match can capture the public imagination and thrust Chess onto the front pages of the world's press. Battles for the World Championship title, often played over several weeks, can become very big news. The various encounters between Bobby Fischer and Boris Spassky in Reykjavik in 1972, Anatoly Karpov and Viktor Korchnoi in the late 1970s, and Garry Kasparov and Anatoly Karpov in the 1980s generated tremendous public interest thanks, in part, to the political subtext of all three clashes. When Garry Kasparov famously lost a six-game match to IBM's Deep Blue computer in May 1997, the moves of the games were relayed in real time on IBM's Chess website. The final and decisive game generated a world record 22 million hits on this site. In comparison, the 1996 Atlanta Olympics attracted a mere 10 million over a three-week period. The IBM record was surpassed only by NASA's reporting of the Mars landing.

## WORLD CHAMPIONS

There has been a recognized World Chess Champion since 1886, and the roll of honor reads as follows.

### WORLD CHAMPIONSHIP ROLL OF HONOUR

| | | |
|---|---|---|
| 1886–1894 | Wilhelm Steinitz | Austria |
| 1894–1921 | Emanuel Lasker | Germany |
| 1921–1927 | José Raoul Capablanca | Cuba |
| 1927–1935 | Alexander Alekhine | USSR and France |
| 1935–1937 | Max Euwe | Holland |
| 1937–1946 | Alexander Alekhine | USSR and France |
| 1948–1957 | Mikhail Botvinnik | USSR |
| 1957–1958 | Vassily Smyslov | USSR |
| 1958–1960 | Mikhail Botvinnik | USSR |
| 1960–1961 | Mikhail Tal | USSR |
| 1961–1963 | Mikhail Botvinnik | USSR |
| 1963–1969 | Tigran Petrosian | USSR |

| 1969–1972 | Boris Spassky | USSR |
| 1972–1975 | Bobby Fischer | USA |
| 1975–1985 | Anatoly Karpov | USSR |
| 1985– | Garry Kasparov | USSR/Russia |

In the years up until the end of 1946, the world champion was expected to play matches to defend the title against the leading challengers of the day. However, there was no formal structure to enable players to qualify for matches against the incumbent champion and this enabled some of the champions to avoid their more dangerous contemporaries or postpone the matches. After Alexander Alekhine's death (while World Champion) in 1946, the World Chess Federation (FIDE) stepped in and organized a five-player tournament, which was won by Mikhail Botvinnik, to determine the new champion. They also established a structure of tournaments and matches to decide a challenger to the champion. In general, this resulted in a match for the World Championship being played every three years.

In 1993, the World Championship cycle was won by Nigel Short of England, who thereby acquired the right to challenge Garry Kasparov for the world title. However, the two players had a dispute with FIDE and therefore broke away to form their own rival organization, the Professional Chess Association. Their 1993 match, which resulted in a comfortable win for Kasparov, was played under the auspices of this new organization. FIDE, meanwhile, organized its own match, contested between the runners-up in the qualifying cycle. This match was between Anatoly Karpov of Russia and Jan Timman of the Netherlands, and was won easily by Karpov.

Kasparov subsequently defended his PCA title against Viswanathan Anand of India in New York in 1995. Kasparov's tournament record demonstrates that he is unquestionably the strongest player in the world, but he is not the world champion of the official governing body. As of early 1998, the PCA has more or less ceased to function, but there has been no rapprochement between Kasparov and FIDE. In late 1997 and early 1998 FIDE organized a World Championship knockout event that resulted in a final between Viswanathan Anand and Anatoly Karpov. The match resulted in a 3-3 tie; Karpov subsequently went on to win the speed play-off 2-0.

## THE BOARD

Chess is played on a board of 64 squares, alternately colored light and dark. The board is always set up with a light square in the lower right-hand corner. In contemporary Chess notation, the squares are referred to using letter and number coordinates. In diagram 1, the square with a black pawn is b5, while the square with a white pawn is f4.

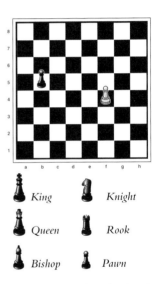

*Diagram 148 The Chessboard and pieces*

There are various other terms used to describe areas of the Chessboard, and it is useful to be aware of these. The lines across the board are known as ranks. For example, the third rank stretches across the board from a3 to h3. The lines running vertically up the board are known as files. For example, the d-file consists of the squares running from d1 up to d8. Additionally, the four left-hand files (i.e. the a-, b-, c-, and d-files) are collectively known as the queenside, while the four right-hand files (i.e. the e-, f-, g- and h-files) are collectively known as the kingside. Therefore, in diagram 148, the square with a black pawn (b5) is on the b-file, the fifth rank, and is also on the queenside.

## THE PIECES

Each player starts the game with one king, one queen, two rooks, two bishops, two knights and eight pawns. The symbols representing the pieces are shown on the previous page. At the start of the game, the pieces are arranged as in diagram 149 (opposite).

In Chess diagrams, it is conventional to display the board from White's point of view. Thus the white pieces start the game along the first and second ranks, while the black pieces start on the seventh and eighth ranks. However, when discussing positions, it is sometimes convenient to refer to, for example, "Black's second rank." This actually means the seventh rank, but from Black's point of view, sitting at the top of the board, it is the second rank.

## BEGINNING TO PLAY

White always moves first and from then on the players move alternately.

## THE MOVES OF THE PIECES

The Chess pieces move around the board in very distinct ways. Some have more mobility than others and this makes them more valuable. A fundamental aim in Chess is to win material by exchanging your lower-ranking pieces for the opponent's more valuable ones. When an opposing piece is captured it is removed from the board.

## THE ROOK

The rook operates along the ranks and files and can move any number of squares, as long as there are no intervening pieces. In diagram 150 (page 231), the black rook has complete freedom of action to operate along the a-file or the eighth rank. The white rook is more restricted, only being able to move as far as g5 along the g-file and c3 along the third rank, where it would capture the black knight. The rook cannot "jump" over intervening pieces, so a3, b3, g7, and g8 are not available.

The white rook could capture the black knight on c3 (the white rook would move to the c3 square and the black knight would be removed from the board), but the g6 square is currently occupied by the white queen and is thus also unavailable. You cannot capture your own pieces.

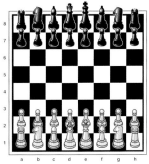

*Diagram 149 Starting position for a game of Chess*

## THE BISHOP

The bishop operates along the diagonals and, like the rook, can move freely as long as there are no other pieces in the way. In diagram 151 (page 231), the black bishop can move to any of the squares d8, c7, a5, a7, c5, d4, e3, f2, and g1. The white bishop has less mobility, only being able to move to g4 or g6, or to capture the black queen on f7. The bishops are permanently restricted to the color of the square on which they start the game. So in this example, Black has a "dark-squared bishop," while White has a "light-squared bishop." Each player starts the game with one dark-squared and one light-squared bishop.

## THE QUEEN

The queen is the most powerful piece on the board, and combines the activities of both the rook and the bishop. The white queen in diagram 152 (page 231) can move as indicated by the arrows and capture the black knight on g5. As with the rook and bishop, the queen cannot jump over pieces and so the squares a5, h5, g2, and h1 are not available.

## THE KNIGHT

Of all the chess pieces, the move of the knight is probably the most difficult to grasp. It moves in an L-shape, two squares along any rank or file and then one square at right angles. Another way to perceive this is to visualize a 3x2 "box" of squares; the knight can move from one corner to an opposite corner. This movement is much easier to understand from a graphical representation rather than a textual one.

In the diagram 153 (opposite) the black knight is able to move to any of the five squares b8, b6, c5, e5, or f6. The f8 square would be available, but it is currently occupied by the black queen. The white knight can move to f3 and h3, or capture the black rook on e2. Note that the knight, unlike other pieces, is not restricted by intervening units of either colour. Thus the presence of the two white pawns on f2 and, g2 and the black bishop on h2 do not prevent the white knight from being able to move to f3 and h3.

## THE PAWN

The pawns are the foot soldiers, or infantry, of Chess. They begin the game on the second row (for White this is the second rank, while for Black it is the seventh rank) and move forward along their respective files. From their initial position, pawns can move either one or two squares, but are then restricted to a move of just one square. So, in diagram 154 (opposite), the white pawn on a2, being on its initial square, can move to either a3 or a4, while the pawn on b3, which has already moved, can only go to b4. Similarly, the black pawn on e3 can advance only to e2, while the pawn on f7 has the option of moving to f6 or f5. The black pawn on h5 is blocked by the white knight and thus has no moves available at all.

The pawns are unique among the Chess forces in that their method of capture differs from the method by which they move. In diagram 154, one might expect that the black pawn on h5 would have been able to capture the white knight on h4, but this is not the case. Pawns capture by moving one square forwards diagonally rather than along a file. So in the diagram 8, the white pawn on b4 can capture either the black queen on a5 or the black knight on c5. The black pawn on h7 can capture the white bishop on g6.

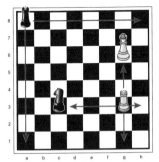

Diagram 150 The rook in action

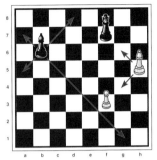

Diagram 151 The bishop in action

Diagram 152 The queen in action

Diagram 153 The knight in action

Diagram 154 The pawns in action

## THE KING

The king is able to move one square in any direction: horizontally, vertically, or diagonally. In diagram 155, the black king can move to g7, g8, and h7. The white king has seven possible moves: six are indicated by the arrows, while it is also possible for the white king to capture the black pawn on f3. If White chose to play this move, the king would come to the f3 square and the black pawn would be removed from the board. The e5 square is

*Diagram 155  The king in action*

not available as this is occupied by one of White's own pieces.

## CHECK AND CHECKMATE

As we shall see later, the fundamental aim in Chess is to capture the opponent's king. Thus whenever the king is threatened by an opposing piece (the king is then said to be "in check") immediate action must be taken to defend against this threat. There are three possible ways to do this:

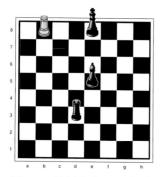

*Diagram 156  Black is in check*

1. The king can move away from the check.
2. The opposing piece can be captured.
3. A piece can intervene to block the check. (Note that if a check is delivered by a knight, then this option is not available, as it is not possible to block a knight move.)

If no such action is possible, and it is inevitable that the king will be captured n the next move, then "checkmate" has occurred and the game is over. In diagram 156 (facing page below), the black king is n check from the white rook on b8.

In this situation all three of the esponses indicated above are possible:

Diagram 157 Black is in checkmate

. The king can move to d7, e7 or f7, escaping from the check. Moving to d8 or f8 is not possible, as the king would then remain in check from the white rook.

2. The black bishop on e5 can capture the white rook.

3. The black rook on d3 can move to d8, blocking the check.

et us now change the situation by adding further pieces. In diagram 157 (above right), Black is still in check, but the options for escape have been removed.

1. The black king cannot move to d7, as this square is threatened by the white pawn on c6 (pawns capture one square diagonally). It cannot go to e7 as this square is threatened by the white knight and the f7 square is now blocked by Black's own rook.

2. The black bishop can no longer capture the white rook as the pawn on c7 is in the way.

3. The black rook on d3 cannot move to d8 to block the check as the white knight on d5 prevents this.

The black king is in check and cannot escape. Black has been checkmated and the game is over.

*Diagram 158  Castling*

## STALEMATE

It sometimes happens – often between expert players – that checkmate is not possible: not enough pieces remain to either player to confine a king in checkmate, or a position has been achieved in which a king is driven in check back and forth onto the same squares in an unending repetition ("perpetual check"). The players have reached a draw, or "stalemate." This may arise, as well, when either player offers a draw, and the other accepts. There is a special rule, too, that allows either player to call, at any time, for "fifty moves"; the game is drawn if checkmate has not occurred within that interval.

## UNUSUAL MOVES

The main moves of the pieces are described above, but there are three other possible moves which do not conform to the above conditions.

### Castling

During the course of the game it is possible to make a move known as "castling," which can occur either on the queenside or kingside. When castling occurs, the king and rook move simultaneously along the back rank. The king always moves two squares and the rook hops over the king to land on the square beyond. Thus, in diagram 158 (above), Black can castle on the queenside by moving the king from e8 to c8 and the rook from a8 to d8. White can castle kingside by moving the king from e1 to g1 and the rook from h1 to f1.

Castling is only permitted if the following conditions apply:

1. The king and rook must not have moved earlier on in the game.

2. The king must not be in check nor must the king pass through check.

In diagram 159 (below), Black cannot castle queenside and white cannot castle kingside. Black is in check from the white queen, while the white king would have to pass through the f1 square, which is controlled by the black bishop. However, White would be able to castle queenside, by moving the king to c1 and the rook to d1. There is no impediment to this move.

## Pawn promotion

As we have seen, the pawn is the weakest of all the pieces, being very restricted in its movements. However, if a pawn manages to break through to the opponent's back rank it "promotes" to a new piece that takes the place of this pawn. The player who promotes a pawn can choose which piece to replace it with. Any piece is possible, with the exception of the king. In almost all cases the player will choose the queen, as this is the most valuable piece.

In diagram 160 (page 236), the white pawn can advance from d7 to d8, when this pawn will be removed from the board and replaced with a

white queen, rook, bishop, or knight, according to the choice of the White player. Similarly, the black pawn can promote on e1, but could alternatively capture the white bishop on f1, when it would also promote.

## En passant

The en passant (French for "in passing") rule is the one that confuses most beginners. It occurs when a pawn advances two squares on its initial move and finds

*Diagram 159 Exceptions to castling*

itself adjacent to an opposing pawn. The opposing pawn then has the option to capture this pawn as if it had only moved one square.

In diagram 161 (opposite), if Black advances the pawn from b7 to b5, White can respond by capturing this pawn as if it had only moved one square, ie from b7 to b6. Similarly, if the white pawn advances from h2 to h4, Black could take as if the pawn had only moved to h3. The en passant capture is only possible if the pawn moves from its initial square. Thus, if the white pawn on f3 moves to f4, the capture is not possible. En passant only applies to pawns and can only be made in immediate response to the advance of the pawn. Thus, if Black did advance the pawn on b7 to b5, but White chose to make a move elsewhere on the board, the chance to make the en passant capture is lost forever. White cannot come back later to make this capture.

## CHESS NOTATION

There is a huge literature on Chess and to understand it successfully it is necessary to understand Chess notation. Fortunately the modern style – algebraic notation – is very straightforward and is now in more or less universal use.

### Algebraic notation

If you have looked through the previous material, you will by now be familiar with the idea of the squares on the Chessboard being referred to by coordinates. The method by which a move is recorded is to give the symbol of the piece followed by the square to which the piece moves. When a pawn is moved, only the square on which the pawn lands is given. The symbols for the pieces are as follows:

*Diagram 160 Pawn promotion*

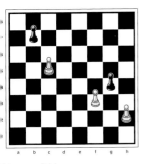

**King      K**
**Queen     Q**
**Rook      R**
**Bishop    B**
**Knight    N**

*Diagram 161*
*The en passant rule*

Thus, starting from the initial position (see diagram 162, page 238), if White opens the game by playing the knight from g1 to f3 and Black responds by playing the pawn from d7 to d5, the "score" of the moves would be written thus: 1 Nf3 d5.

The "1" designates the first move of the game and, conventionally, White moves first. When a capture is made, an "x" is introduced, and when a move results in check a "+" is added to the move.

Consider the position in diagram 163 on page 239. Here, White captures the pawn on e4 with the bishop and Black replies by taking the knight on a5, giving check. This sequence would be recorded as 1 Bxe4 bxa5+.

Note that with a pawn capture, the file from which the pawn has moved is given.

Occasionally, a position arises where a little extra information is required to avoid any ambiguity. For example, if White has rooks on a1 and f1 and moves the a1 rook to d1, writing 1 Rd1 will not yield sufficient information to recreate the move, as the other rook could also have moved to d1. In this case, the file from which the piece moves is added, ie 1 Rad1.

Two other moves need a mention. Castling on the kingside (for either color) is denoted by 0–0, while castling on the queenside is given by 0–0–0. When a pawn promotes, the piece for which it is exchanged is given at the end of the move, eg 1 e8Q or 1 b8N.

## CHESS SYMBOLS

Many theoretical works on Chess are sold around the world and these often use a completely languageless notation to describe the game. To the untutored eye, such texts can look like hieroglyphics with strange symbols denoting factors such as "small advantage to White," "Black is winning," or even "space advantage and the two bishops." However, the following special symbols, attached to individual moves, are much more common and would be used in Chess columns in the general press:

| ... | Black move follows |
| ! | Good move |
| !! | Excellent move |
| ? | Bad move |
| ?? | Blunder |
| !? | Interesting move |
| ?! | Dubious move |

*Diagram 162 Starting position for a game*

## THE VALUES OF THE PIECES

Before one can make any attempt to play a game of Chess with any degree of competence, it is important to be aware of the value of the different pieces. Opportunities constantly crop up to exchange pieces, and a knowledge of their relative values is essential to gain an insight into whether a particular trade is a particularly good idea.

As the pawn is the basic unit in Chess, it is convenient to assess all other pieces relative to the pawn. The following is a good rule of thumb. Remember that the king can never be exchanged, as checkmating the king ends the game, so assigning it a value has no meaning.

| Piece | Value in Pawns |
| Knight | 3 |

| | |
|---|---|
| Bishop | 3 |
| Rook | 5 |
| Queen | 9 |
| King | Not applicable |

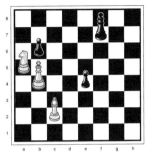

*Diagram 163 An endgame position*

From this table, we can conclude that, all other things being equal, knights and bishops have approximately equal value. A rook is worth a knight or a bishop plus two pawns, and a queen is worth a rook, a bishop (or a knight) plus one pawn. Knights and bishops are known in chess as minor pieces, while the rooks and queens are referred to as major pieces. Another typical chess term is the "exchange." A player who has won a rook for a bishop is said to be "the exchange up."

Although the ultimate aim of the game is to checkmate the opponent's king, a more typical method of winning a game is to gain material. Even the advantage of a single pawn is often enough to decide a game. Remember that when a pawn reaches the opponent's back row it can promote to queen, thus creating a huge material balance in favor of the player who has just achieved this.

## CHESS TACTICS

There are various fundamental tactics that enable a player to win material, and the following are typical examples.

### The fork

A fork occurs when one player attacks two pieces simultaneously, of which only one can be saved. Consider the positions in diagram 164 (page 240). On the queenside, White is attacking the black bishop and knight with the pawn on b3. Black can only move one of these and so the other will be lost. 1 … Bxb3 will not help as White could recapture 2 axb3 and still win a piece. On the kingside, Black has forked the white queen and rook with the knight. Both of White's pieces are more valuable than Black's and so the impending trade will favor Black.

## The skewer

A skewer is a device whereby two pieces along the same line are threatened and one cannot move without exposing the

*Diagram 164 The fork*

other. On the queenside, White has checked the black king, which will be obliged to vacate the diagonal, allowing the white bishop to capture the black queen. On the kingside, the two white knights have been skewered by the black rook.

In diagram 166 (opposite above), very favorable exchanges result from pinning a piece against the king – a "theme" used quite often in Chess.

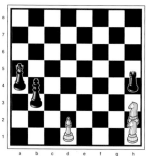

*Diagram 165 The skewer*

### WINNING THE GAME

The ultimate aim in Chess is to checkmate the opponent's king. As with tactics, there are various checkmating situations that arise again and again in Chess. The following is a typical, but by no means comprehensive, selection.

(a) The white queen single-handedly covers all the black king's escape squares. The black king cannot capture the queen as it is protected by the pawn.

(b) The white rook and bishop combine to take away all the flight squares from the black king.

(c) The white king has been smothered by its own pieces and cannot escape the check from the black knight.

(d) Having three pawns in front of the king (a typical situation when one has castled) is good for protecting the king from frontal attacks. However, it does leave a weakness on the back row which an enemy major piece can sometimes exploit. Here White needs to move the king to the second rank to escape from the black rook, but all these squares are taken by White's own pawns.

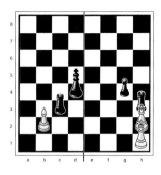

*Diagram 166 The pin*

## CHESS CLOCKS

Social Chess games are most often played with just a board and the 32 pieces, but all tournament games are nowadays played with the aid of a chess clock. Even social players would do well to consider using a clock, as this limits the amount of time that can be spent on a game.

The Chess clock is a clever device which actually consists of two clocks, one for each player. They are linked in such a way that the starting of one clock automatically stops the other and vice versa. Thus only one player's clock is running at any one time. Each player has a set period of time to complete either a certain number of moves or the entire game. Failure to

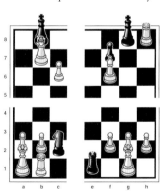

*Diagram 167 Four possible checkmating positions*

comply to the time control, as it is known, results in automatic loss of the game, regardless of the position on the board. The most common version of the Chess clock has a flag which is pushed up by the minute hand as it approaches the hour mark. When the hand passes the hour mark, the flag falls and time is deemed to be up. This mechanical, and perhaps slightly unreliable, version of the clock is gradually being replaced by digital models.

In international events, the time control is typically two hours for the first 40 moves of the game, one hour for the next 20 moves and then a further half an hour to complete the game. If this time allowance were used in full, each player would have three and a half hours thinking time for the game. However, as the clocks do not run simultaneously, this would mean that the game lasted seven hours.

Events which are played at faster time limits are becoming more and more popular. Typical time controls in such events are 30 minutes, 15 minutes or even just five minutes per player for the entire game. The Chess clock is a very efficient method of timing a two-player game and these clocks are used in many other competitive games such as Scrabble, Checkers, and Go.

## PROGRESSIVE CHESS

This is probably the most widely played variant of the parent game. Progressive Chess provides an interesting challenge that rewards creativity and imagination.

*Players:* two
*Equipment:* board and Chess pieces
*Difficulty:* anyone who can play Chess can easily master Progressive Chess
*Duration:* between 10 and 20 minutes

### BEGINNING TO PLAY

The pieces are set up as for normal Chess.

### MOVING

White moves first and plays as in normal Chess. Black then replies by having two moves. White then plays three, Black four, and so on, the number being incremented by one on each turn. A player may only give check on the last move of his sequence and if a player is in check, the first move of his sequence must be to escape from the check. If a player gives check before his move is complete, then the check ends his sequence. Pawn promotion is perfectly valid.

*Diagram 168 A typical Progressive Chess game*

### WINNING THE GAME

A game will typically last around seven or eight moves and is won, as in normal Chess, by delivering checkmate. If you are unable to deliver checkmate, often the best plan is to take as many of your opponent's pieces as you can and to give your king as much air as possible. This will make it harder for your opponent to deliver checkmate on their next turn. A useful trick is to keep the king on the back row, as this makes it more difficult for your opponent to promote a pawn (promoting to a queen or rook will give check – only permissible on the final move of the sequence).

Diagram 168 (above) shows a typical progressive Chess game. The pieces start as in normal Chess and the notation is the same: 1 d4 2 d5, Nh6 3 Nc3, Nf3, Bxh6 4 Bg4, Bxf3, Bxe2, Bxd1. Black's last move was a mistake. White's reply shows the drawback of not creating flight squares for the king: 5 Nb5, Bc4, Bb3, Ba4, Nxc7 checkmate.

# CHECKERS (DRAUGHTS)

Checkers (Draughts in the United Kingdom) is perhaps the world's best-known board game. The attraction of the game is that, despite the simplicity of the rules, complex play can result.

*Players:* two
*Equipment:* *board and 12 pieces. Tournament games also use a clock*
*Difficulty:* *the rules of Checkers are very simple and the game can be enjoyed by players of almost any age*
*Duration:* *tournament games will typically last between one and two hours. A social game will probably take between 10 minutes and half an hour.*

## BRIEF HISTORY

Checkers may well be a very old game, as a typical board and pieces have been discovered that date back to Egypt in the period 1600 BC. However it is not clear that these were necessarily used to play a game that would be familiar as a precursor to Checkers as it is played today. The modern game had its beginnings in Spain in the sixteenth century and spread, via France, to the rest of Europe. In 1688, a manual on Checkers, *Jeu des Dames,* was published in France. The key publication in Great Britain followed in 1756 – *Treatise on the Game of Draughts* by William Payne. This contained much fundamental analysis on endgame positions and demonstrates that even 250 years ago, there was a great deal of knowledge about Checkers.

The modern era of Checkers features one of the most dominant champions ever of any mental sport – Dr Marion Tinsley. Tinsley was born in Ohio in 1927 and died in 1994. He was the best player in the world for 40 years, during which time he lost the incredibly small total of just seven games.

## THE BOARD AND PIECES

Checkers is played on a standard Chessboard, using only the dark squares. Each side starts the game with 12 pieces, as indicated in diagram 169 (top right). Unlike Chess, Black is conventionally shown as starting from the lower end off the board. In a further divergence from Chess, Black always moves first.

## THE AIM OF THE GAME

The aim in Checkers is to capture all the opponent's pieces or render them unable to move. It sometimes happens that both sides are reduced to a small number of pieces and these are unable to attack the opposition successfully. The pieces will

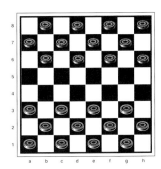

*Diagram 169   Starting position for a game of Checkers*

then circle around each other endlessly with no hope of a decisive result. In such situations the players can agree to a draw (in fact the players can, by mutual consent, agree to a draw at anytime during the game). Draws are very common in Checkers, especially at a high level. For example, when Dr Tinsley played the computer program Chinook in London in 1992, the result was four wins for Tinsley, two for Chinook and 33 draws.

## MOVING AND CAPTURING

The pieces can move one square in a forward diagonal direction. For example, in the starting position Black can move the piece on c3 to either b4 or d4. The White piece on h6 can only move to g5. The eight pieces that each side has on the back two rows cannot, for the moment at least, move anywhere at all.

Checkers pieces capture by jumping over an enemy piece to the square beyond. The enemy piece is then removed from

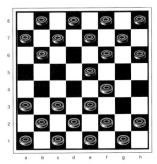

*Diagram 170   The position after Black's opening move and White's response*

the board. For example, if Black opens the game by moving the piece on g3 to f4 and White responds by moving from d6 to e5, we arrive at the position in diagram 170 (page 245).

Now Black captures the White piece on e5 by jumping with his own piece on f4 to d6.

White now has a choice of recaptures, either by jumping from c7 to e5, or e7 to c5. In Checkers, unlike Chess, captures are obligatory. If you are in a position to capture an enemy piece, you must do so. If you have a choice of captures, you are free to choose which one you want to make. It is also possible to capture more than one piece as in diagram 172 (opposite).

If it is Black's turn to move, the piece on g1 can make a triple capture, jumping from g1-e3-g5-e7, taking all three White pieces in the process.

If you have a choice between captures and one move involves capturing more pieces than the other, you are still free to choose which play to make – you are not obliged to make the capture that removes most of the opponent's pieces.

## PROMOTION

When a piece fights its way through to the opponent's back rank, it promotes to become a king. A king is the same as a normal piece, except that it can move and capture both forwards and backwards. A king is represented by two pieces on a square.

In diagram 173 (opposite), Black can move the piece on c7 to either b8 or d8 and promote this piece to a king. If it were White's turn he could jump from g3 to e1, capturing the Black piece on f2 and simultaneously promoting to a king. Diagram 174 (opposite) illustrates the power of the king.

The White king on f2 can move, like a normal piece, to e3 or g3. However, the added option of moving backwards means that the squares e1 and g1 are also available. The Black king on f6 demonstrates the

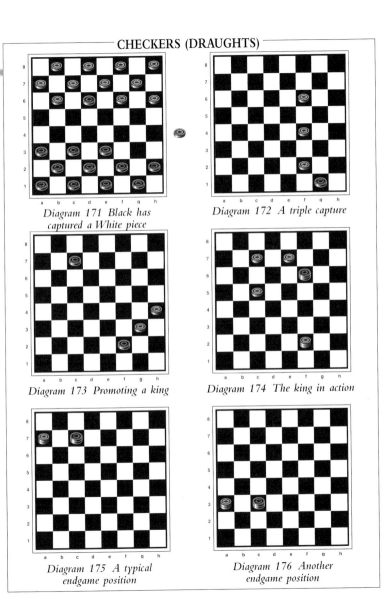

# CHECKERS (DRAUGHTS)

*Diagram 171 Black has captured a White piece*

*Diagram 172 A triple capture*

*Diagram 173 Promoting a king*

*Diagram 174 The king in action*

*Diagram 175 A typical endgame position*

*Diagram 176 Another endgame position*

capturing power of a king. The added direction of movement means that this piece is able to jump from f6 to d8 to b6 to d4, capturing the three White pieces in the process.

## THE ENDGAME

The endgame in Checkers can be very subtle and is often finely balanced between a win and a draw. Consider the position in diagrams 175 and 176 (page 247).

In the upper half of the board, White can move safely by playing a7-b8. If Black responds with c7-b6, White can simply go back with b8-a7 and the position is a draw. In the lower half, the White king is stymied and any move is met by immediate capture. However, if it were Black's turn to play, then Black would not be able to maintain the blockade and the game would be a draw.

Here, Black has a king and White only a piece. If it is White to play, for example, d4-e3 h4-g3 e3-d2 g3-f2 d2-c1/K f2-e1 c1-b2 e1-d2 b2-a3 d2-c3, the White

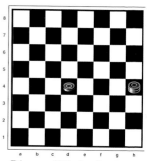

*Diagram 177 Another endgame position*

king is trapped as in the previous example. However, if it is Black to play, then the timing is wrong and the game will be a draw. Try it and see!

## TACTICS

The fact that captures are obligatory in Checkers creates many opportunities for tactical play. Pieces are often sacrificed in order to create opportunities to make multiple jumps and recapture many pieces at once. Diagram 178 (opposite top) shows a typical example. Black wins the game with a neat combination by playing the king from d4 to c3. White is now obligated to capture this piece with b4 x d2 (the 'x' signifying a capture). Now Black plays the killer blow, f2-e1.

White now has only one move. He is forced to play his king from c1 to b2, when Black wins the game with the double jump, e1 x c3 x a1 (diagram 179, below).

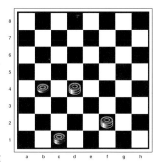

Diagram 178 *An example of sacrifice play*

## DIFFERENT METHODS OF PLAY

As Checkers has been studied to a deeper and deeper level, the theory of the opening moves has become increasingly well understood. This presents a problem for expert players, because many of the openings are now known to fizzle out to drawn positions. This is unsatisfactory for tournament play, because weak players would have the chance to make easy draws with their stronger opponents simply by playing out a drawing sequence. Three main styles of play have been developed to combat this problem.

## GO AS YOU PLEASE (GAYP)

This is not a solution to the problem; in fact, it completely ignores it. Both players can make any move they wish. Playing like this is perfectly satisfactory for social players or club players who are less well versed in the subtle nuances of the game.

## ELEVEN-MAN-BALLOT

In this version, each players starts with 11 pieces, rather than the standard 12. The missing piece is selected by ballot and is the same for each player.

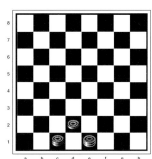

Diagram 179 *Black wins with a double jump*

## THREE-MOVE-BALLOT

This is by far the most popular solution to the problem. A number of three-move sequences (Black's opening move, White's reply and Black's second move) are written on cards, one of which is drawn at random. The players then play two games, each taking one Black and one White, using this opening sequence. If the sequence is favourable for one side, then this becomes like serving at tennis and then having to receive the serve. This is by far the most popular form of the game and is used in almost all major tournaments and championship matches.

## LOSING CHECKERS (DRAUGHTS)

In Losing (or Giveaway) Checkers, the winner is the first player to get rid of all their pieces. It is an amusing variation that particularly appeals to young players.

*Players: two*
*Equipment: board and 24 pieces*
*Difficulty: easy to grasp strategy*
*Duration: usually less than 20 minutes*

### BEGINNING TO PLAY

The board and pieces are arranged in the same way as for Checkers, and the rules are the same.

### MOVING

Just as in the parent game, players are obliged to capture if they can. If a player fails to capture an opponent's piece when it is possible to do so, the opponent can insist on the move being replayed and the capture made. After the opening stages, it is desirable for players to move their nen out from the back rank, leaving spaces between those pieces and the ones in front, since of course it is almost always fatal to make a king.

## WINNING THE GAME

The player who is first to get rid of all their pieces or be placed in a position in which they cannot move is the winner.

## ITALIAN CHECKERS (DRAUGHTS)

Italian Checkers is almost identical to the British and US version, with slightly differing rules on captures, and is known to date from at least the sixteenth century.

*Players: two*
*Equipment: board and 24 pieces*
*Difficulty: strategic*
*Duration: usually about one hour*

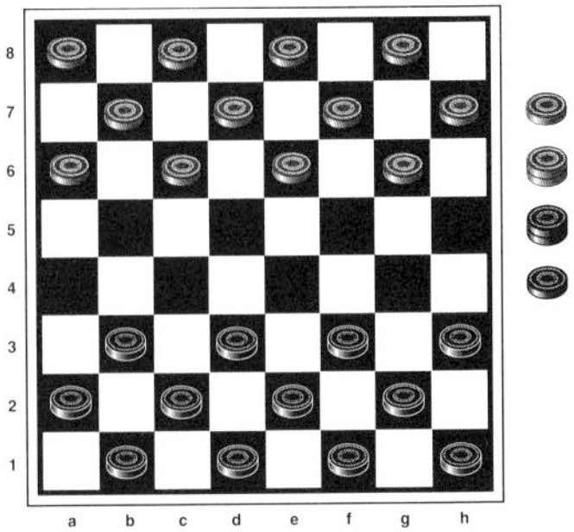

*Diagram 180 Starting position for a game of Italian Checkers*

## BEGINNING TO PLAY

The board and starting position are identical to British and American Checkers, except that the board is placed with a white square in the bottom left-hand corner. Play still takes place on the black squares.

## MOVING

The moves in Italian Checkers are exactly the same as in the conventional version, except that there are slightly different rules for captures. In Italian Checkers kings cannot be captured by uncrowned pieces. In addition, a player who has a choice between two or more captures must make the move that captures the greater number of pieces. If the number of pieces is equal, but a player faces a choice between capturing a king and an uncrowned piece, they must capture the king.

### WINNING THE GAME

Just as in conventional Checkers, the winner is the player who captures all the opponent's pieces or immobilizes those that remain.

## SPANISH CHECKERS (DRAUGHTS)

Spanish Checkers is identical to Italian Checkers, except for the power of the king, who can move any distance along a diagonal and can land beyond the captured piece any distance. Spanish Checkers can also be traced back to the sixteenth century.

*Players:* two
*Equipment:* board and 24 pieces
*Difficulty:* strategic
*Duration:* usually about one hour

### BEGINNING TO PLAY

The board and pieces are arranged in exactly the same way as for a game of Italian Checkers.

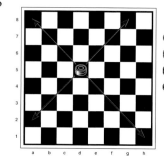

*Diagram 181 King captures in Spanish Checkers*

### MOVING

The rules are the same as for Italian Checkers, except in relation to the king. In Spanish Checkers a king can move any number of squares along a diagonal, as long as it is unobstructed by its own pieces. If there is an opposing piece on that diagonal, it can be captured provided that there are no pieces in front of it and that there are one or more squares immediately beyond it for the king to land on. The king may land on any of the vacant squares beyond the captured piece, but having made that capture, the king must capture another piece on a different diagonal if it is possible to do so. The move is only completed once the king has made all the captures it can. The captured pieces are removed from the board once the move is completed, but the king can jump over each of them only once – dead pieces form an impassable barrier.

## WINNING THE GAME

Just as in conventional Checkers, the winner is the player who captures all the opponent's pieces or immobilizes those that remain.

# GERMAN CHECKERS (DRAUGHTS)

German Checkers is identical to Spanish Checkers except in relation to the capturing powers of uncrowned pieces. The pieces are arranged in the standard way on a 64-square board. Instead of being made kings, pieces that land on the opponent's back row are made queens or dames.

*Players:* two
*Equipment:* board and 24 pieces
*Difficulty:* strategic
*Duration:* usually about one hour

## BEGINNING TO PLAY

The board and pieces are arranged in exactly the same way as for a game of Spanish Checkers.

# GERMAN CHECKERS (DRAUGHTS)

## MOVING

The rules of German Checkers are identical to those of Spanish Checkers apart from one very important aspect: in German Checkers uncrowned pieces can capture in both a forward and backward direction. Furthermore an uncrowned piece's move is not necessarily completed if it reaches the coronation square. If it can then capture other pieces by moving backwards it must do so. In that case, it does not promote to a king on that move.

## WINNING THE GAME

Just as in conventional checkers, the winner is the player who captures all the opponent's pieces or immobilizes those that remain.

# RUSSIAN CHECKERS (DRAUGHTS)

Russian Checkers is very similar to German Checkers, but with slight rule variations for capturing and promotion. Capturing is not compulsory, and the moment a piece hits the king's row, it is crowned.

*Players:* two
*Equipment:* board and 24 pieces
*Difficulty:* strategic
*Duration:* usually about one hour

## BEGINNING TO PLAY

The board and pieces are arranged in exactly the same way as for a game of German Checkers.

## MOVING

There are two rules that distinguish Russian and German Checkers. First, when a piece reaches the coronation square it cannot again capture backwards, but in Russian Checkers it does become a king. Second, when there is a choice between two capturing moves, there is no obligation to choose the move that captures the highest number of pieces.

## WINNING THE GAME

Just as in conventional Checkers, the winner is the player who captures all the opponent's pieces or immobilizes those that remain

## ——— POLISH CHECKERS (DRAUGHTS) ———

Polish or Continental Checkers, which was developed around 1725, is identical to German Checkers, but is played with a larger board and more pieces. Nowadays, it is the form of Checkers played in France, Belgium, Holland, and the French-speaking cantons of Switzerland.

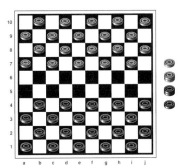

Diagram 182 *Starting position for a game of Polish Checkers*

*Players:* two
*Equipment:* board and 40 pieces
*Difficulty:* strategic
*Duration:* usually about one hour

## BEGINNING TO PLAY

In Polish Checkers the board and pieces are arranged in exactly the same way as for a game of German Checkers, but on a 10x10 board with a white square in the bottom right-hand corner. Each player starts with 20 pieces, five on each of the first four rows.

# POLISH CHECKERS (DRAUGHTS)

### MOVING
The rules for Polish Checkers are identical to those of German Checkers. Interestingly, crowned pieces are known as queens rather than kings in Polish Checkers.

### WINNING THE GAME
Just as in conventional Checkers, the winner is the player who captures all the opponent's pieces or immobilizes those that remain.

# CANADIAN CHECKERS (DRAUGHTS)

Canadian Checkers is identical to German and Polish Checkers, but with an even larger board and more pieces. It was devised by the French settlers of Quebec, who called it the Grand Jeu de Dames.

*Players:* two
*Equipment:* board and 60 pieces
*Difficulty:* strategic
*Duration:* usually about one hour

### BEGINNING TO PLAY
The board and pieces are arranged in exactly the same way as for a game of German Checkers, but on a 12x12 board. Each player starts with 30 pieces, six on each of the first five rows.

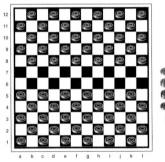

*Diagram 183 Starting position for a game of Canadian Checkers*

### MOVING
The rules for Canadian Checkers are identical to those of German Checkers.

# CANADIAN CHECKERS (DRAUGHTS)

## WINNING THE GAME

Just as in conventional Checkers, the winner is the player who captures all the opponent's pieces or succeeds in immobilizing all those that remain.

# TURKISH CHECKERS (DRAUGHTS)

In the Turkish form of Checkers play takes place on both the white and black squares, and pieces can move forwards or sideways, but not diagonally.

*Players:* two
*Equipment:* board and 32 pieces
*Difficulty:* strategic
*Duration:* usually about one hour

## BEGINNING TO PLAY

The pieces are lined up side by side on the second and third ranks of a standard Chessboard.

## MOVING

Unlike other forms of Checkers, a move in Turkish Checkers can be forwards, lateral or backwards (for the kings) but not diagonal. Uncrowned pieces can move one square in a forward or lateral direction. They capture by jumping over the opponent's pieces, again either forwards or laterally. On reaching the other side of the board, a piece becomes a king, after which it can move any number of squares forwards, backwards or sideways (but not diagonally) and capture by moving forwards, backwards or sideways in similar fashion to a king in Spanish Checkers. Captured pieces are removed from the board immediately, and cannot impede further captures. Just as in Spanish Checkers, it is compulsory to capture a piece if it is possible to do so and, given a choice of captures, the move that involves the greatest number of captures must be made.

## WINNING THE GAME
As in conventional Checkers, the winner is the player who captures all the opponent's pieces or immobilizes those that remain. However, it is also possible to win by reducing one's opponent to a single uncrowned piece.

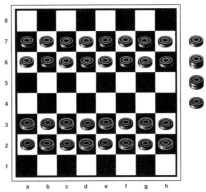

*Diagram 184  Starting position for a game of Turkish Checkers*

# GO

Go is the ultimate territory game. Players take it in turns to place stones on the board, attempting to surround territory. The apparent simplicity of the game is deceptive and even the very strongest computers only play at the level of a competent beginner. Go has been compared to playing five games of Chess simultaneously – one in the center and one in each corner.

*Players:* two
*Equipment:* *Go board and Go stones. Tournament games also use a clock*
*Difficulty:* *the rules of Go are very simple and the game can quickly be enjoyed by anybody. However, the intricacies of the game take decades to master*
*Duration:* *tournament games can last a day or more. However, a leisurely social game will probably take between 30 minutes and one hour*

## BRIEF HISTORY

The origin of Go is steeped in mystery and legend, but the game almost certainly developed several thousand years ago in China. The most popular story is that Go was invented by the Chinese Emperor Shun to "strengthen his son's weak mind." From China, Go spread to Japan and Korea and eventually throughout the rest of the world. It is revered in Eastern tradition in much the same way as the physical sport of Sumo. In fact, even though Go is not a physical sport, it is categorized as a martial art because study of the game is regarded as a process of self-development.

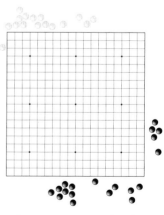

Diagram 185 *A Go board and stones*

Although there has been a recent upsurge in interest in the United Kingdom and United States, the game remains most popular in the East, where the top Go players are huge stars. For example, Lee Chang-Ho, a brilliant young player from Korea, was ranked as the eighth most recognized person in the world in a survey in Korea.

## THE GO BOARD AND STONES

The classic game of Go is played on a 19x19 board as shown in diagram 185 (page 259).

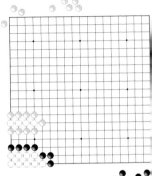

*Diagram 186*
*Capturing territory*

There are 19 horizontal and 19 vertical lines on a standard board, yielding 361 intersections, called "points." The nine darker points are reference markers and are used to locate your position. As a game on the full-size board can take a great deal of time, the game is also often played on a smaller 13x13 board. Beginners can also play on a further reduced 9x9 board. The game obviously simplifies as the size of the board decreases, but all the rules and the basic principles remain the same.

The game is played by the two players ("White" and "Black") taking turns to place stones on the board. The stronger player takes White, as Black plays first and thus holds a small advantage. The stones are placed on the intersections and not the squares themselves. The traditional nature of the game of Go can be discerned from the fact that players are expected to place the stones by using the index and middle fingers. At the start of the game the board is empty, unless one player is far superior to the other, in which case a handicap system may be used. The weaker player takes Black and can receive a head start of up to nine stones. These stones are placed on the star points, White plays first and the game continues as for an even game. Once the stones have been placed on the board, they cannot be moved. The play consists only of adding further stones to the board on unoccupied points.

## THE AIM OF THE GAME

The aim of Go is extremely simple – it is to capture territory. At the end of the game, the size of the Black and White territories are compared. Whoever has captured more is the winner. Territory is defined as points surrounded by stones of the same color. For example, in diagram 186 (opposite), White has succeeded in capturing four points, while Black has done better with nine. If the game were now concluded, then Black, having captured more territory, would win.

## RULES OF PLAY

In the battle to capture territory, it is possible that your stones may be captured, or you may capture those of the opponent. A key concept in the fight to capture stones is that of "liberties." A stone's liberties are adjacent points horizontally and vertically.

A stone in the center of the board has four liberties (see the White stone in diagram 187, right), while ones on the edge or in the corner have three and two, respectively (see the Black stones). When enemy stones block all the liberties of a stone, the stone is surrounded, deemed to be captured, and then removed from the board.

In diagram 188 (over page), the White stone in mid-board has been captured, and will be removed from the board. The same applies to the Black stones on the edge.

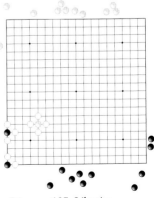

*Diagram 187 Liberties*

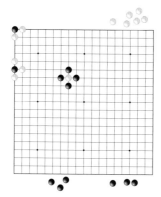

*Diagram 188 Captured stones*

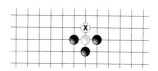

*Diagram 189 White is threatened with capture*

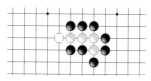

*Diagram 190 Capturing a number of stones*

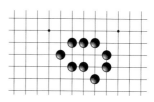

*Diagram 191 The White stones have been captured*

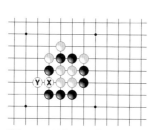

*Diagram 192 Attack and counterattack*

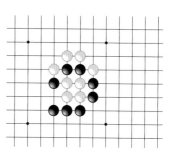

*Diagram 193 White captures the Black stones*

A captured stone is a prisoner-of-war. It has value at the end of the game because it can be used to "fill in" points that the opponent has gained, thus reducing his territory.

## ATARI

Stones that are threatened with imminent capture are said to be in "atari." In diagram 189 (opposite), three of the White stone's liberties are already blocked. If Black were now to play a stone on the point marked with an "x," the White stone would be captured. The White stone is therefore in atari. However, it is White's turn to play and save the situation, temporarily at least, by playing a stone to the "x." Black cannot now capture both stones.

Regardless of how many stones there are in a group (see diagram 190, opposite), if all their liberties are taken away, the stones are captured.

If Black now plays a stone as indicated, the four White stones will have been deprived of all their liberties and the result is shown in diagram 191 (opposite). Black has captured four White stones and gained four points of territory.

As play in the game progresses and the stones become intertwined the possibilities for capturing, both stones and territory, can become complex. In diagram 192 (opposite), the group of four white stones in the lower half of the board are in atari and seem to be in trouble. White could try to keep these alive by playing on "x," but then Black would play on "y" and the stones would still be captured.

However, White has a much better move. In diagram 193 (opposite), the two highest black stones are captured and removed from the board. The lower group of four white stones is thus no longer in atari.

## LEGAL AND ILLEGAL MOVES

You may only place a stone on the board if that stone will have liberties. In diagram 194 (over page), White cannot place a stone on the point marked with an "x" because this stone will have no liberties and will simply be removed from the board by Black. However, the white stone marked with a triangle is not the same. It is connected to other white stones and thus shares liberties with them. White would not place a stone here – this would make no sense as the stone would simply reduce White's territory – but if this configuration arose during play, there would be no problem.

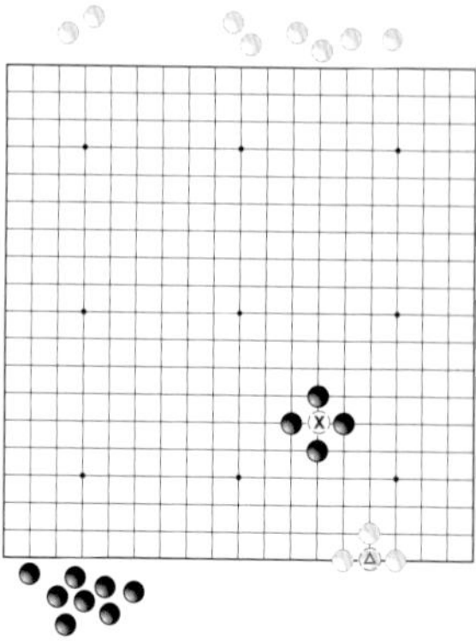

However, you are allowed to place a stone on a point where it has no liberties if, by doing so, you capture enemy stones and thus create liberties. In the upper group of diagram 195 (below top), Black cannot place a stone at "x" as this stone would be part of a group

*Diagram 194 Legal and illegal moves*

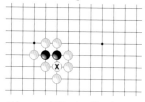

*Diagram 195 An illegal move*

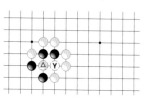

*Diagram 196 A legal move: Black captures a White stone*

that has no liberties. However, in diagram 196 (below bottom), Black can play at "y," as, by so doing, he would capture the white stone marked with a triangle. His group of stones would then have liberties.

## LIFE AND DEATH

A key element in the strategy of Go is whether a group of stones are alive or dead. If a group of stones is dead, they will be picked off, and any territory they have gained will be transferred to the opponent. If a group is alive this will not happen. Ensuring that your groups are alive is crucial. In diagram 197 (opposite top right), the group of Black stones has been completely surrounded, but White will never be able to capture these stones. It is not possible to play a stone to either of the points marked "x," as they have no liberties. The Black group is "alive."

The situation in diagram 198 (below) is different. Here, although the Black group has two points of territory, the stones can nevertheless be captured. White is able to play a stone to either "x" or "y," as these points have liberties. Let us assume that White plays to "x." White now threatens to play to "y" and capture the group. Black could capture the white stone by playing to "y," but now the position in diagram 198 (below) arises.

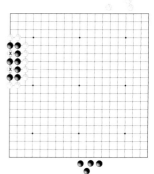

Diagram 197 The Black stones are alive

Now White hits back by playing to "x" and killing off the Black group. In fact, in the original position, White is in no hurry to attack this group, as it is defenseless. This group of stones is "dead."

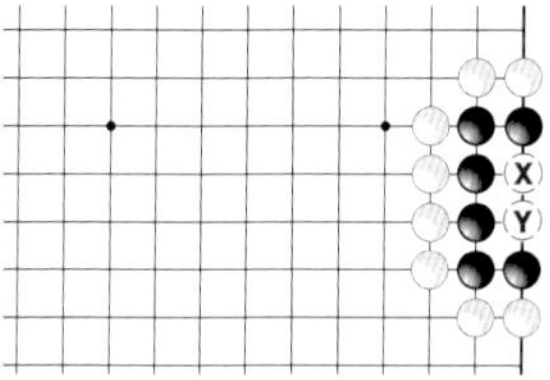

### THE RULE OF KO

The rule of Ko is important in Go because it prevents a situation where the game could have no resolution. Consider the position in diagram 200 (page 267).

Diagram 198 The Black stones are dead

The White stone to the right of the group is in atari, so Black can play to "x" and capture this stone. The position in diagram 201 (page 267) results.

Now, however, the Black stone that has just made the capture is itself in atari, so White can perform the same manoeuver and capture in return.

This leads to the position illustrated in diagram 202 (opposite). We are now back where we started.

Between two particularly stubborn players, it is possible that this little exchange of captures could continue indefinitely. However, the rule of Ko (*Ko* is, in fact, the Japanese word for "eternity") prevents this. When a stone captures in Ko, it may not be captured immediately. In our previous example, Black played to "x," capturing the White stone and leaving the position in diagram 203 (opposite).

White is not now allowed to play to "y," but must play elsewhere on the board. If White plays as marked by the triangle and Black does the same, White can now return to the point "y" and make the capture. White has captured in Ko, and now it is Black's turn to find something else to do.

## STRATEGY

A basic element of Go strategy is to form strong chains of stones. Such stones are said to be connected. If stones are prevented from connecting, they are weak and can become vulnerable to capture. Stones are strongest when they are connected in a straight line.

The upper group of stones in diagram 204 (opposite) is very secure. It is very difficult for White to mount an attack against them and they can form the basis of plans to gain territory. Any group of stones which is connected horizontally or vertically constitutes a powerful unit. Groups which contain a diagonal connection, as in the lower group in diagram 204, are less secure.

The key point here is "x." If Black can play to "x," this will make a strong connected group of stones. However, if White plays to "x," the black stones are "cut," and more vulnerable to attack.

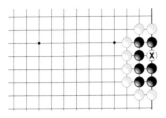

*Diagram 199 White captures the Black stones*

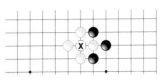

*Diagram 200 A White stone is in atari*

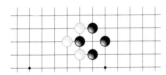

*Diagram 201 Black captures the White stone*

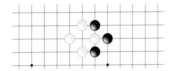

*Diagram 202 White recaptures*

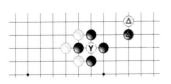

*Diagram 203 The rule of Ko*

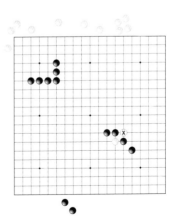

*Diagram 204 Connecting and cutting*

The simple game of Horseshoe is played in many parts of the world, including China.

*Players: two*
*Equipment: board and four counters (two black and two white)*
*Difficulty: easy-to-grasp strategy*
*Duration: less than 10 minutes per game*

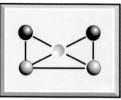

*Diagram 205 Starting position for a game of Horseshoe*

## BEGINNING TO PLAY

The Horseshoe board can easily be drawn on a sheet of paper. Diagram 205 (above right) shows the starting position.

## MOVING

The game starts with one player moving their counter to the center point. The opponent must now move one of their counters to the point vacated by the first player. Play then continues alternately, with each player in turn moving one of their counters to the vacant point.

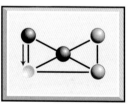

*Diagram 206 Achieving a winning position in Horseshoe*

## WINNING THE GAME

The player who manages to block the opponent so that they cannot move either of their counters achieves victory. In Diagram 206 (left), Black can achieve a winning position by moving the counter in the direction of the arrow.

Four Field Kono is one of a family of Korean games that includes Five Field Kono and Six Field Kono. It takes its name from the fact that it is played on a 4x4 board, which creates 16 intersections.

*Players: two*
*Equipment: board and 16 counters (eight each of two different colors)*
*Difficulty: mainly strategy*
*Duration: usually less than half an hour per game*

## BEGINNING TO PLAY

Four Field Kono is played on a square board of 16 points. Each player has eight counters, arranged in the starting position shown in diagram 207 (below).

## MOVING

The players move in alternate turns. If a counter is able to jump over another counter of the same color and land on an opponent's counter, it can capture the latter. If no capturing moves are possible, a counter may only move to an adjacent point along one of the lines.

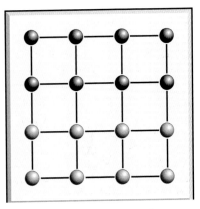

## WINNING THE GAME

The winner is the player who is able to capture all the opponent's counters or block them so that they cannot move.

*Diagram 207 Starting position for a game of Four Field Kono*

Nine Men's Morris (known as "Mill" in the United States) is one of the oldest board games in the world.

*Players:* two
*Equipment:* board and 18 counters (nine black and nine white)
*Difficulty:* requires good strategy
*Duration:* usually less than half an hour per game

## BRIEF HISTORY

Nine Men's Morris reached a peak of popularity in Europe in the Middle Ages, when the grid was often marked out with a trowel on the turf. It was probably to this in fact that Shakespeare was referring in *A Midsummer Night's Dream* (II, I, 96–8):

> *The folds stand empty in the drowned field,*
> *And crows are fatter with the murrion flock*
> *The nine men's morris is filled up with mud.*

Today, the board is usually made of wood or pasteboard. It comprises three squares, one inside the other, linked by four lines, two horizontal and two vertical (see diagram 208, opposite).

## BEGINNING TO PLAY

Each player starts with nine men, which they take turns to place on any vacant point of intersection on the board. If one of the players manages to achieve a row of three counters, known as a "mill," they can remove one of the opponent's counters from the board, but not one that itself stands in a mill – unless there are no other men available. Once counters have been removed from the board they are then deemed to be "dead."

Diagram 209 (opposite) shows the position after one counter has been introduced by each side, Black moving first. After two moves each

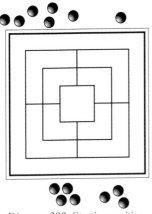

Diagram 208 *Starting position for a game of Nine Men's Morris*

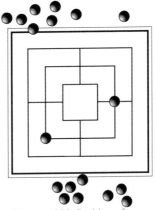

Diagram 209 *Position after one move each*

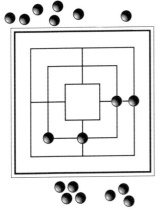

Diagram 210 *Position after two moves each*

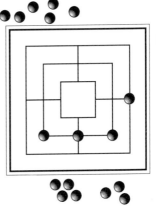

Diagram 211 *Position after Black's third move (forming a mill and capturing a white piece)*

(diagram 210, page 271) both sides are close to forming a mill. However, Black moves first and is able to form a mill, thereby removing one of White's counters from the board (diagram 211, page 271).

## MOVING

Once all the counters have been placed on the board, the players continue in alternate turns by moving a piece to an adjacent vacant point along a line, attempting to create a mill. A mill can be made and broken any number of times, an enemy counter being removed each time a mill is formed. It is particularly desirable to set up a double mill, whereby a counter can oscillate from one mill to another and then back again, capturing an opposing counter on every turn.

## THE HOP

This common optional variation is often used to prolong the game. If used, it enables a player with only three men left to hop one of their pieces to any point on the board, rather than being restricted to adjacent points. This is a big advantage and often enables a player to regain a great deal of lost ground. Of course, if the opponent is then reduced to three men, they are also entitled to hop. (It is interesting to note that centuries later this idea of hopping re-emerged in the late 1970s in the guise of "hyperspace" in video arcade games.)

## WINNING THE GAME

The winner is the player who manages to leave their opponent with only two men. If hopping is not allowed, victory can also be achieved by blocking the opponent's men so that they cannot be moved.

Hex was invented by the Danish mathematician and poet Piet Hein in the 1940s. Although relatively little known nowadays, it is simple to play and has an elegant and intriguing cut and thrust.

*Players:* two
*Equipment:* board and 122 counters
*Difficulty:* very strategic
*Duration:* usually less than one hour per game

## BEGINNING TO PLAY

Hex is played on a diamond-shaped board ruled into equilateral triangles. The standard size board has 10 triangles along each edge (see diagram 212, below). Just as in Go, play takes place on the points of intersection between the triangles, and not within the triangles themselves. Sometimes the board is shown instead as a series of adjoining hexagons (hence the name "Hex"), as in diagram 213 (below), but this is harder to draw. In the hexagonal version, play takes place on each of the hexagons.

## MOVING

Like Go, the game starts with the players alternately placing counters on any vacant point,

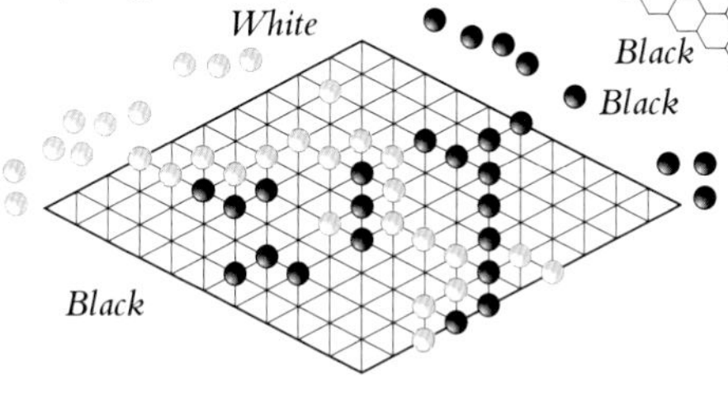

Diagram 212 A game of Hex (triangle version)

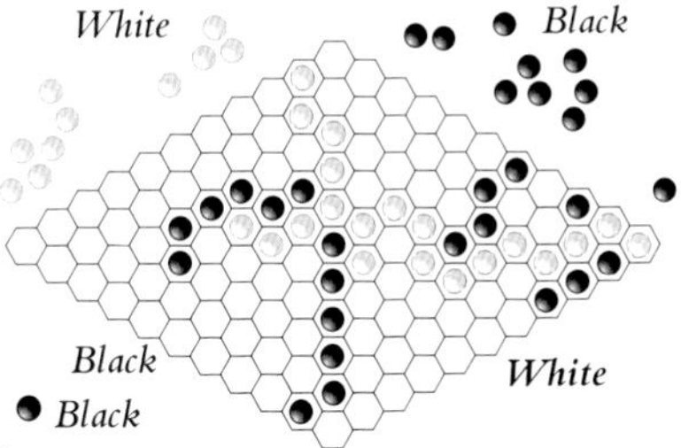

Diagram 213 A game of Hex (hexagonal version)

Black moving first. Once these counters have been placed, they remain in that position for the whole game. Counters cannot be moved or captured.

## WINNING THE GAME

The winner is the first player to complete a continuous line of counters from one of the sides marked with their colour to the other. A winning chain can be of any length and can turn and double back on itself as many times as it likes provided that there are no gaps. Note that the four corner points belong to both players.

## ALQUERQUE

**Alquerque is a board game for two, similar to Checkers (Draughts).**

*Players:* two
*Equipment:* board and 24 counters
*Difficulty:* mainly strategy
*Duration:* usually less than half an hour per game

## BRIEF HISTORY

Introduced into Europe by the Moors, Alquerque is thought to have originated in Ancient Egypt. Originally, boards would have been made out of stone, marble, wood, or some other material, and the lines would have been incised. Alquerque's game board is incised into the roof tiles of the ancient temple at Kurna – an honor it shares with Nine Men's Morris.

## BEGINNING TO PLAY

The board consists of 25 points connected by diagonal, horizontal, and vertical lines. Each player begins with 12 counters, which at the start of the game are arranged on the board as shown in diagram 214 (opposite).

## MOVING

Play is by alternate moves. On their turn, players may move one counter to any adjacent empty point. If an adjacent point is occupied by an enemy piece and the point beyond it is empty, a player may jump over that counter, capturing it in the process and removing it from the board. If a second counter can then be taken in the same fashion, this may also be removed, even if it involves a change of direction. Further captures may be made in the same way. A turn is completed when a counter is moved to an adjacent empty point or when all captures by that counter have been exhausted. In many variations of the game, it is compulsory for a piece to capture if it can do so, otherwise the offending counter is "huffed," and removed from the board.

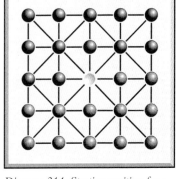

*Diagram 214 Starting position for a game of Alquerque*

## WINNING THE GAME

The game is won by capturing all the opponent's counters.

# OWARI

Owari originated in West Africa several thousand years ago.

*Players: two*
*Equipment: board and 48 stones or beans*
*Difficulty: easy-to-grasp strategy, but requires great skill to play well*
*Duration: usually less than 20 minutes per game*

## BRIEF HISTORY

Owari, sometimes called "Oware," "Wari," or "Ware," can be played by marking boards out in the sand and using seashells as pieces. Boards are often beautifully carved; smooth stones or beans are usually used as pieces. Also known as Mancala in the United States.

## BEGINNING TO PLAY

The Owari board comprises 12 cups arranged in two parallel rows, with an additional large cup at each end for each player to store captured stones. At the start of the game, four stones are placed in each of the cups on both sides of the board, leaving the large cups at each end empty (see diagram 215, opposite). Each player has control of the six cups on their side of the board and may not move any of the stones in the other player's cups, although they may add stones to them, as we shall see.

## MOVING

The first player starts the game by lifting all the stones from any one cup on their side of the board and, in a counter-clockwise direction, 'sowing' one stone in each successive cup, starting immediately to the right of the emptied cup and continuing into the opponent's territory, if necessary, until all the stones from that cup have been sown. The second player then does the same, picking up all the stones from a cup on their side of the board and sowing the stones around the board. The players take it in turns to move until one of the players manages to place the last stone in a sowing sequence into a cup on the opponent's side of the board containing only one or two stones (i.e. two or three stones after the sowing has been completed). That player captures all the stones in that cup and places them in the cup to their right. If there are either two or three stones in the preceding cup, these are also captured, and so on with the cup before that. However, if there are fewer than two or more than three stones in a cup, these are not captured and that player's turn ends.

There are very few other rules. First, if there are more than 11 stones in a cup, a whole circuit of the board will be carried out when these are sown. In that case, the original cup from which the pieces are being sown remains empty and the player skips that cup and continues sowing around the board. Finally, it is not permissible to leave your opponent with no stones to sow on their side of the board; if it is possible to give them a stone to sow, you must do so. If this is not possible and the opponent cannot move, all the remaining stones are captured by the first player. If both sides have stones left, but no further captures are possible, the remaining stones are shared.

## STRATEGY

The first thing that you will notice is that it is dangerous to leave cups with only one or two stones on your side of the board. If your opponent has a cup with the correct number of stones, these will be captured. If you have a vulnerable cup, you should either empty that cup to distribute the stones, empty another cup in such a way as to add a stone to it, thereby making it impregnable, or empty another cup in such a way as to cause the enemy cup to overshoot its target. By building up your right-hand cups, it is sometimes possible to mount simultaneous attacks on your opponent's cups. However, if these cups become too full, they end up being sown into your own territory and are thus harmless.

## WINNING THE GAME

The winner is the player who has captured the most stones at the end of the game.

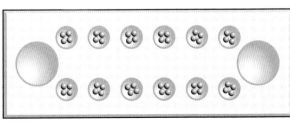

*Diagram 215  Starting position for a game of Owari*

# DOMINO GAMES

Before beginning a game of Dominoes, it is advisable to give some thought as to where you are going to play. At a glance, 28 bones may not look like much, but they do take up a lot of space. Avoid soft surfaces such as a rug on the floor.

To start a game, each player draws the required number of bones at random from the pool. The bones are set out on edge so that the other players cannot see them, rather like holding a hand of cards. (Some people hold as many bones as possible in one hand, but few can manage more than five or six.) Bones that remain facedown after the draw are known as the "boneyard." Players who cannot play from their hand must take a bone from the boneyard, much the same as drawing from the stockpile in card games.

The basic rules of Dominoes are simple: players have to match the end of one of their bones with one end of the bones on the table. Depending on the game, they either have to match suits (for example, playing a 1 from hand against a 1 on the table), or make matches that add up to a given number, such as 5. Play moves clockwise around the table as the chain, or layout, of bones grows. Traditionally, doubles are laid crosswise to the other bones.

There are two basic types of domino game: block games, where the sole aim is to get rid of your bones before your opponent; and point games, where you also score points at the same time. Both types of game are usually played up to a total of a specified number of points. The first to play all his bones declares 'Domino!', which means finished. If the game is blocked, which means no one can make another move, the other players add up the spots still in their hands. The winner is the one with the lowest, or lightest, total.

This is the basic game of Dominoes – the best way to learn the fundamental rules of play.

*Players:* two to five
*Equipment:* one set of double sixes (28 bones)
*Difficulty:* ideal for children; adults may play more strategically
*Duration:* half an hour upwards

### BEGINNING TO PLAY

Turn all the bones facedown on the table and shuffle them. With two or three players, each takes seven dominoes; four or five players take five each. The player with the highest doublet begins, or "sets," laying the doublet face up on the table. Play moves to the player on the left, who adds a bone that matches it, at right angles to the doublet. The third player then plays a bone that matches one of the two open ends of the layout. Play continues clockwise round the table, each player in turn matching one of the two open ends of the layout.

In diagram 216 (below), the highest doublet drawn, 5-5, was set vertically and 5-1 played against it. The third player had the option of either matching the 1 or the 5 on the other side of the doublet, and played a 5-3.

### RULES OF PLAY

A player who cannot match either end of the layout must take bones from the boneyard until a match is drawn. If all the dominoes are drawn and there is still no match, the player must pass and wait for his next turn.

*Diagram 216 Setting the bones*

### WINNING THE GAME

The first player to get rid of all his bones calls "Domino!" and wins the hand. Otherwise, the game continues until no player can make another move. This impasse is known as a blocked game.

### SCORING

When a player calls "Domino!", the other players add up the spots on the dominoes still in their hands (blanks score zero) and this total is the winner's score. If the game is blocked and nobody can move, the players add up the spots on their dominoes and the player with the lowest total wins. The winner calculates his or her score by subtracting the total number of points in his or her hand from the number in each of the losers' hands, then adding the resulting totals together. So, if one player has won a blocked game with a final total of 11, and the two other players have 13 and 15, respectively, the winner's score is 6. The first player to reach 100 wins the game (or 50 for a shorter game).

### STRATEGIC TIPS

Once you have mastered the basic rules, you can think about developing a strategy. In many hands, there will be only one possible play, but, if there is a choice of play, skill can be used. For example, if you hold four or more dominoes in one suit, try to leave both open ends in that suit because your opponents are less likely to have any. Then they will have to empty the boneyard – when the game is closed you may gain a high score!

Dig in the boneyard early on in the game to supplement your hand, but as the game proceeds, do your best to offload your highest scoring dominoes, particularly if your hand appears weak after several plays, because otherwise they will mount up as penalty points to be added against you when someone else goes 'Domino!' If your hand seems strong, play to go out. When an opponent plays sets a doublet, aim to cover it as soon as possible – chances are that he has at least one other bone to play on it.

# BLOCK DOMINOES

An easy version of Dominoes that is suitable for young children. It eliminates the draw (from the boneyard), the remaining bones being distributed after reshuffling.

The player with the highest doublet starts and the others follow in turn. Reshuffle the bones and divide them between the players. If there are two players, they take 13 each; three players take 8 and four players take 5. Any remaining dominoes are left out of play. Take turns to lay down bones until "Domino!" is called or the game is blocked. This is a game of pure luck, because chance decides whether the dominoes needed to unblock the game remain in the boneyard – or in the other players' hands.

# CROSS DOMINOES

A game with more options than Block and Draw dominoes, and which has the added advantage of taking up less space.

The player with the highest doublet starts, then for the next four turns players have to match dominoes to form a cross. In diagram 2, a double 4 was set to start, then the next players laid down a 4-3, 4-6, 4-1 and 4-5 to create four open ends with 3, 6, 1 and 5 available for play. No other dominoes can be played until the cross has been created. Play then continues as in Block and Draw Dominoes.

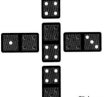

*Diagram 217 Forming a cross to start the game*

# DOUBLE CROSS DOMINOES

This game is not – as its name might suggest – a game of double dealing and deception, but is instead a variation on Cross Dominoes.

This is played in the same way as Cross Dominoes, with the exception that a doublet must be played on one of the arms before play can continue on the four open ends. In diagram 218 (right), a double 3 started the game, then 6-3, 1-3, 5-3, 3-2 were played. After that, a doublet has to be played on one end of the cross (players often have to draw from the boneyard for this), in this case a double 2, before play can continue as for Block and Draw Dominoes.

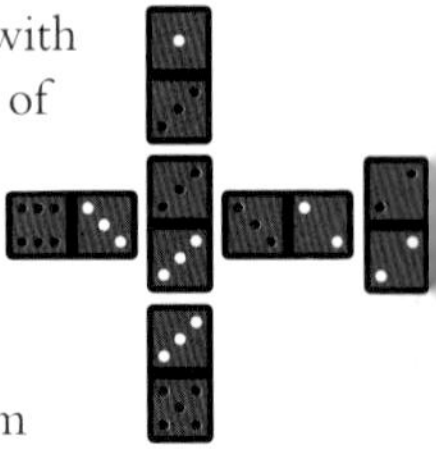

*Diagram 218
Forming a
double cross*

# MALTESE CROSS DOMINOES

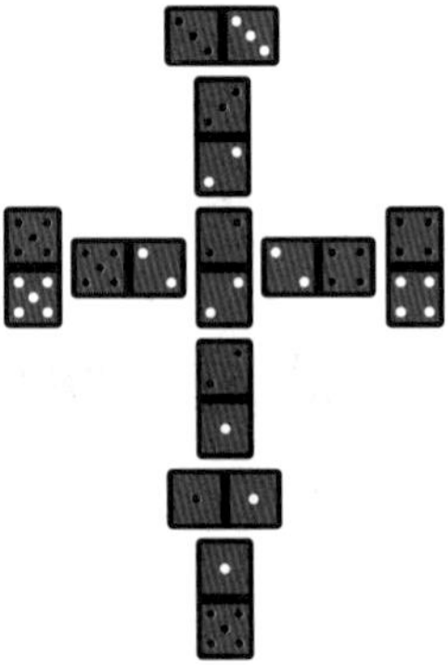

Another variation, this time a tricky one, on Cross Dominoes.

After a doublet has been set to start, it must be matched by four dominoes, and then four doublets played at each arm of the cross before play can proceed. In diagram 219 (left), before the 1-5 could be played, doublets had to be placed at the ends of the cross. Often players have to dig deep into the boneyard to get the game going!

*Diagram 219 Forming
a Maltese cross*

# DOUBLE NINE CROSS DOMINOES

A family game requiring a set of double nines (55 dominoes).

With two to three players, seven dominoes are drawn; four or more players draw five each. The player with the highest doublet starts, then dominoes are matched to the two ends and two sides, as in Cross Dominoes. As play proceeds, every time a doublet is played two more ends are opened for play. In the game shown in diagram 220 (right), the double 4 was played first, then dominoes were laid at the four sides of this doublet. After the double 9 was played, 9-1 followed it and players can lay down a domino on either side, such as 9-3 as illustrated.

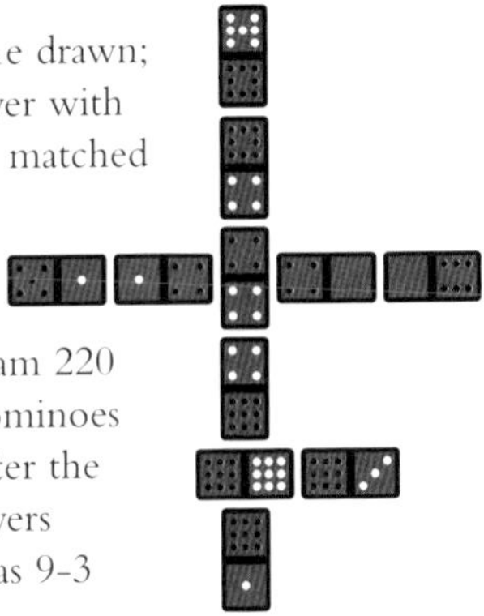

*Diagram 220 A game of Double Nine Cross Dominoes in progress*

# CYPRUS

This game also uses a set of double nines. It is good for four or more.

Once the dominoes have been shuffled, four players draw 13 each, five draw 11 each, six draw 9 each, seven draw 7, eight or nine draw 6, and ten draw 5 each. The player with the double 9 starts (if no-one has drawn the double 9, the dominoes are reshuffled and drawn again). After the double 9 is played, the domino must be matched on both sides and ends to make a cross, and then diagonally to make an eight-pointed star. Play proceeds clockwise and, when the star has been created, the ends of the nines already played can be matched. Play continues as for Block and Draw Dominoes.

*Diagram 221 The eight-pointed star of Cyprus*

The most popular form of Dominoes in the United States, this game is also known as the Five Game or Muggins. Players score not only by winning hands but also by scoring points during play.

*Players:* *two to four*
*Equipment:* *one set of double sixes (28 bones)*
*Difficulty:* *not as difficult as Five Up, but needs some arithmetical ability and keen observation*
*Duration:* *about half an hour*

### BEGINNING TO PLAY

After the bones have been shuffled, each player draws five dominoes, whether it is a two-, three- or four-handed game. The player with the highest doublet begins, then play continues clockwise around the table, players drawing from the boneyard when they cannot match the ends with the same suit.

### RULES OF PLAY

Whenever possible a player should try to make the open ends of the layout add up to 5, 10, 15, or 20. As is usual, doublets are laid crosswise and count their full value. For example, in diagram 222 (below), Player 1 sets 5-5 and scores because the domino totals 10. Player 2 plays 5-0 and also scores because the total is still 10, the blank scoring 0, but the doublet still making 5+5. Player 1 then adds 5-3, and does not score because the total of the ends is now 3 (3+0). Player 2 plays 0-3 and does not score because the total of spots on the ends is now 6 (3+3). Player 2 next adds a 3-3, but still does not score because this only totals 9 (3+3+3). Player 1 plays a 3-4,

*Diagram 222 A game of All Fives*

making 10 (3+3+4) and Player 2 adds a 3-6, also making 10 (4+6).

It is essential to keep your eyes on the game because if a

player makes a multiple of 10 and does not declare it, any player can call "Muggins" as soon as the next play is made and score the points himself. Players may draw from the boneyard if they cannot play, but the last two bones in it are left unplayed.

## WINNING THE GAME

The first player to go out by getting rid of all his bones calls "Domino!" otherwise the game may end when no one can make another move, in which case the player with the lightest hand wins.

## SCORING

Players score the total value of each multiple of five made. For example, if one end of the layout is a 5 and a player lays another 5 on the other end, he scores 10, and so on.

After a hand is finished, players who still have bones each total up their spots and round the number to the nearest multiple of five (for example, downward for scores which end in 1 or 2, upward for scores with 3 or 4). The player who has called "Domino!" wins the opponents' adjusted points. In a blocked game, the player with the lightest hand wins and scores the difference between his spot total and that of his opponents – all scores rounded to the nearest multiple of five. The player who reaches 100 first is the winner. A cribbage board or single stroke scoring (see Five Up for description) is the best way of keeping the score.

## STRATEGIC TIPS

It is difficult to score after one player has made a multiple of five because it is unlikely that the next player will have a bone that will turn the open ends into another multiple of five. Keep an eye out for the 6-1, 5-5, and 5-0, however, as they can help you score, as can the 0-0. As this is a points game, if you have a good hand do not try to finish too quickly but try to score as many points as possible to help you toward the all-decisive 100.

Developed in San Francisco early in the twentieth century, this popular game demands skill and perseverance, plus the ability to add up quickly!

*Players: four, playing as partners*
*Equipment: one set of double sixes (28 bones)*
*Difficulty: easy to learn, but difficult to become proficient. Not suitable for young children, as scoring is complicated*
*Duration: about half an hour*

## BEGINNING TO PLAY

After the tiles have been shuffled, the four players draw for partners, the two with the heaviest bones playing together. The player with the heaviest bone (the one with the highest total of spots, or, in the event of a tie, the highest number on one end) starts. Play then continues in a clockwise direction.

After the draw for partners the bones are reshuffled, each player drawing five bones. The game begins with the first player setting any bone. The next players then match ends to suits, but, as often as possible, make the open ends add up to five or multiples of five.

## RULES OF PLAY

In the usual fashion of dominoes, doublets are always laid crosswise on the chain. When another bone is laid against a doublet on the other side, the doublet becomes a spinner. This means that tiles can be played to either end, in effect, sprouting off the double to form a cross pattern – although each end can only be included in the score if a bone has been played to it. In diagram 223 (page 288), the first player lays the 3-1, and the second player lays 1-1, making a total of five (see section on scoring, below) totaling the two ends (3+1+1). The third player lays 1-2 and also scores five (3+2). The fourth player lays 5-1 against the double and scores en (3+5+2). When 2-3 is laid, this totals 11 (3+5+3), so the player does not score. Next, 6-2 is laid, so the total from all four ends is 17 (6+3+5+3), and no score is recorded. From this point, as the spinner has had bones added to each crosswise end, four numbers must be included for each score, and each double added can become a spinner, opening more and more ends for scoring.

Players draw from the boneyard until a playable bone is found, although one bone is always left facedown. When this stage is reached, players who cannot play must pass. The hand is over when one player calls "Domino!" or when play is blocked.

## SCORING

Each multiple of five scores 1; 10 counts as 2; 15 counts as 3; 20 counts as 4; and so on. Many players find it easiest to keep the score for this game on a cribbage board, or by recording a single stroke on a pad of paper for each 5 points.

If no one notices a score before the next player begins his turn, then no points are awarded, so all players are advised to be as observant as possible. However, if the opponents notice, they can say "Muggins" and score the other team's points.

Each team's points can be added together after each hand. The first player to declare 'Domino!' scores points for the tiles remaining in the opponents' hands. These points are scored just like the multiples of five above, but if the total ends in 1 or 2, they are rounded down to the nearest multiple of five (so 11 rounds down to 10 and two points are awarded). If the total ends in 3 or 4, it is rounded up (24 rounds up to 25 and five points are scored).

If play is blocked and no player can proceed, the team with the lowest combined number of points in hand wins and scores one point for every five spots left in the losers' hands. Play continues until one team has reached a total of 61.

## STRATEGIC TIPS

Try to play bones that will force the opponents to draw from the boneyard, and try to go out first so that they will be left with a handful of bones. Hold onto tiles, known as kickers, which automatically score after an opponent scores – the double blank, and 5-5, for instance, as well as tiles that can be played off their own doubles to score (1-2, 2-4, 3-1, 4-3, 5-0, and 6-2). Try to play these to your best advantage.

Keep a close eye on the tiles being played to make sure that you are not left with an unplayable doublet after all the tiles in that suit have been played. One way of making sure that play comes back to you is to play a doublet if you have tiles of a matching suit for the next go. As in Five Up, there are four playable faces on every doublet, so you will be able to play one of your bones.

Keep a constant check on the total of the open ends – this will let you know instantly which of your bones can score and helps you catch any scores that your opponents miss, which you can then claim for yourself.

## VARIATION

In Five Up for two players, each player draws five tiles to begin. The game is usually played to 21, and two tiles must remain in the boneyard.

*Diagram 223  A game of Five Up in progress*

Sometimes referred to as "the Bergen game," this point-scoring game may have originated in either Norway or the Netherlands.

*Players:* two to four
*Equipment:* one set of double sixes (28 bones)
*Difficulty:* fairly easy
*Duration:* about half an hour

## STARTING TO PLAY

After the bones have been shuffled, if there are two players they draw six bones each; three or four players draw five each. The player with the lowest doublet sets.

## RULES OF PLAY

If a player does not have a suitable bone, he can draw one (no more) from the boneyard. Two bones must always remain in the boneyard. Play is otherwise the same as in Block and Draw Dominoes, but points are given for leaving both ends open in the same suit (known as a double header), or leaving one open end in the same suit as a doublet on the other (a triple header). In diagram 224 (page 290), Player 1 scores for his first play of 2-2, a doublet. Player 2 lays down 2-1 and does not score; nor does Player 1 who next lays 4-2. Player 2 then adds 1-4 and scores a double header, as there is a 4 at the other open end. Player 1 tops this by adding a doublet, a 4-4, and scores a triple header, having a doublet and an open end all of the same suit.

## SCORING

Score 2 points for a doublet, 2 points for a double header, and 3 points for a triple header. A player calling "Domino!" scores 1 point. If the game is closed (no one can move) the player with no doublets wins 1 point or, alternatively, the player with the lightest doublet wins the game point. If no one has a doublet in their hand, the lightest hand wins 1 point. The first player to score 15 points wins.

## STRATEGIC TIPS

You should get into the habit of counting the number of occurrences of a suit in the layout. Each suit appears eight times at the ends of bones, so half of the available matching ends are used up at each doublet. Doublets are important and you should hold them as long as possible to get a valuable triple header.

## VARIATION

Because the total number of spots is not used for scoring, Bergen can be played by young children using picture dominoes. In the event of a blocked game, you can adjust the rules so that if, say, animal dominoes are used, the player with the doublet containing the smallest animal wins. If nobody has a doublet the player with the fewest number of dominoes wins.

*Diagram 224  A two-handed game of Bergen*

# MATADOR

This game of skill, which makes use of "wild" bones, is also known as Russian Dominoes or All Sevens.

*Players:* two to four
*Equipment:* one set of double sixes
(28 bones)
*Difficulty:* strategic skill needed
*Duration:* about half an hour

*Diagram 225 Matadors*

## STARTING TO PLAY
First shuffle the bones. If there are two players, each draws seven dominoes; three or four players, each draws five. The player with the highest doublet sets, and play continues clockwise around the table.

## RULES OF THE GAME
Matador differs in several ways from other domino games:

1. A player can draw from the boneyard even when he has a playable bone. However, if he cannot play a bone he must draw from the boneyard until he gets one, or until the boneyard is empty of all but two bones.
2. Players must match adjacent ends so that they add up to seven, rather than matching ends to suits. For example, an open end with a 6 calls for a 1; a 5 calls for a 2; a 4 calls for a 3 and so on.
3. Doublets are always laid end-to-end, rather than crosswise. The bones that add up to 7 (3-4, 5-2, 6-1) and the double blank are known as matadors (see diagram 225, above). They are played like wild cards or trumps – that is, a matador can be played at any time and is the only bone that can unblock an end which has been closed with a blank. In diagram 226 (page 292), 3-2 has been set, and the next player must add a bone that totals 7, so a 4-4 is laid against the 3 (4+3), making

the required 7. Several moves later, a 2-0 is played and the only way to continue playing against this bone is to add a matador, in this case 4-3.

## WINNING THE GAME

As is usual in Domino games, either the first player to get rid of all his or her bones and call "Domino!" wins, or the game cannot continue when it is blocked.

## SCORING

Making adjacent tiles add up to 7 does not score any points – it is the basic requirement of the game. Scoring is the same as in Block and Draw Dominoes: the player who calls "Domino!" wins the total of all the spots left in opponents' hands. If the game is blocked, the player with the lightest hand wins and scores the difference between his spot total and each opponent's. The first to reach the agreed 50 or 100 points is the winner.

*Diagram 226 Making a Matador*

This is a fast and fun game in which no one gets to see their hand before the start of play.

*Players:* *two to five*
*Equipment:* *one set of double sixes (28 bones)*
*Difficulty:* *great for kids because it's all luck and no strategy!*
*Duration:* *about half an hour*

### STARTING TO PLAY

The bones are shuffled facedown, then players draw to see who will play first, the heaviest bone winning. After reshuffling, all the bones are dealt equally between the players: 14 each to two players; 9 each to three players (the one left over is not played); 7 each to four players; 5 each to five players (three left over). The players do not look at their bones, but arrange them face-down in a vertical row. If there are leftover bones, one of them is played (with two or four players, the first player lays any bone), then the first player turns over the top bone in his row and plays it if possible. If not, the bone is put facedown at the bottom of the row. If an unplayable doublet is turned up, this is put at the bottom of the row, but it remains face-up so that everyone can see it, as shown in diagram 227 (right). The next player then takes his turn.

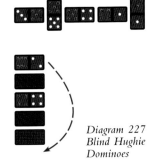

### WINNING THE GAME

Play continues clockwise around the table, until either a player gets rid of all his bones and calls "Domino!" or the game is blocked. In this case, the player with the lightest hand wins and scores the difference between his hand and each opponent's hand. The first to reach the agreed 50 or 100 wins.

*Diagram 227*
*Blind Hughie*
*Dominoes*

Mah-Jongg, which originated in China, is a fascinating and elaborate game. It is not, however, quite as difficult to learn as it may seem.

*Players: best with four; two or three can play but the game will not be as good*
*Equipment: 144 Mah-Jongg tiles, two dice, four wind disks and counters for scoring, four racks for holding each player's tiles upright*
*Difficulty: because of the exotic Chinese pieces, Mah-Jongg looks daunting, but the basic game can be learned in an hour*
*Duration: experienced players can play a hand in five minutes, but beginners should set aside an hour for a hand, an evening for a game*

### THE TILES

Before you play, it is a good idea to familiarize yourself with the 144 Mah-Jongg tiles. Basically, they are divided into three categories: 28 honor tiles, 108 suit tiles, and 8 optional flower tiles (see Diagram 228, page 296).

The honor tiles consist of four Green Dragons, four Red Dragons, four White Dragons, four North Winds, four East Winds, four South Winds and four West Winds.

The suit tiles consist of three different suits of 36 tiles. Each tile is numbered from 1 to 9, and there are four of each number. The three suits are Bamboos, Circles, and Characters. Bamboos are sometimes called Bams or Sticks, Circles are also called Dots or Balls, and Characters are also known as Cracks. Individual tiles are referred to as 1-Bamboo, 4-Circles, 7-Characters, and so on. The 1 and 9 of each suit (known as head tiles) are worth more than tiles 2–8 (known as middle tiles).

Some sets of Mah-Jongg come with eight optional Flower tiles (sometimes called Seasons), consisting of either four Seasons and four Flower tiles or eight of one type. These are essentially wild cards. Beginners are advised to learn the basic game before including these tiles in their play, and use of them will be discussed under Variations.

Apart from the tiles, a Mah-Jongg set includes four wind disks (marked N, S, E, W), which decide the seating arrangements of the players, two dice and counters (usually dyed bars and disks) that represent different points.

## AIM OF THE GAME

There are no partners in Mah-Jongg – each player is on his own. The aim of the game is to collect "sets" of tiles, of which there are three different kinds:

1. Chow: A sequence, or run, of three tiles in the same suit. For example, 2-3-4 Characters or 6-7-8 Circles. Only three tiles are allowed in a sequence.
2. Pung: Three of a kind, for example, three 4-Bamboos or three Green Dragons or three South Winds.
3. Kong: Four of a kind, for example, four 8-Characters or four White Dragons.

A player aims to collect four of these sets and a pair for a complete hand (also known as a 'woo'). Although any sets can help the player to go out, some carry higher points than others. For example, Chows are worth nothing in points, while Pungs consisting of middle tiles score only half as much as three of a kind with head tiles. (It is a good idea to keep the scoring system close to hand when you start to play, to help to remind you of which sets score most.)

## PREPARING FOR THE GAME

Before you start to play, there is a formal ritual that determines where each player sits around the table. However, beginners may find it easier to use this simplified method: each player throws the dice, and the highest score takes the East Wind disk. The player to the right becomes the South Wind. North Wind is on the left, while West sits opposite. The East Wind always starts.

Before play begins, each player should take counters to the value of 2000 points: two 500-point bones; nine 100-point bones; eight 10-point bones; and ten 2-point bones. In a game for beginners, remove the eight Flower tiles if they are present in the set, then turn the Mah-Jongg tiles facedown and shuffle them in the same way as for dominoes. At the same time each player should take a rack and position it in front of them.

Each of the four players picks 34 tiles, and without looking at them, stacks them facedown to make a wall that is 17 tiles long and two tiles deep. The four walls are then pushed together with the help of the racks to form a hollow square in the middle of the table.

### BEGINNING TO PLAY

Every Mah-Jongg game begins with the opening of the wall. East Wind throws the dice to decide which side of the wall is to be breached. This is arrived at by counting to the right and taking East Wind's wall as

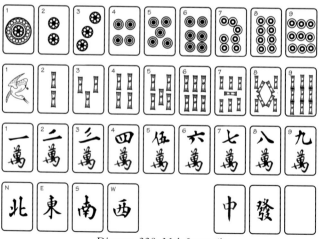

*Diagram 228  Mah-Jongg tiles*

"one," South Wind's wall as "two," and so on, until the number shown on the dice is reached. The player designated by the end of the count throws the dice again and adds the total of this second throw to the total of the first throw. Starting at the right-hand corner of the wall, the player counts left the number of tiles indicated by this final total. For example, if East Wind's first throw was 4-1 (5) and the second was 5-3 (8), the total is 13 (5+8). Starting at the right-hand corner of the chosen wall, the player counts 13 from right to left and removes the thirteenth pair of tiles from the wall and places them facedown on top of the wall to the right of the opening. (These are known as loose tiles and when both have been taken, the next stack of two to the right of the break is set on the wall and become loose tiles.) If the total number from the two dice throws is more than 17, the player rounds the corner and opens the wall of the player on the left. At this point, traditionally, East Wind picks up the dice and places them in his rack, as they will not be needed until the next hand.

Now that the wall has been opened, the draw begins from the left side of the wall opening. East Wind goes first, taking two pairs of tiles from the opening. Moving counterclockwise around the table, each player does the same, drawing four tiles at a time, until each player has drawn three times and has 12 tiles. Then players draw one more tile each, and East Wind draws one last tile. This means that by the end of the draw East Wind has 14 tiles and North, West and South have 13 tiles each. Players then arrange their tiles in suits and decide what kind of sets they will try to collect.

## RULES OF PLAY

Players now try to collect a complete hand by drawing new tiles from the wall and discarding unusable ones into the hollow center. East Wind begins by discarding a tile face-up into the center, naming it while doing so: for example, "6-Circle." (All players should do this when they discard.)

Next, South Wind may either take the discard or draw one from the wall, discarding a tile from hand. Play continues counterclockwise to West Wind and North Wind, each player either drawing from the wall, or picking up the last discard (none of the other discards are ever picked up), before discarding a tile.

The rules relating to the picking up of discards are as follows: a player may pick up the last discarded tile only if it can be used to make a Pung (three of a kind) or a Chow (a sequence). When the discard is picked up, it must be added to the relevant two other tiles in hand and the set immediately laid face-up on the table. The player now has an exposed hand (the set on the table) as well as a concealed hand. As the scoring system shows, sets in the concealed hand are worth more than sets in the exposed hand. After laying down a Pung or Chow, the player discards so that the number of tiles in both exposed and concealed hands still totals 13.

A player may Pung out of turn if a tile is discarded that completes three of a kind in their hand. The player simply calls : "Pung!" and takes the discarded tile. Furthermore, if a player picks up a discard intending to Chow, and another player says "Pung!", the second player gets the tile even if the opponent has already picked up the tile. If the opponent has already revealed the tiles for the Chow, however, the tile in question can be kept.

Declaring a Kong, which is four of a kind, obeys different rules. A completed hand that contains a Kong must contain extra tiles. (A completed hand with 1 Kong = 15 tiles; 2 Kongs = 16 tiles; 3 Kongs = 17 tiles.) To make sure that the correct number of tiles are maintained in hand a player making a Kong draws an extra tile from the loose tiles on top of the wall. For example, to convert a Pung into a Kong, a player can pick up the relevant discard and lay a Kong face-up on the table, then draw the first loose tile on the top of the wall before discarding a tile.

Another way to convert a Pung into a Kong occurs when a player draws a tile from the wall that matches an already exposed Pung. The player can simply add the single tile to the Pung, then draw a loose tile and discard another. A player who has a Kong need not necessarily declare it. It can be saved and one of the four tiles can be used in a Chow (sequence). However, during any turn, a player must never declare a Kong after announcing a Chow or a Pung.

## WINNING THE GAME

When a player has collected four sets and a pair, either by drawing the final necessary tile or by Punging or Chowing a discard from the table, they declare "Mah-Jongg!" and lay the concealed hand face-up by the exposed hand.

You can also declare "Mah-Jongg" by picking up a discarded tile. This can be done out-of-turn by any player who is one tile short of declaring "Mah-Jongg," even if the tile is to be used in a Chow or a Pung.

A player cannot discard after declaring "Mah- Jongg." Nor can a player complete a Kong and win, because a loose tile must always be drawn afterward. Furthermore, if a player declares a Kong by drawing a fourth tile to add to an exposed Pung, another player may steal the fourth tile (known as stealing the fourth, this move carries bonus points) and make Mah-Jongg. If no-one declares "Mah-Jongg," the game may be said to be a draw when the wall is reduced to the last 14 tiles. In this case, no scores count, the tiles are reshuffled, and a new hand is played. The same player remains East Wind.

When each game is over, the East Wind disk and all the other Wind disks pass to the right. The tiles are turned facedown and shuffled before a new game begins. In Mah Jongg, several games, known as "rounds," are usually played until each player has had a turn as East Wind.

## SCORING

The value of the winning hand is calculated first with the help of the scoring table, adding in any bonus points and doubling. Each other player pays this amount in counters to the winner. If East Wind wins, the other players always pay double. The values of the losers' hands are then calculated and each player pays each other player who has a higher score than he does the difference between their scores.

Winning hands tend to average about 40 points, but bonuses can send scores rocketing, so a limit of 300 or 500 per hand is usually established before the game starts.

## SCORING SYSTEM
*Exposed combinations*

| (completed from discards) | points |
|---|---|
| Three of a kind (middle tiles 2-8) | 2 |
| Three of a kind (head tiles 1 and 9) | 4 |
| Three of a kind any Winds | 4 |
| Three of a kind any Dragons | 4 |
| Four of a kind (middle tiles) | 8 |
| Four of a kind (head tiles) | 16 |
| Four of a kind any Winds | 16 |
| Four of a kind any Dragons | 16 |
| Pair of any Dragons or player's own Wind | 2 |

*Concealed combinations*

| (completed by drawing from the wall) | points |
|---|---|
| Three of a kind (middle tiles 2-8) | 4 |
| Three of a kind (head tiles 1 and 9) | 8 |
| Three of a kind any Winds | 8 |
| Three of a kind any Dragons | 8 |
| Four of a kind (middle tiles) | 16 |
| Four of a kind (head tiles) | 32 |
| Four of a kind any Winds | 32 |
| Four of a kind any Dragons | 32 |
| Pair of any Dragons or player's own Wind | 2 |

*Bonus scores*

| | points |
|---|---|
| (for the winning hand only) | |
| Mah-Jongg (for winning the hand) | 20 |
| Drawing winning tile (rather than discard) | 2 |
| Drawing winning loose tile | 10★ |
| No score other than Mah-Jongg | 10 |
| No Chow, concealed or exposed | 10 |
| Stealing fourth to win | 10 |
| Mah-Jongg on the last tile drawn | 10 |

(★ score this or the previous bonus, not both)

*Double honor scores (applies to all hands; calculated last)*

Three or four of your own Wind, concealed or exposed: Double total score

Three or four Dragons, concealed or exposed: Double total score

Hand all one suit except for Dragons and Winds: Double total score

Hand all one suit: Double total score three times

Hand entirely honor tiles (Winds and Dragons, no suits): Double total score three times

## STRATEGIC TIPS

Make sure you maintain 13 tiles (plus one extra for each Kong) in your hand at all times, otherwise you cannot complete a Mah-Jongg and your hand will score zero. Try to assess both your chances of scoring high and your chances of making a Mah-Jongg at the beginning of the game. For example, if the original draw provides you with six or more single tiles, the chances are you won't declare Mah-Jongg. If the tiles that you draw do not improve, avoid Chows and go for high-scoring Pungs. Watch for combinations that can be completed in as many ways as possible: for example, a Chow that is open at both ends 3-4 or 6-7, rather than 8-9. Discard your least useful tiles, such as single suits and nines of a suit, because they can be difficult to combine in a run. Keep your eye on the discard pile, calculating which tiles are dead and which have yet to appear. Try to collect the pair that is necessary to complete your hand early on, because this is the most difficult part of the hand to complete.

## VARIATIONS
### Flowers and Seasons
The eight optional Flowers and Seasons tiles (two series of four tiles), are numbered 1 to 4, each series in a different colour. Each player has their own Flower and Season: East is 1, South is 2, West is 3, and North is 4. When a player draws a Flower or Season, it cannot be discarded and must be immediately declared and exposed, or laid face-up. The player then draws a tile from the dead portion of the wall to replace it. Each Flower or Season scores 4 points. If a player holds one of their own Flowers or Seasons, their total score is doubled; if they hold two, the total score is doubled twice. And should they be so lucky as to hold all four Flowers and Seasons of one colour, the total score is doubled three times!

### Limit Hands
When you gain more experience, you can incorporate the special limit hands listed on below. A player who has collected a group of them and declares "Mah-Jongg!" gets the maximum points.

*Limit hand scoring system*
**Hand from heaven:** East picks up a complete Mah-Jongg in his or her 14 tiles at the beginning of the game and scores the limit (300).
**Hand from earth:** If any player other than East picks up a set hand of 13 tiles and pungs East's first discard for Mah-Jongg, this scores half the limit (150).
**Lucky thirteen:** If a player picks up a set hand and cannot complete it with the first discard, he or she can declare the set hand before

making the first draw. Provided none of the original 13 tiles are discarded, this scores one-third of the limit (100) when the player finally draws or pungs the necessary tile.

**Snake:** 1 to 9 of a suit plus one of each of the Winds with any tile paired. All tiles but the last must be drawn from the wall. This scores the limit (300).

**Thirteen hidden orphans:** Thirteen single tiles concealed in the hand – each one of the four Winds, the three Dragons and one head tile from each suit – all drawn from the wall. Drawing one matching tile completes the hand, and it scores the limit (300). If that one tile is not drawn, the hand scores nothing.

**Seven twins:** Any seven pairs, making 14 tiles in all. The fourteenth can be drawn or punged, and the complete hand scores half the limit (150).

**Three Great Scholars:** A Pung or Kong of one of the Dragons (Red, White or Green), plus any Chow or Pung, and a pair, scores the limit (300).

# INDEX

# INDEX

# INDEX

## HALF HOUR GAMES

# INDEX